IMAGES
of America

GOLD HILL

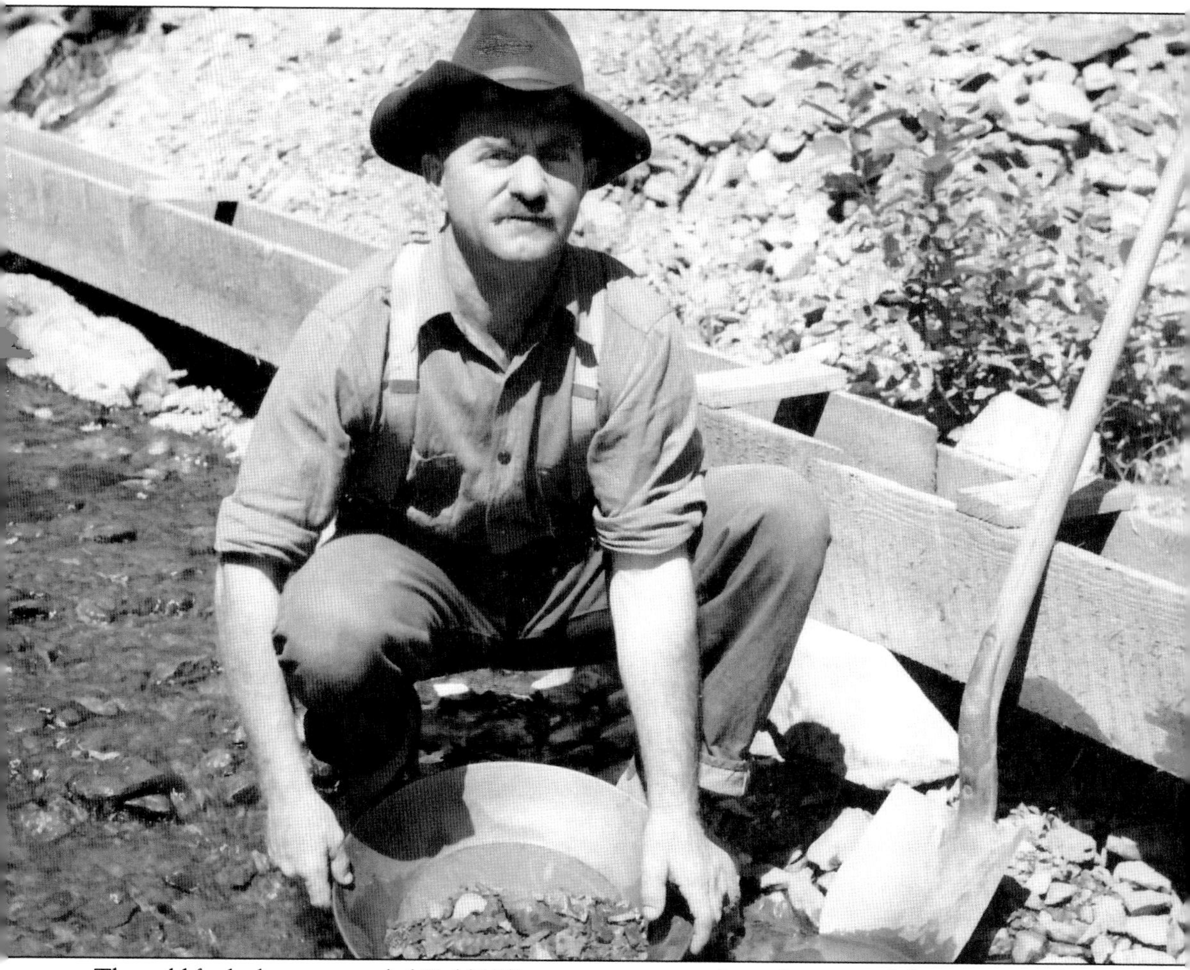

The gold finds that surrounded Gold Hill were extensive, rich, and supported the town in different times. The lure of striking it rich drove men and their families to great sacrifices. The historical society's Ted Wharton wrote about the "chaos of riches and broken dreams where many mines were bought and sold, or outright stolen, and many leads and veins fizzled out." They did. But the lure continues today. Shorty Berrow, pictured here, was one of the many prospectors who heard this tune. Behind him is a sluice box with wooden riffles, allowing the gold in the water to settle out in the riffles' eddies.

On the Cover: This early 1900s photograph shows the sizeable crew at the Hammersly Placer Mine, located above the two forks of Sardine Creek. Hammersly owned the ground and the "old Maybright ditch," which gave a 75-foot pressure although located more than a quarter of a mile from the claim's lower end. At the upper end was a natural reservoir site. (SOHS.)

IMAGES
of America

GOLD HILL

Dennis Powers of the Gold Hill Historical Society

ARCADIA
PUBLISHING

ISBN 978-0-7385-8179-8

Published by Arcadia Publishing
Charleston, South Carolina

Printed in the United States of America

Library of Congress Control Number: 2010932151

For all general information, please contact Arcadia Publishing:
Telephone 843-853-2070
Fax 843-853-0044
E-mail sales@arcadiapublishing.com
For customer service and orders:
Toll-Free 1-888-313-2665

Visit us on the Internet at www.arcadiapublishing.com

This book is dedicated to all who have lived in the Gold Hill area and made it the special place that it is. This is also to my parents, Dorothy and Edwin Powers, and their guidance from the past.

CONTENTS

ACKNOWLEDGMENTS

Although properly acknowledging everyone who contributed over time to the Gold Hill Historical Society (GHHS) and its acquisitions is difficult, there are areas and individuals that stand out. The GHHS Board of Directors was very supportive: Rene Webb, Marge Martin, Glenn and Gloria Ray, Janet Sessions, and officers Anita Brown (president), Sherry Verstrate (vice president), Maureen Smith (treasurer), and Morgan Smith (secretary).

In perusing the historical society's extensive photograph files, I was amazed at the extent and quality. This was due to outstanding volunteer efforts over the years, such as those by Ted Wharton, who created and built the image acquisition files, among other noticeable efforts, along with Linda M. Genaw and her hard work.

Many individuals donated or worked on GHHS's artifact and image collections. Although it is impossible to recognize everyone who so contributed, the following made notable donations: Ted Wharton, Greg Applen, Linda Genaw, Cindy Tilley Faubion, the H. Thompson Mayer estate, Mary Truax Hendricks, and Pearl Walker, among others. Further contributions were made by Winona Shoemaker Nichols, Tom Cushman, the Lyman estate, Alyce Bottelson, Pearl and Delos Walker, Linda Walker Turner, Jack Martin, Evalyn Christensen Kile, and Philip Thompson.

Janet Sessions stands out with her extraordinary help on this book and its research, not to mention her wonderful enthusiasm and support. Thanks, Janet! Past historical facts can be difficult to precisely pin down. Ted Wharton, Linda Genaw, Charles Johnson, Marge Martin, Joyce Wayland, Sherry Verstrate, and Rene Webb contributed with background research—past and present—and have our appreciation.

On the photographs appearing in this book: unless otherwise noted, all images appear courtesy of the Gold Hill Historical Society. The Southern Oregon Historical Society (SOHS) granted permission to use several images, and Recreation Guide (RG) with Bob Howe (Howe) also furnished images. We also thank Linda Walker Turner, Pearl Walker, Sherry and Dick Verstrate, Becky Estremado, Maria Cooper, and Ted Wharton (again) who directly furnished images.

The professionalism of Arcadia Publishing, especially Devon Weston and my sharp editor Donna Libert, stood out. Last but never least, I am so thankful for the support and boundless energy of my wife Judy, who was instrumental in helping to bring this book to reality.

On behalf of the Gold Hill Historical Society, thank you all!

INTRODUCTION

When the news reached north of the 1848 gold discovery at Sutter's Mill in California, numerous settlers left to seek their fortunes there. On the way down, they panned and searched for gold, and a few stayed in Southern Oregon.

The early 1852 news of gold discovered at Rich Gulch in what is now Jacksonville brought miners into the area from all over. Among them was William T'Vault, who built a log cabin with a post office that year at Dardanelles as the first settlement, becoming the first postmaster in Southern Oregon, among other credits. Located across the Rogue River from what later became Gold Hill, the name Dardanelles apparently came from the strait between the Black and Mediterranean Seas. Although T'Vault moved to nearby Jacksonville in 1857, Dr. George Ambrose, John Swinden, and a few others settled around Dardanelles with their families. Sparsely populated at the time, two tiny settlements with stagecoach stops then existed on opposite banks of the mighty Rogue, Dardanelles and Rock Point. In 1852, John B. White had established this tiny settlement named for the huge rocks at its point on the Rogue's banks. Rock Point had its own hotel, a general store, blacksmith shop, and residences, and was quite similar to Dardanelles.

In the 1850s, prospectors began discovering gold on the nearby creeks that fed into the Rogue, including Galls, Sardine, Foots, and Kane Creeks—with the precious metal found in 1857 on Sardine Creek. Both Galls and Foots Creeks were named after the specific pioneer who settled on that particular tributary, Sardine Creek probably came from the many miners who packed its banks, and although originally named T-Vault Creek, that tributary's name was changed to Kane Creek in honor of a Dr. Kane, another settler there. All the area creeks and watersheds—and indeed nearly all in Jackson and adjacent Josephine County—produced gold. Some would stand far above the others.

As more miners and settlers moved in, conflict grew between pioneers and Native Americans. There were bitter skirmishes, several major battles, and violent brutality on both sides. In 1856, the Indians were removed from the Rogue Valley to southeastern Oregon. Located 5 miles northeast of Gold Hill, Sams Valley is named for Chief Sam of the Rogue River Indians, who signed the peace treaty. The rich lands of these plains supplied excess grains, livestock, and dairy products that helped support the area.

In 1857, 41-year-old Irish immigrant Thomas Chavner (pronounced "kav-ner") purchased a donation land claim near Dardanelles and later acquired a ranch on the same side. In January 1860, as the story goes, two ranch hands were searching for stray horses in the hills above Chavner's property on the Gold Hill side. One of the men, James Willis "Bill" Hay, sat down to look around. He became fascinated by a "dull, yellowish something" embedded throughout the rock he was sitting on, and noticed that the surrounding outcropping was littered with rocky yellow streaks. Hay later showed a piece of the brilliant white rock to his boss, Thomas Chavner, who immediately recognized it as being houndstooth quartz heavily laced with gold!

Five men—partners George Ish, James Hay, O. J. Graham, A. J. Long, and Thomas Chavner—quickly filed the first gold mine claim, but by the following night—owing to one partner having a strong liking for liquor—150 men had staked claims with roped sections over the entire mountain. Cries of "Gold! Gold! Gold!" filled the air, and the gold rush was on. The mine became known as the Gold Hill Pocket (on Gold Hill Mountain), located above the present town site. This discovery near the hill's top was probably the most famous of the regional gold pocket discoveries. The ore was white, almost transparent quartz, and the pocket was heavy with free gold. Some rock was so knit together with threads of gold that pieces would not separate when hit by a sledgehammer. A total of $700,000 ($40 million in today's dollars) was carried out in fine jewelry-like gold and quartz nuggets over nine months, but the pocket soon became exhausted; subsequent operations failed to find further paying rock.

Miners and their families swarmed around like bees, and the town of Gold Hill quickly arose. The first steam quartz mill to reduce the rock was brought to Dardanelles, and numerous sightseers came daily to see the new machinery. A daily stage run from Jacksonville was started. When the nearby gold strike dissipated, however, and numbers of stamp mills came into existence, Dardanelles lost its influence. The rough miners fished the Rogue River for salmon, drank hard whiskey, bartered with gold, and resolved their differences indifferently or by bare knuckles and bottles. Stagecoaches rattled by, blacksmiths hammered, stamp mills clattered, and sawmills screeched.

An astute businessman, Chavner had bought out most of his partners early on, and with his share of the profits—along with foreclosing on unpaid land loans—he acquired nearly 2,000 acres of prime land along the Rogue River. He diversified into operating hotels, saloons, general stores, and extensive ranching operations, and it was said he owned 3 miles of land to what is now Central Point. He caused the Centennial Toll Bridge to be built across the Rogue in 1876, which he operated until selling it to the county 12 years later. When the Oregon and California Railroad came to Jackson County, it was Chavner who sold the land in 1883 for its right-of-way and depot, located across the Rogue from Dardanelles. He and his wife Rosa recorded the plat map in January 1884 for the town of Gold Hill, laying it out with lots of 50 feet by 100 feet. Deeding the streets and alleyways to the public, the Chavners sold off land parcels for homes and buildings to start the new town.

The railroad's choice of Gold Hill for a center depot drew people away from the neighboring settlements of Rock Point, Dardenelles, and Sams Valley. To appease nearby Rock Point, the railway sponsored a contest to name the new town, with the prize being a building lot. John Griffiths, brother of Margaret Griffiths Patrick (who would have a school named after her), submitted the name of Gold Hill for the prominent feature above the town. Gold Hill quickly developed into a bustling town with homes, bars, hotels, restaurants, warehouses, and numerous merchants. With the railroad in Gold Hill, residents of Rock Point—just three miles away—slowly moved there; Dardanelles also passed into oblivion.

Thomas Chavner died on his ranch in 1888 at age 72, leaving four adult children. On February 12, 1895, the City of Gold Hill was incorporated. The Rogue River Telephone Company built telephone lines in 1895, and the *Gold Hill News* was established in 1897. A fire department was organized one year later. The 1890s also brought schools and more gold discoveries, along with new methods in deep-mining techniques. The 20th century gave rise to a sewer system, electric lights, a city waterworks project, and Gold Ray Dam.

In 1900, Col. Frank H. Ray persuaded his brother, Dr. C. R. Ray, to inspect a gold mine in Southern Oregon. With a positive report, the two brothers bought the Braden Mine near the town, along with land and the rights to a power site to be constructed on the Rogue River. A wealthy New Yorker, Colonel Ray was an organizer and vice president of the American Tobacco Company and easily raised the necessary money to build the power station. The capital came not only from the company but also by selling securities on the New York Stock Exchange. They chose Tolo as the site for the dam—4 miles above the city, where the river leaves the valley basin. In 1902, work began on the original dam as a cofferdam was constructed to divert the rushing river. Laborers next jammed large timbers into bedrock and backfilled this with rocks to create a solid log barrier that held back the water. When completed, the log dam was 17 feet tall and 350 feet long. The impounded river lifted the Rogue's surface enough to divert it through a powerhouse, whose unique rope-driven turbines created the first hydroelectric power in Southern Oregon. Seeing the potential in selling electricity throughout the area, along with powering the gold mines and mills, starting in 1904 the Rays' Condor Water and Power Company furnished power to Grants Pass, Gold Hill, Medford, Jacksonville, Central Point, and Ashland. With different owners, the plant produced hydroelectric power for the area for nearly 70 years.

During the early 1900s, gold mining continued as an important commercial activity surrounding Gold Hill. Miners and their families came to town from the surrounding creeks and hills for their supplies, goods, and entertainment. The local *Gold Hill News* was filled with stories about new strikes. It was run for a time by Ben Hur Lampman, future longtime editor of *The Oregonian* and poet laureate of Oregon. In 1910, a brick schoolhouse—later named Hanby School in honor of longtime teacher A. J. Hanby—was constructed. First serving all 12 grades, it later became the high school; over 100 years later, the building is still used as an administrative office.

The town was busy and prosperous. A dramatic fire nearly destroyed Gold Hill's business center in 1915 (caught by a photographer), but the townsfolk quickly rebuilt. By the mid-1920s, the gold mines had played out, but the employment slack was taken up by Del Rio Orchards at Rock Point, a tile factory, and the operations of a large cement plant, constructed in 1915 by the Beaver Portland Cement Company. Employing up to 150 people primarily from the Gold Hill area, these operations continued for 60 years.

Located strategically between Grants Pass and Ashland—and the site of the county's regional airport in 1930—nearby Medford had already become the county seat and the region's major city. Although the timber dam had been replaced with a concrete one in 1941, Pacific Power closed the Gold Ray Dam facility in 1972, deeding the facilities and acreage to the county. The cement plant's closing in 1967 caused a shock to the close-knit community, and some years would pass before Gold Hill stabilized. With cutbacks also in lumbering and milling activity, Gold Hill struggled to retain its residents. The Jeddeloh Brothers Sweed Mills, which first manufactured sawmill equipment, developed over time into the successful Sweed Machinery operations. This enterprise is located in the heart of the town and is the only major manufacturing industry left. Rock Point changed from a third-generation pear orchard in the early 1990s to the extensive winery and grapevines of Del Rio Vineyards. Where thirsty stagecoach passengers were once served shots of whiskey, the historical Rock Point Hotel now offers premium wines for tourists to taste. T'Vault's Dardanelles is now marked only by a plaque; Tolo has disappeared.

Although it would eliminate an environmentally sensitive slough, in 2010 the Jackson County commissioners agreed to remove Gold Ray Dam; its demolition is now complete. The population of Gold Hill is 1,100, about what it was a century ago. In recent years, folks attracted by small-town life, the exquisite surroundings, and the legendary Rogue River have discovered Gold Hill. Its charm and history cannot be denied.

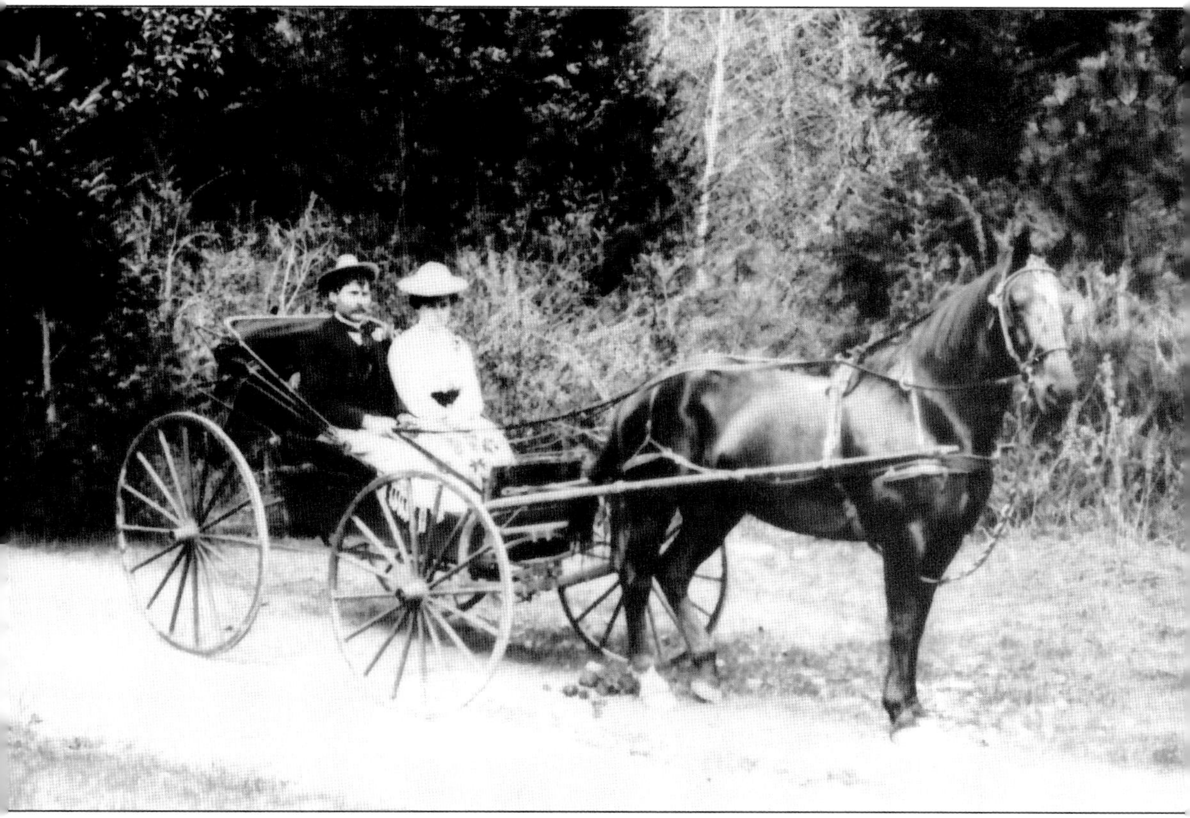

Many images in this book date from a time when horses and buggies were used for transportation, and gold nuggets could buy dinner. Although life was simpler then, physical labor and long hours were the rule. Relaxation meant a ride in the country, going to a dance, or listening to a band. In this photograph, Toots and Lulu Dusenberry are out for a ride in 1902—before their marriage on Sardine Creek, 2 miles from Gold Hill.

One

The Chavners and Other Pioneer Families

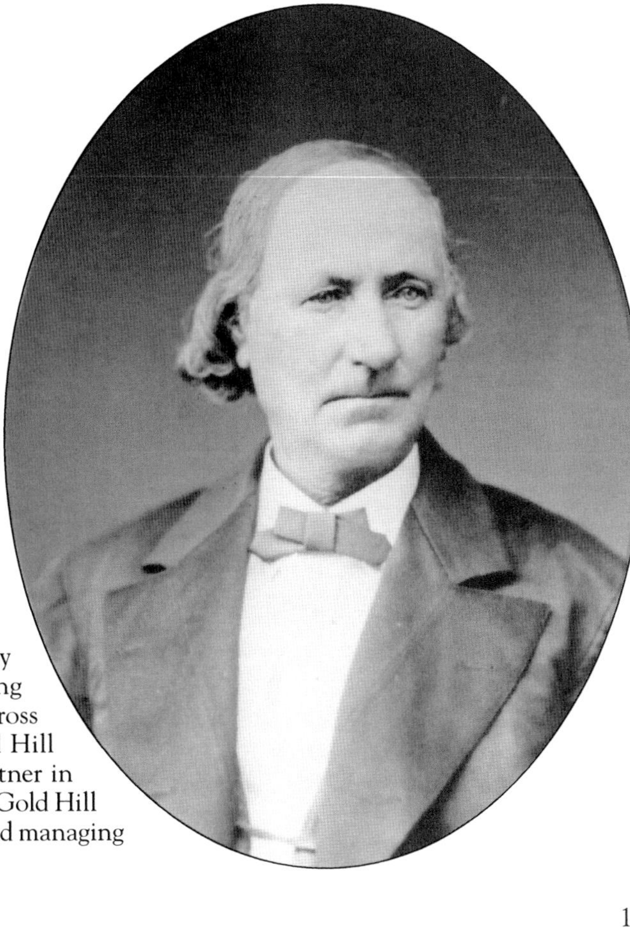

Founder of Gold Hill and pioneer Thomas Chavner had lived an adventurous life even before migrating to the area. Born in Ireland in 1814, he had been a cabin boy on riverboats, a trapper with Kit Carson, a Comanche interpreter, and a fighter in the Mexican War. Chavner arrived in the Rogue Valley in 1856. He soon started acquiring land near Dardanelles, directly across the Rogue River from where Gold Hill is now. He had both luck (as a partner in the first major gold strike, the 1860 Gold Hill Pocket) and skill (acquiring lands and managing various business operations).

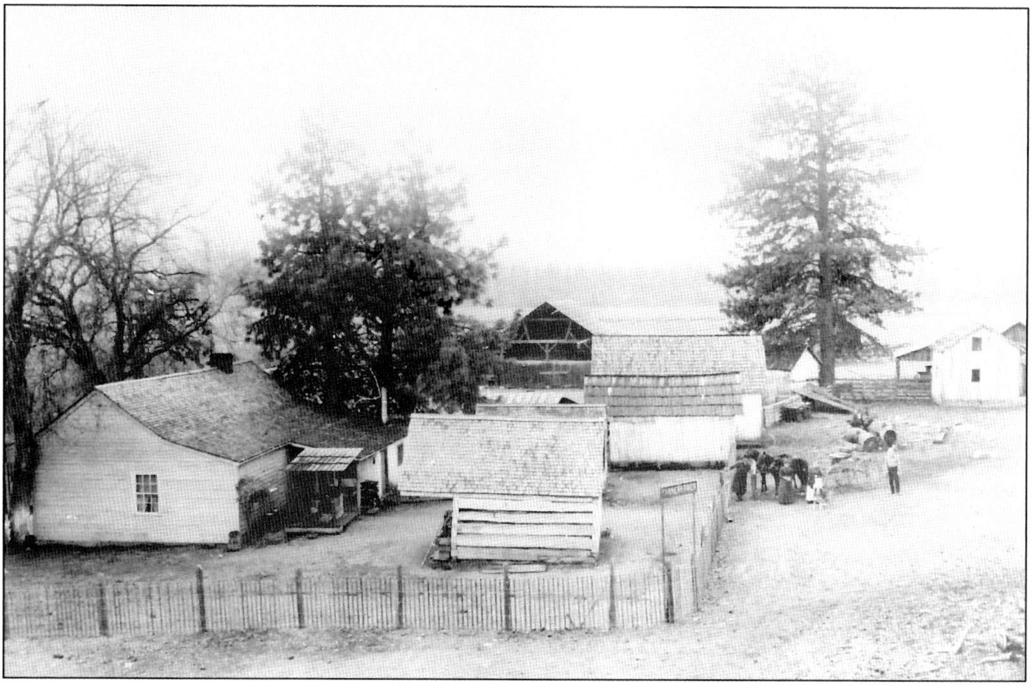

Built in the early 1850s, this home site by the Dardanelles was acquired by Thomas Chavner in 1857. With his acumen, money from the gold find found its way into more land holdings. Ranchers came to Chavner for loans, which he kindly granted. If they did not or could not repay, he expected their acreage and foreclosed. By both this method and straight purchase, Chavner acquired large blocks of land.

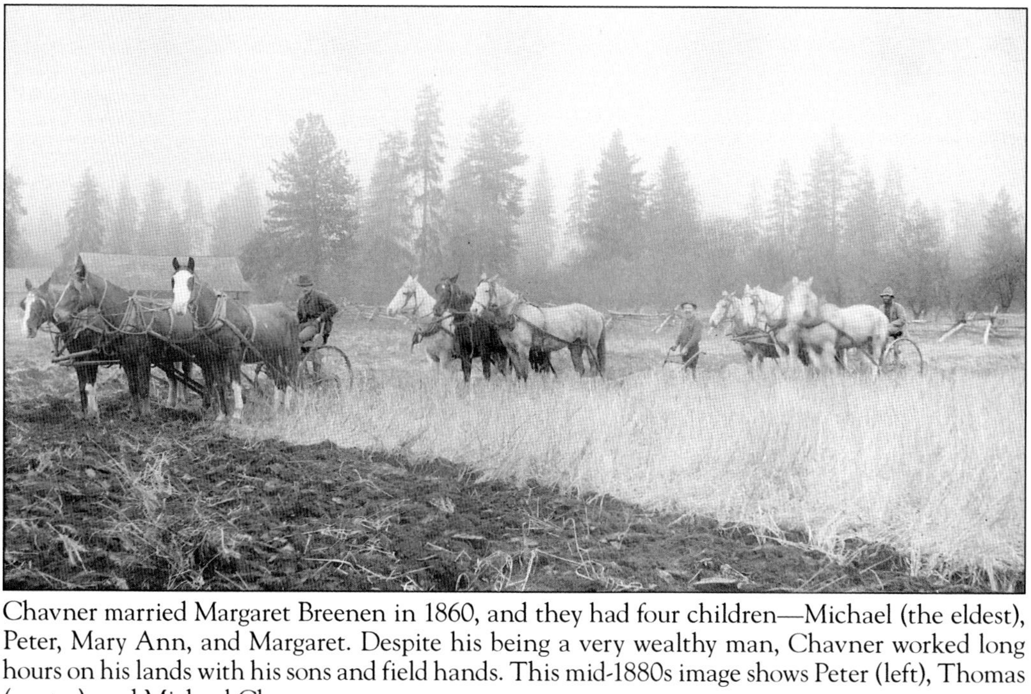

Chavner married Margaret Breenen in 1860, and they had four children—Michael (the eldest), Peter, Mary Ann, and Margaret. Despite his being a very wealthy man, Chavner worked long hours on his lands with his sons and field hands. This mid-1880s image shows Peter (left), Thomas (center), and Michael Chavner.

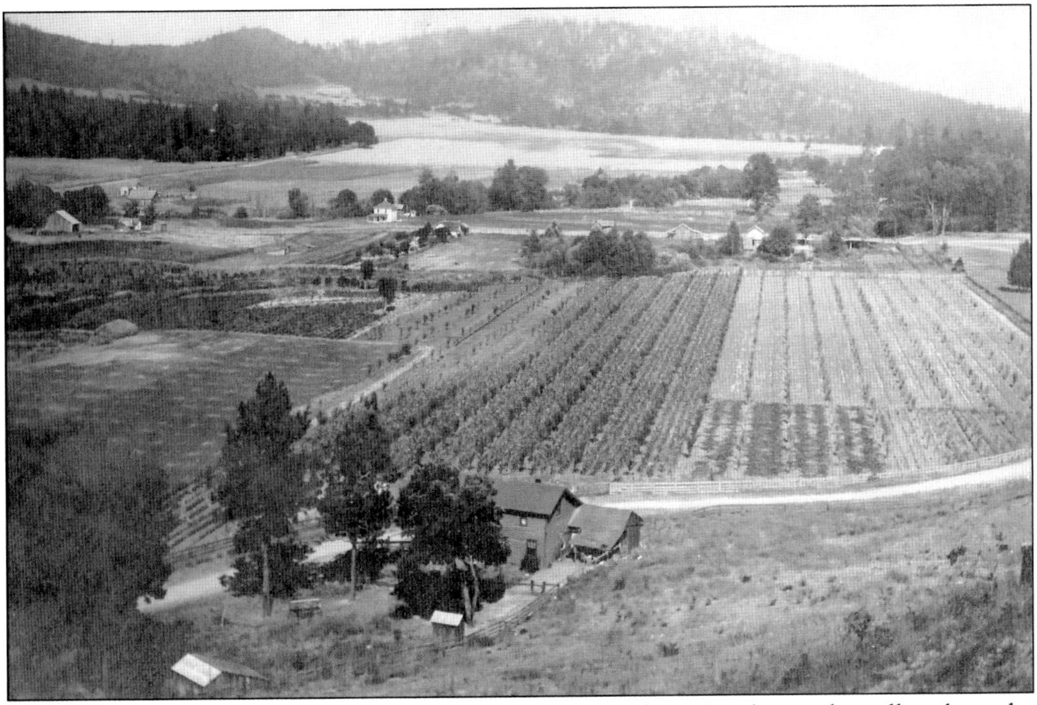

Chavner's land holding grew to 2,000 acres by 1880, stretching 3 miles up the valley along the Rogue River to Central Point. He owned farms, ranches, orchards, and different businesses, from toll bridges and blacksmith shops to hotels and bars. This is one of his orchards around 1904. Since the 1950s, Interstate 5 cuts through the middle. Dardanelles is to the right.

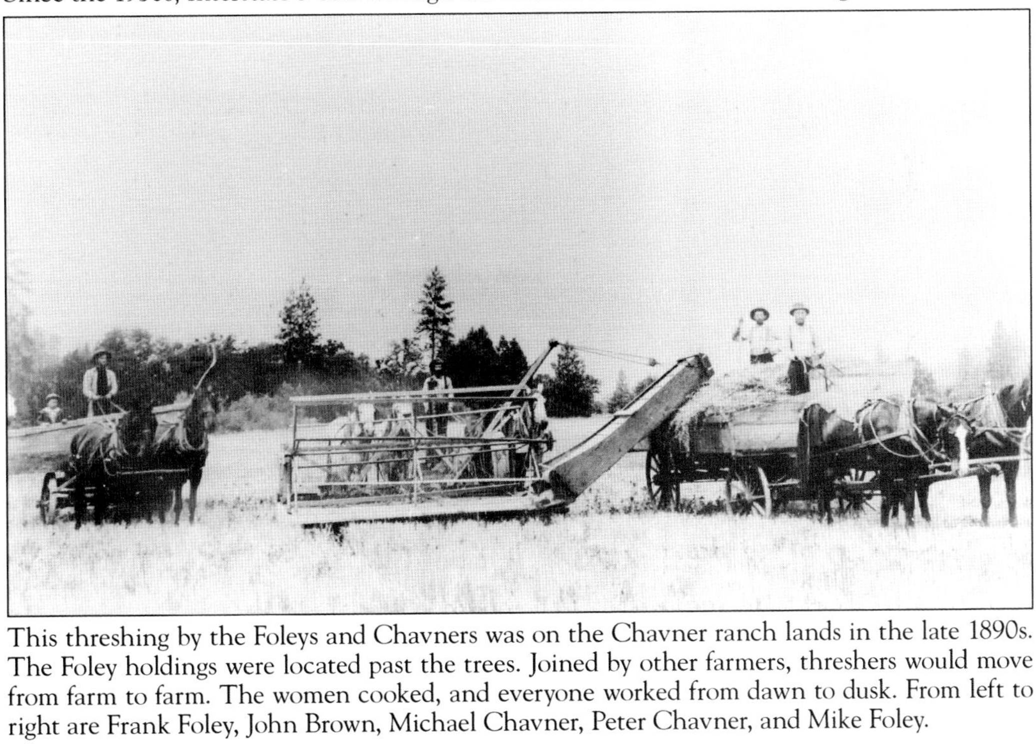

This threshing by the Foleys and Chavners was on the Chavner ranch lands in the late 1890s. The Foley holdings were located past the trees. Joined by other farmers, threshers would move from farm to farm. The women cooked, and everyone worked from dawn to dusk. From left to right are Frank Foley, John Brown, Michael Chavner, Peter Chavner, and Mike Foley.

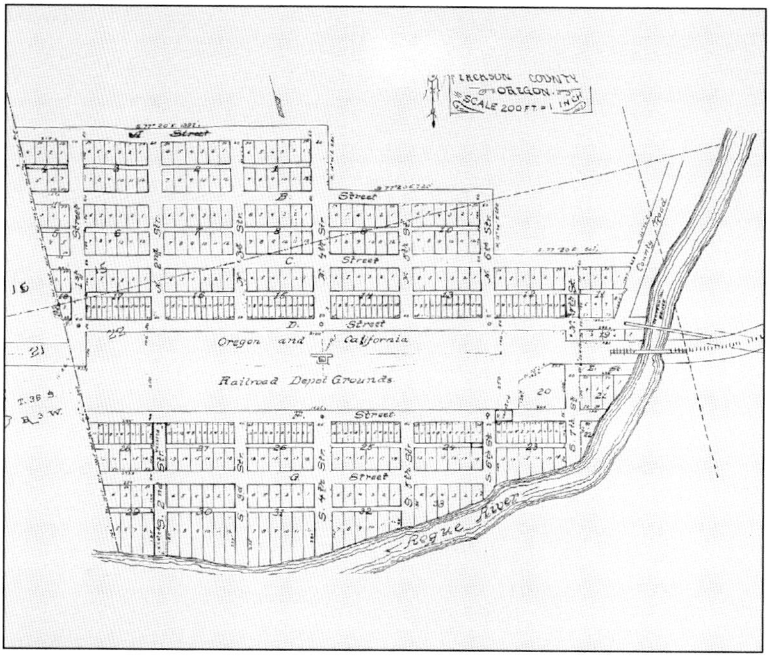

Margaret Breenen Chavner died in 1880, and two years later Thomas Chavner married Rosa Riley. In 1883, he sold 17 acres of land to the railroad for the Gold Hill depot, right-of-way, freight office, and stockyard. On January 7, 1884, the Chavners recorded this plat map survey on another 80 acres for the town, donating the streets and alleys to the public and selling individual lots to people.

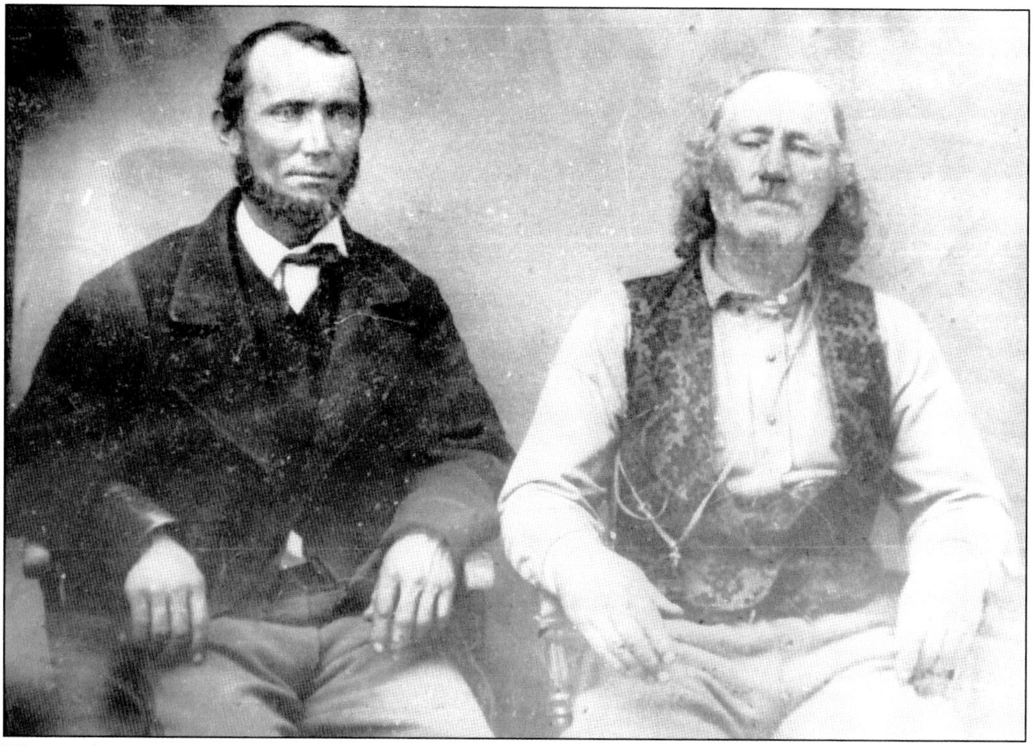

This mid-1880's image shows Michael, the eldest son of Thomas Chavner, with his father. Neither Michael nor Peter Chavner married, and both lived on the Chavner ranch. Their farming lives were obviously satisfying, as Michael lived to 85 and Peter to 77. Thomas Chavner died on September 8, 1888, missing the later prosperity that the town experienced with a renewed interest in hard rock mining.

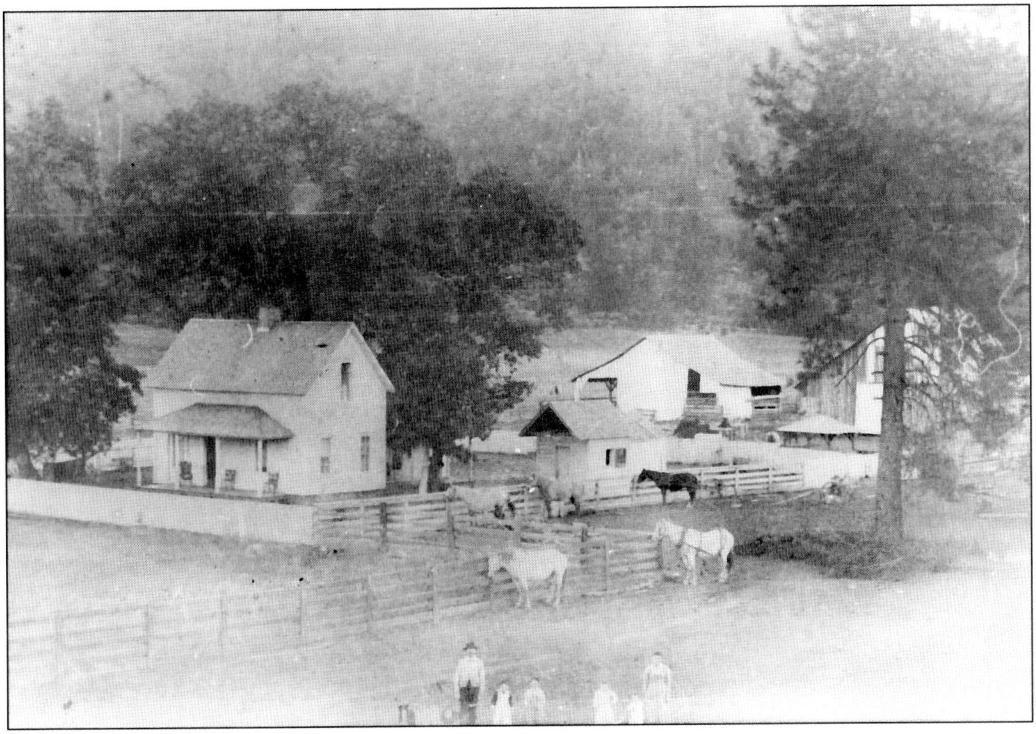

In 1888, Mike Foley bought his farm for $1,200 along what is now Foley Lane by the Dardanelles, building the main house later. The land encompassed over 150 acres, and the Foleys were also early cattle ranchers. This picture was taken in 1899. At the bottom are Mike Foley and his wife Alice, along with their children.

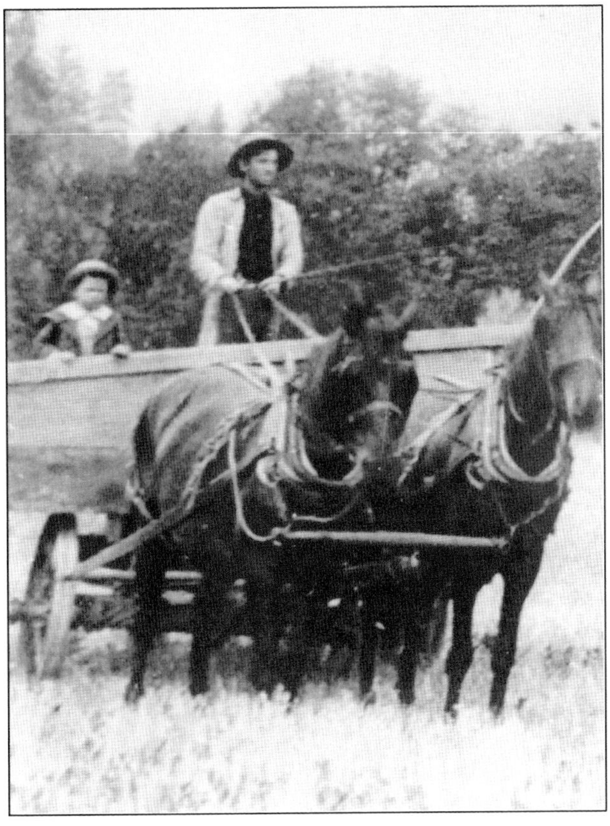

As with other nearby farmers and ranchers, families like the Foleys, Chavners, and others worked and traded services to help each other out. In this close-up view of a horse team used to mow and thresh the Foley fields in 1897, a neighbor of the Foleys and Chavners—John Brown—was helping out as a driver. The small boy is believed to be one of the Foley sons, Frank Foley.

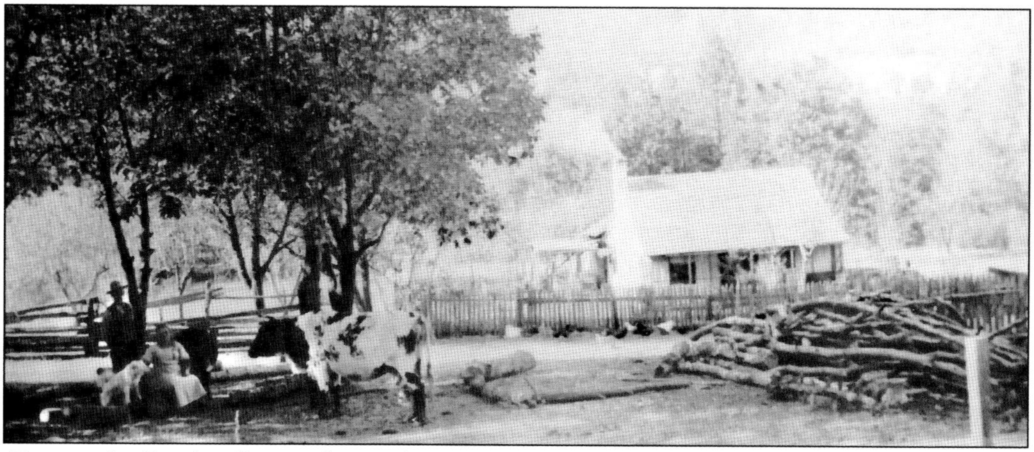

Close to the Dardanelles, Galls Creek emptied into the Rogue River opposite Gold Hill. The Steelman homestead on Galls Creek is shown in this 1880s image. An inscription on the back reads, "Winona & Wesley & Dog in picture, plus the cow. This is our ranch house after Wes fixed it up & don't seem very plain."

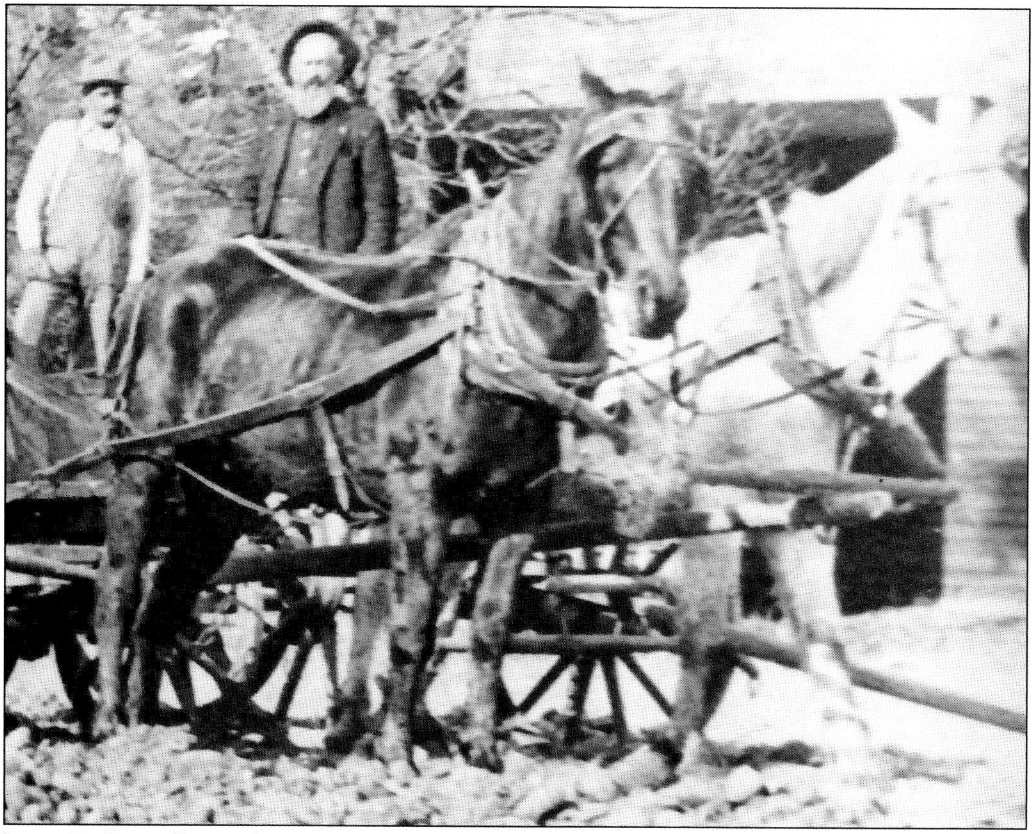

James Willis "Bill" Hay (center) discovered the fabled Gold Hill Pocket in 1860 while working for Thomas Chavner. He soon accepted $5,000 (a large sum at the time) for his share and bought a ranch. Later Hay built a blacksmith shop at Rock Point and shoed horses for the stagecoach line that ran to Northern California and back. In the early 1900s, he moved to Gold Hill and started another blacksmith shop.

Three generations are shown in this early 1900s picture of the Cook family. Clockwise from lower left are Robert A. "Bob" Cook, his sons John and Bob, and his grandson Alva. The Cooks lived on Foots Creek and were known for their placer mining operations. Son Bob was a miner, blacksmith, member of the school board, and two-term mayor of Gold Hill. He built suction dredges for the local miners.

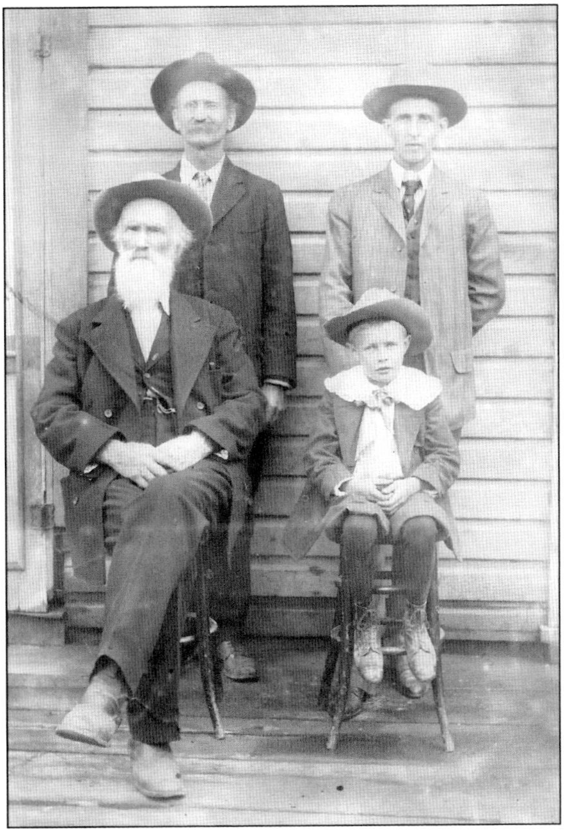

William Richard "Dick" Walker (far right) was another Gold Hill blacksmith in the early 1900s; his daughter Della is the background. When stagecoaches or buggies had mechanical problems, blacksmiths repaired the wooden wheels, shod horses, and repaired the ironwork. This type of labor declined when the railroads put stagecoach lines out of business. Blacksmiths also forged metal items from fire pokers to metal spikes and repaired miners' equipment, including pickaxes, sledgehammers, and stamp mills.

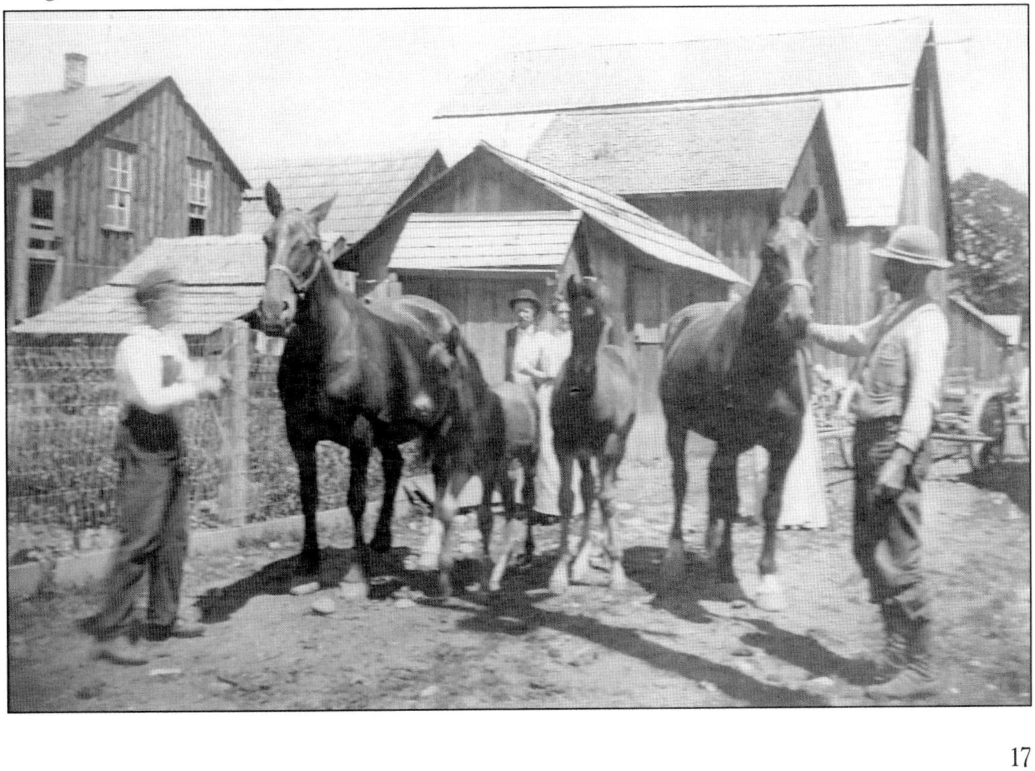

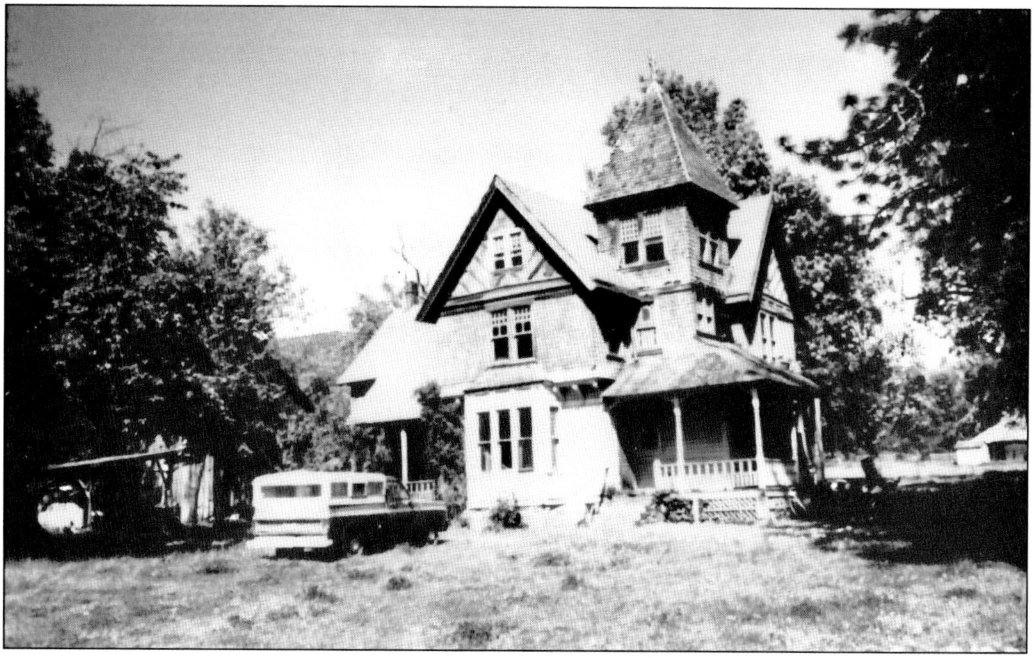

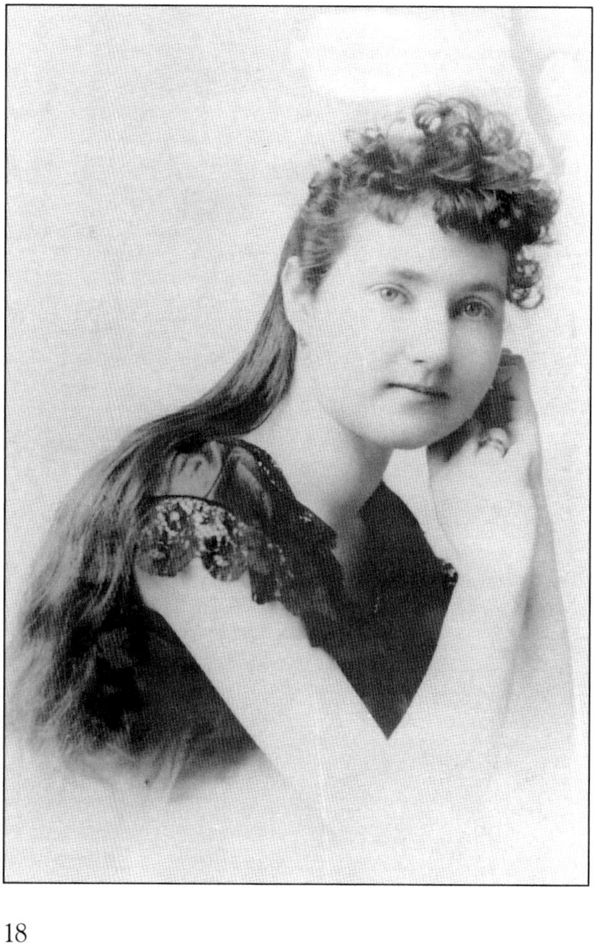

After Thomas Chavner's death, the family ordered a home from a catalog and had it shipped by wagon to be assembled. This beautiful Queen Anne house was then built in 1892 on Blackwell Road close to Gold Hill. Listed on the National Register of Historic Places, the house is occupied today and in exquisite condition, including a beautifully renovated interior. Mary Ann Chavner primarily lived here; after studying art "back east," she returned and used the tower room as her studio.

When her first husband died suddenly after one year of marriage, Mary Ann Chavner never remarried and lived out her life on the Blackwell estate until dying at age 80 in 1946. Early on, her younger sister Margaret split the lands and built an exquisite Queen Anne cottage. She lived in this separate dwelling, both sisters having their own tastes and individuality.

After her father's death, Margaret Chavner studied music at the Cincinnati Conservatory and Boston's New England Conservatory of Music. She played the piano for one Chautauqua season in Ashland and gave piano lessons. After her first husband died, Margaret married William Thompson in 1906. This photograph is from the late 1880s.

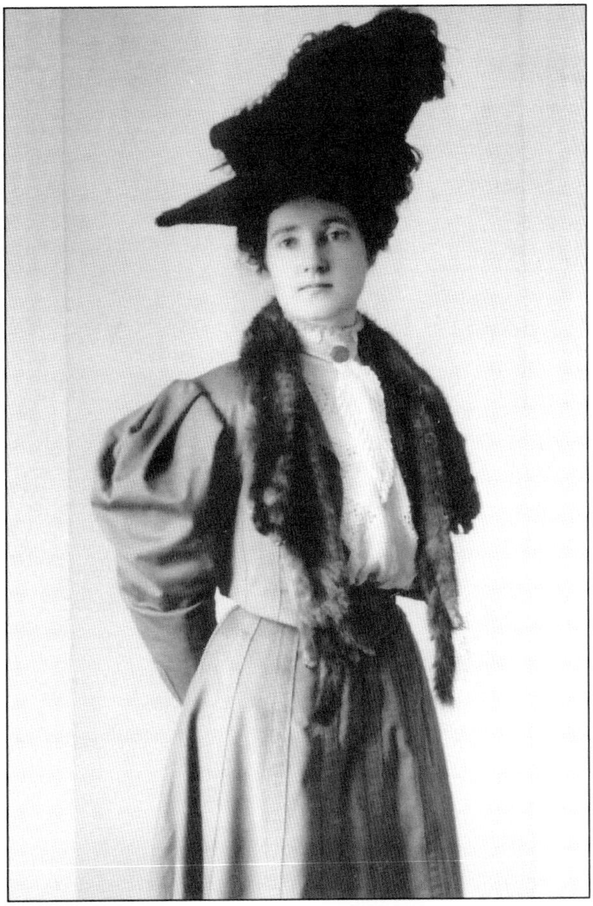

William Thompson had an interest in the Blue Ledge Mine, 4 miles south of the California state line in the upper Applegate River watershed, where he and Margaret spent their honeymoon and first year of marriage. Thompson (left) is driving his buggy from town to the copper mine in 1906 with his partner, a Mr. Waley.

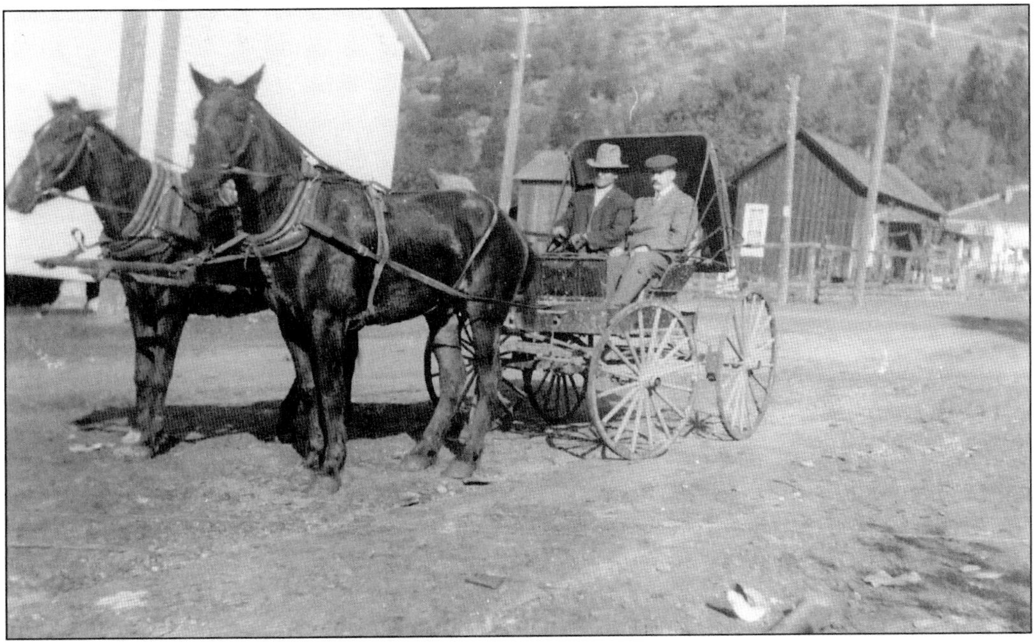

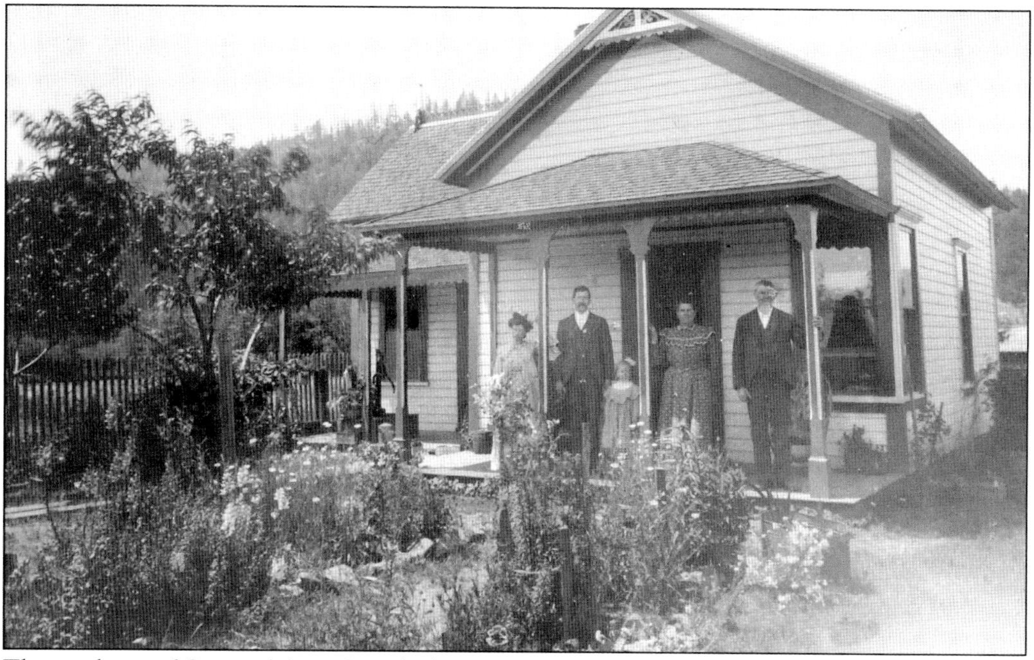

The residence of Oris and Amy Crawford in summer 1903 was in the uphill section above Fourth Avenue. The Crawfords seen here are, from left to right, Amy, Oris, their child Juanita, and Minna and Joshua Crawford (Oris's father and Juanita's grandfather). Although modest in size by today's standards, these residences were felt to be quite sufficient.

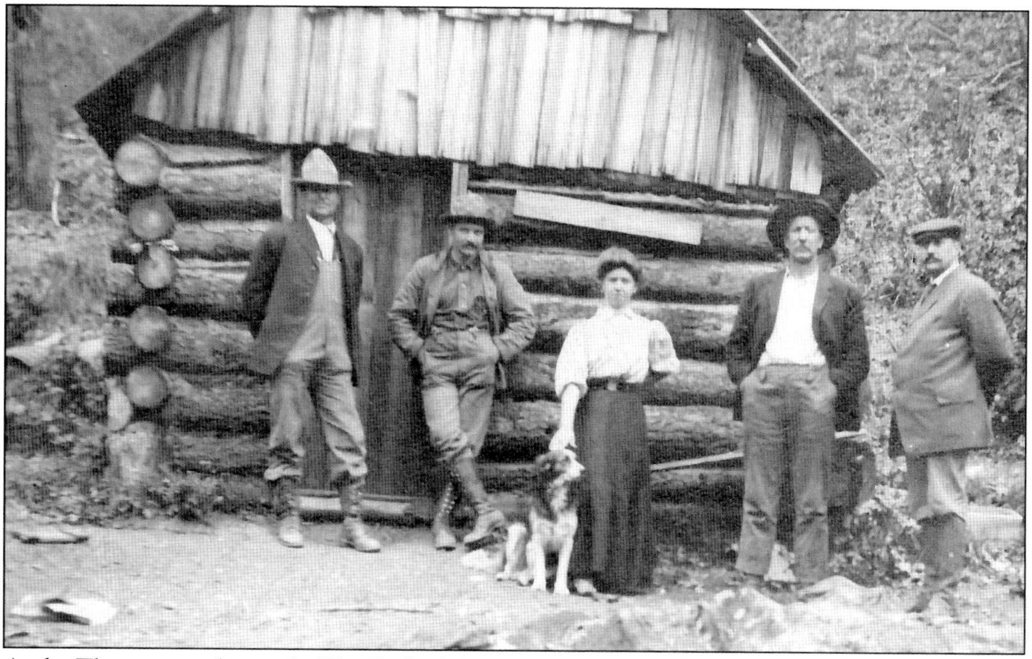

At the Thompson cabin at the Blue Ledge Mine in 1906 are, from left to right, William Thompson, unidentified, Margaret Chavner Thompson, unidentified, and Mr. Waley. The mine was named for the characteristic blue sheen of the copper ore, and it continued operating through 1919, when low copper prices forced its shutdown. Limited spurts of activity occurred in the late 1920s and 1940s.

Two

Prospecting and Gold Mining

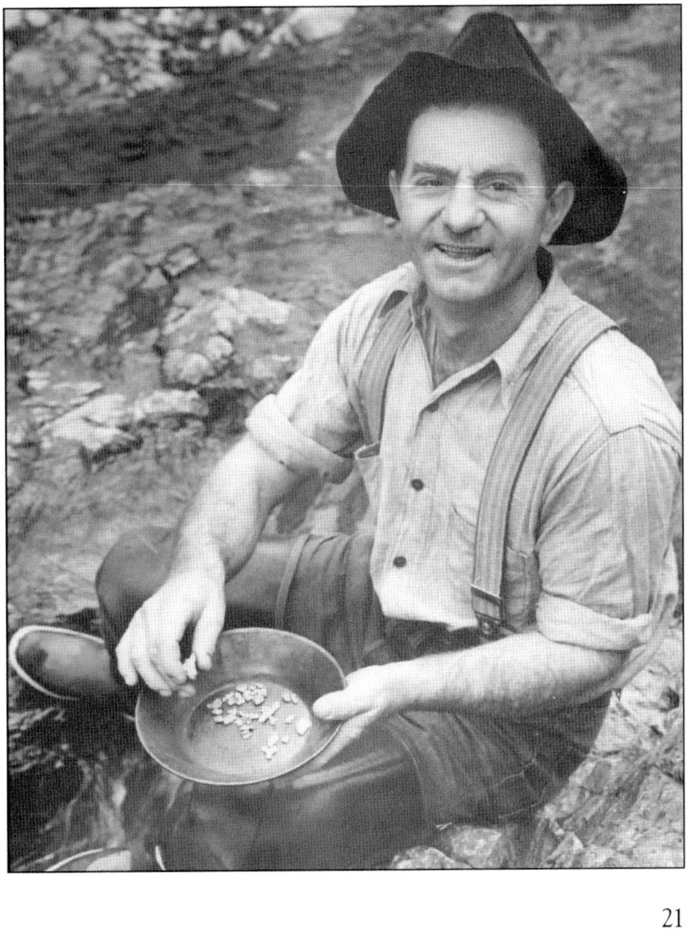

Gold prospecting was hard, risky work. Lester Foley wrote in 1931, "After seventeen years, I'm a little weary, hungry. I'm reduced to Spartan austerity. Have a depressed feeling. Am on a diet of beans. After 17 years my pocket averaged $2.30 a year, excluding expenses; but included frost-bite, fly-bite, and rattlesnake bite; included bleeding fingers, an aching back, a frosted lung, and pain." This 1930s placer miner was Shorty Berrow. Although a sizeable poke is shown in his pan, the amount of gold indicates he is posing. Normally, this much gold was not found in one day.

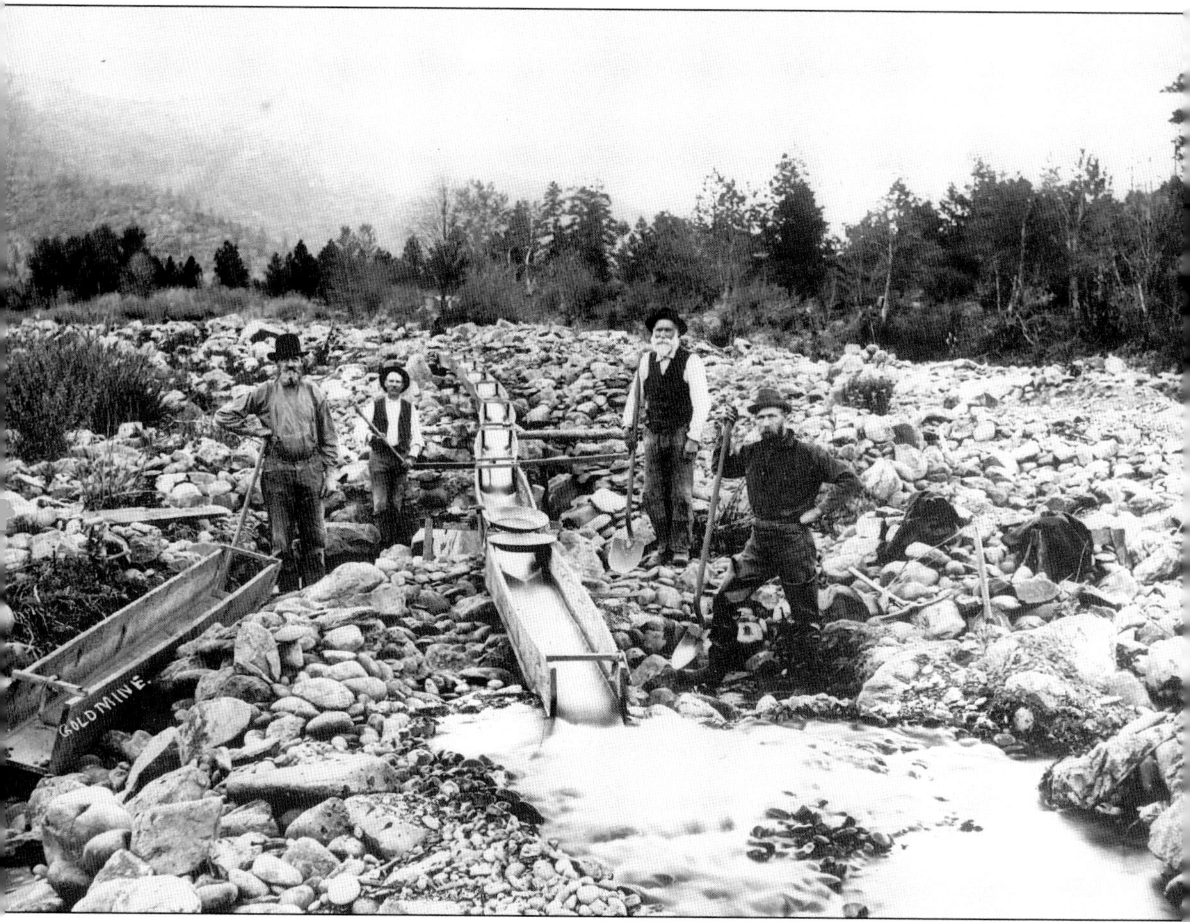

The rich 1860 Gold Hill lode discovery brought an influx of prospectors and their families. Lured by rich prospects, men swarmed along the streams, gullies, and ridges. Pick axes and shovels were about all the tools required—along with water. Getting to the deep gold veins, however, required hard tunneling with numerous exploration shafts. During the 1860s, numbers of new quartz ledges were discovered around the town. Interest died down as people discovered how difficult mining really was. In 1890, however, finds such as the Lucky Bart and Sylvanite mines brought renewed interest, including eastern and international financing of deep-rock mining. These joined other rich mines over time, such as the Braden, Smuggler, and Revenue Pocket, among others. This 1894 placer mine is along the Rogue River, half a mile above Gold Hill. In this photograph, from left to right, are Mr. Potter, Mr. Neff, Sampson McConnell Sr., and Mr. Dearmond. To the left is a sluice box to wash away lighter material, leaving behind gold flakes and gravel to pan. The flume in the middle brought the vital water in from above. (SOHS.)

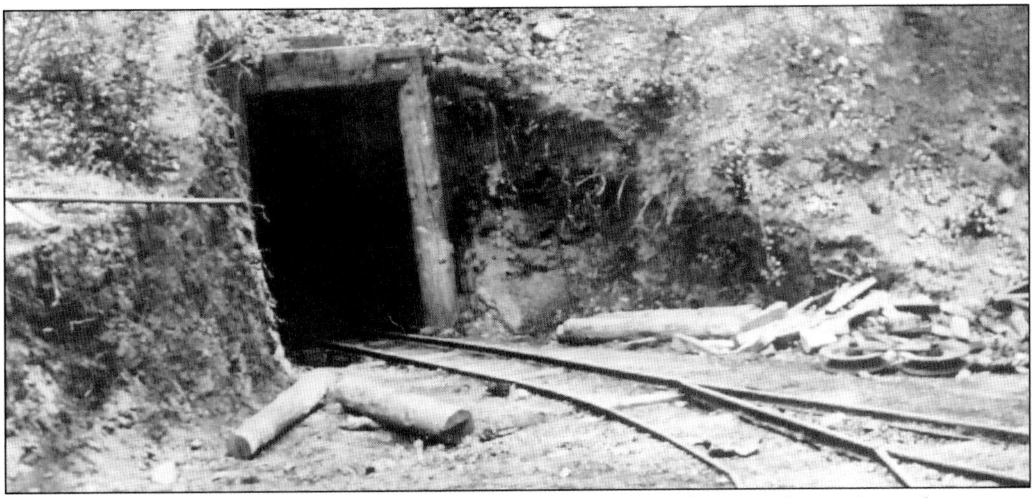

The Grey Eagle mine was located on the left, or west fork, of Sardine Creek just above the present site of the House of Mystery. The lower tunnel of the mine is shown above, and an ore car is inside the tunnel. Although the entrance seems limiting, an entrance tunnel can run hundreds of feet with honeycombed laterals (horizontal openings), crosscuts (at right angles to the strike), raises (openings driven upwards), or winzes (driven down). The mill building below had a jaw crusher and stamp mill inside. Owner William Van Houten is to the far right, directing his workers in setting up a boiler. Deep mining beneath bedrock was much more complicated, expensive, and time-consuming than placer surface work. Both photographs are *c.* 1910

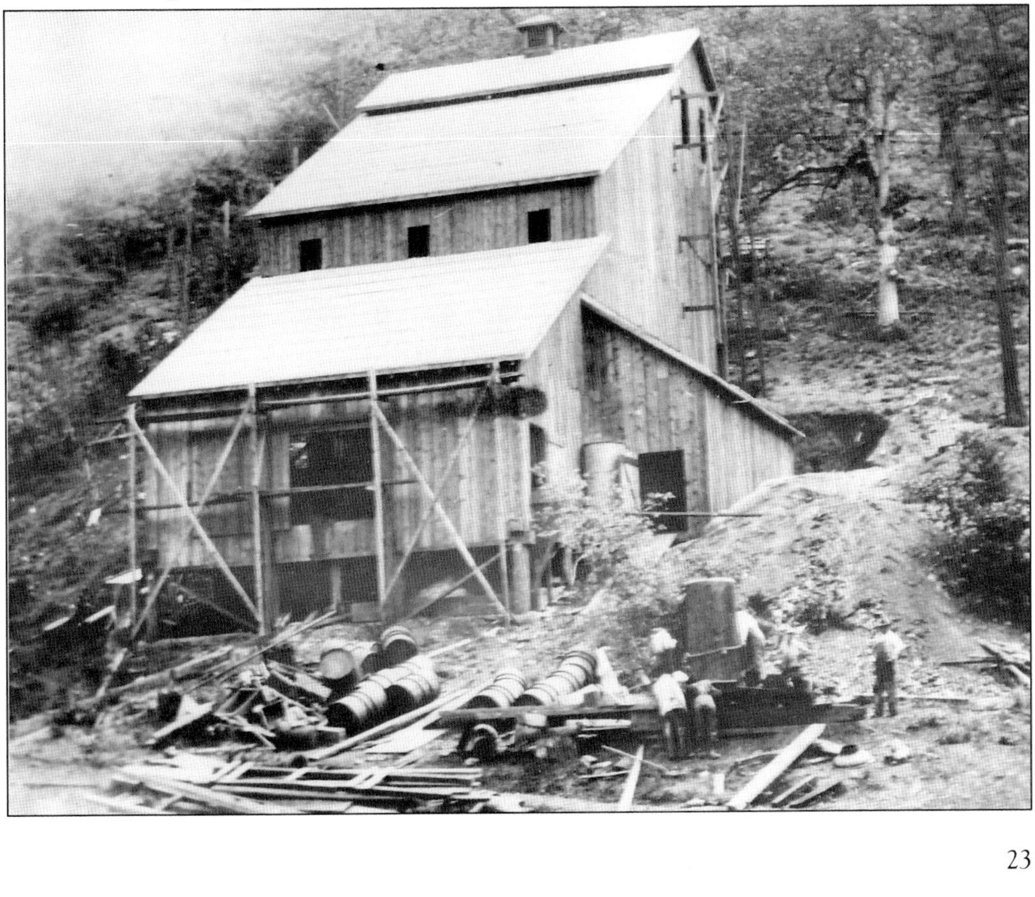

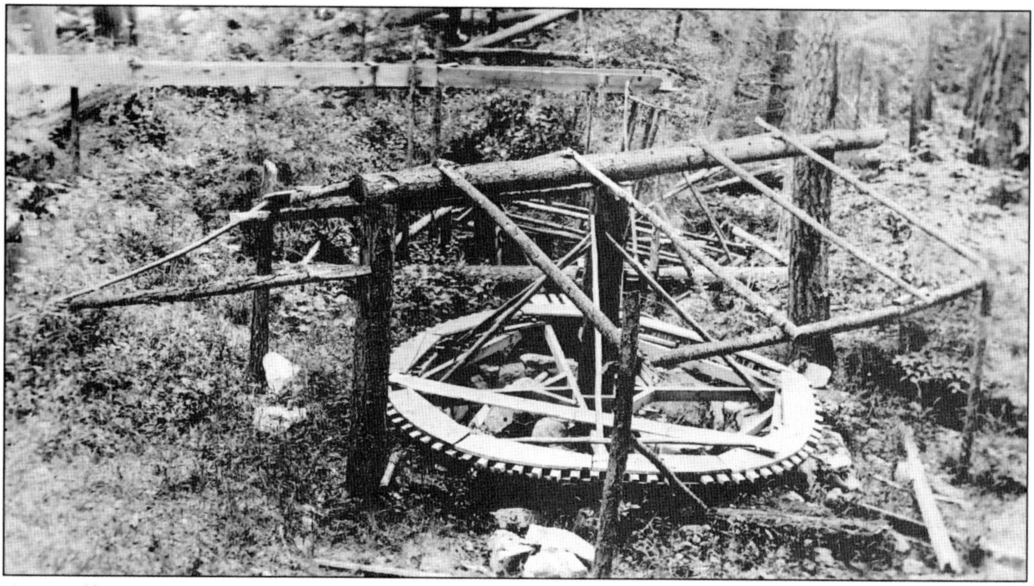

An inefficient but inexpensive way to crush quartz for gold was the arrastra. Workers positioned a circular track of level stones with a low wall built around. A post was positioned in the middle with a horizontal shaft bolted to it. One or more large stones were attached to the shaft, which horses pulled to grind and crack the quartz. Extensive treatments were then needed to separate the gold. (SOHS.)

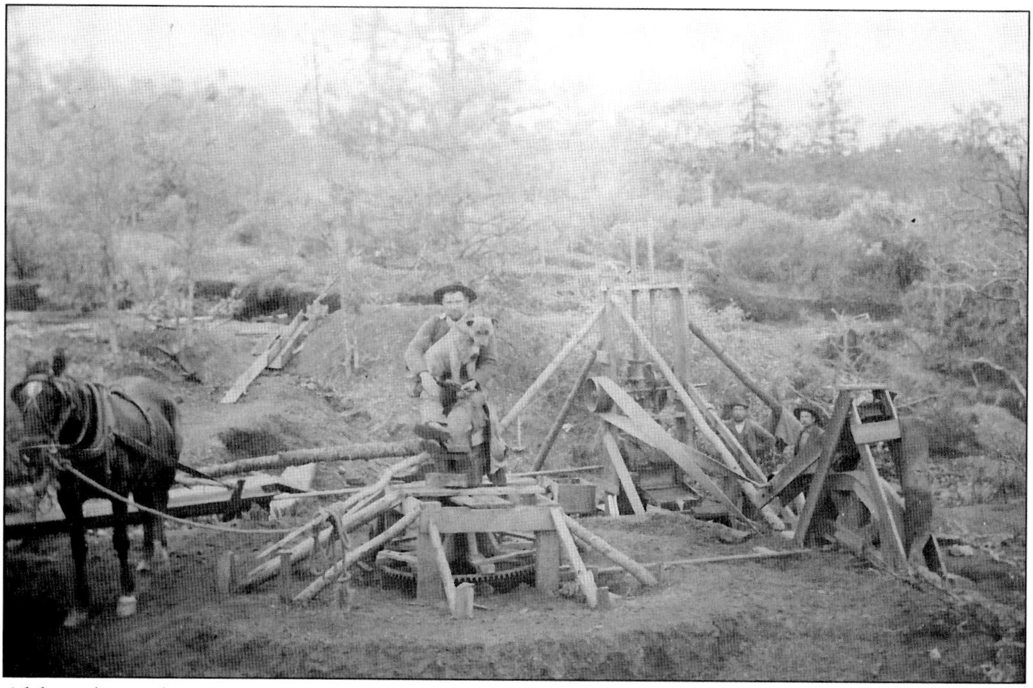

Although much more expensive and requiring a steam engine or electricity, stamp mills soon proliferated around the area. The number of cast iron stamps used to crush the ore categorized them. Run by a one horsepower steam engine, this small, two-stamp mill was used by George Ross in 1897 in the Kane Creek drainage area close to Gold Hill.

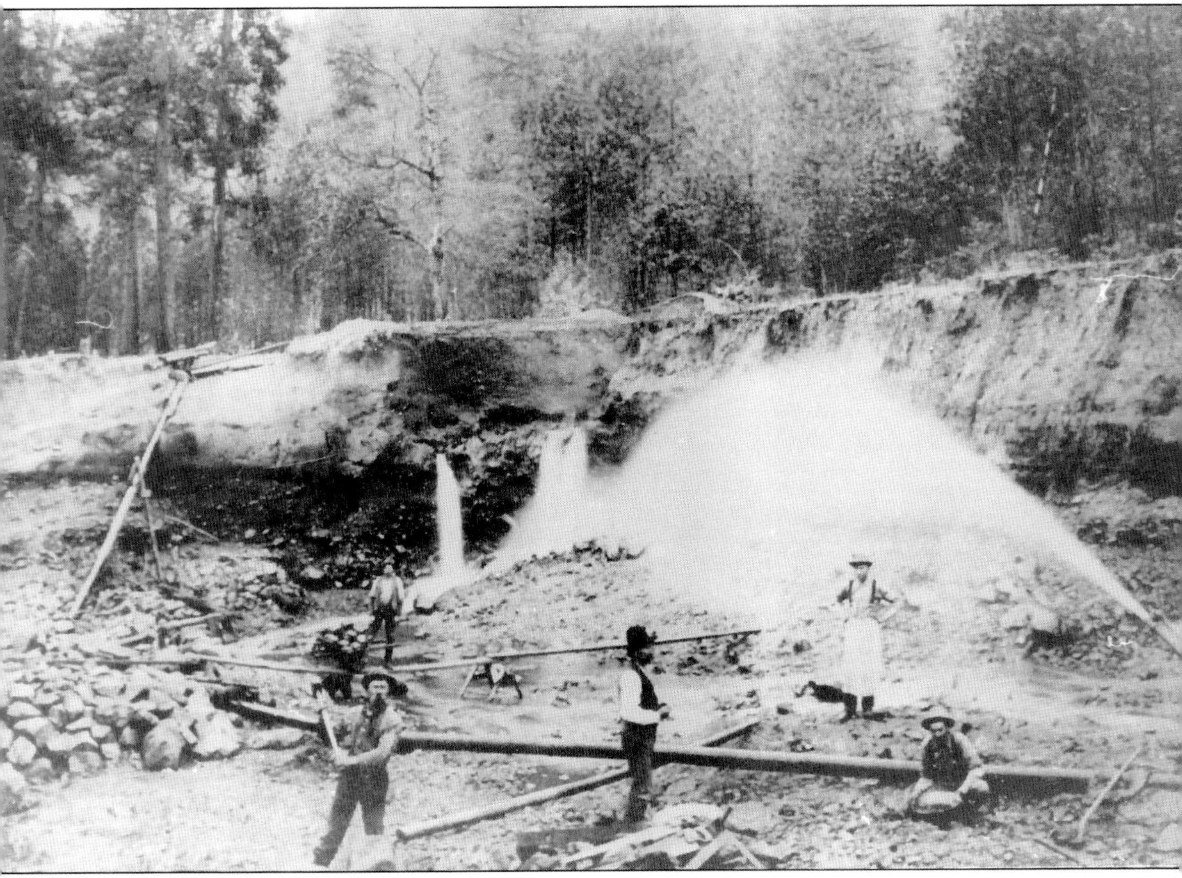

Here the Dusenberry family is working a large hydraulic mining operation on Sardine Creek in 1904. They are, from left to right, Ralph, Joe, Robert L. (father), Cal, Robert, and Sam. The Dusenberry property consisted of 360 acres of deeded land that controlled 1.5 miles of Sardine Creek; a 2.5-mile ditch out of Sardine Creek provided water for the placer operations. The area is now completely hidden and grown over. Hydraulic mining is typically used on gravel banks where pressurized water can break up the gravel, wash it down, and carry it beyond the pit by way of sluices. "Water under a high head" is required. Ground sluicing is another method of washing away the gravel to reveal gold, whereby a stream is diverted against placer ground to erode and wash it through box sluices.

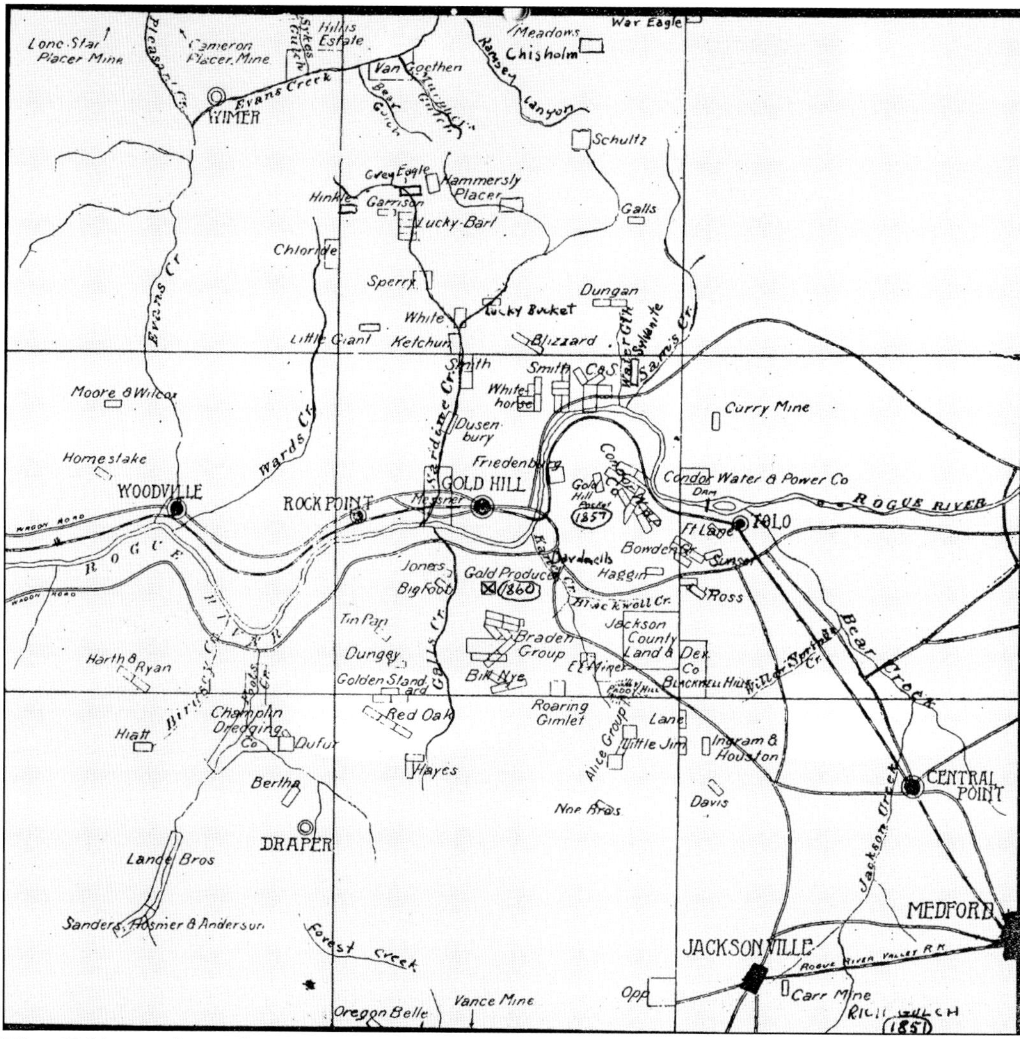

This 1904 map shows the mining operations in the Gold Hill District. Within a 10-mile radius of Gold Hill, numbers of mines came, flourished, and eventually dissipated over time. In the early 1900s, Sardine Creek, Birdseye Creek, Foots Creek, Galls Creek, Kane Creek—all tributaries of the Rogue River—and the Rogue itself had almost countless mining operations. Mines such as Dusenberry were on Sardine Creek, with the Sperry, Lucky Bart, and Grey Eagle on the left fork, while the Hammersly Placer was off the right, or east fork. The Champlin Dredge Company, Dufur, and others were on Foots Creek. The Big Foot, Tin Pan, Golden Stand, and more were around Galls Creek. The Braden Group, Gold Producer, Alice, and Bill Nye mines were on the mountains close or adjacent to Kane Creek, with others such as the Ingram and Houston plus Roaring Gimlet on the southwestern side. The Fredenburg works were just above Gold Hill close to the river, not to mention the "mountain of gold" overlooking the city.

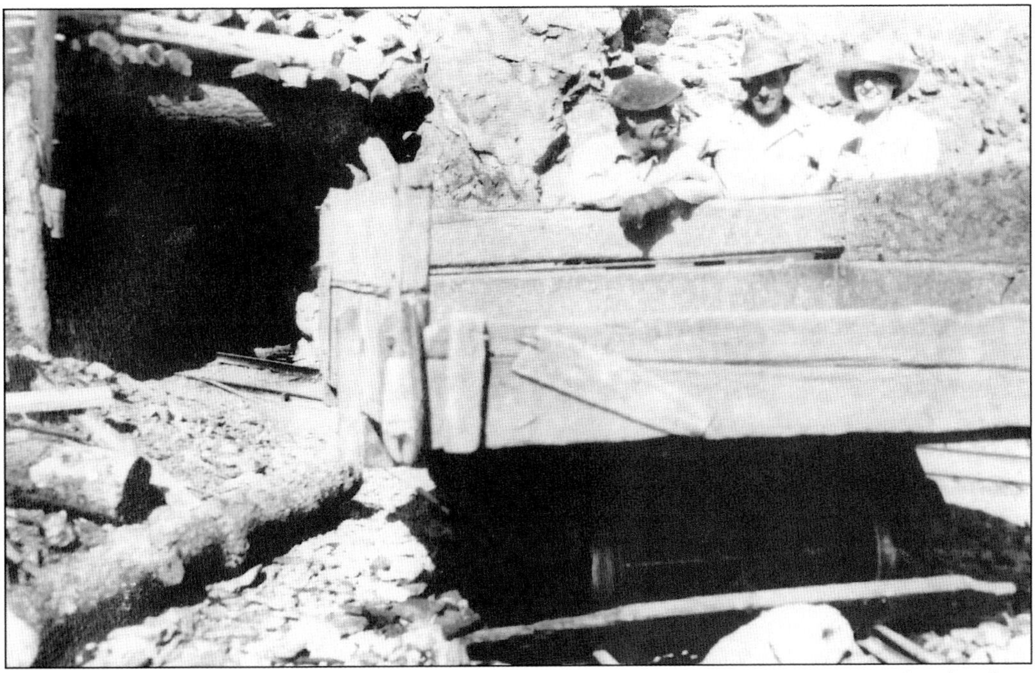

The discoverer of this rich deposit, B. A. Knotts, sold his holdings to Dr. James Braden; he then sold the mining operations in 1900 to the Condor Water and Power Company and C. R. Ray, whose later Gold Ray Dam electrified the entire area, including the Braden Mine as the first all-electric mine in the region. From left to right are Perry Knotts, John Lansden, and Evalynna Stumbo.

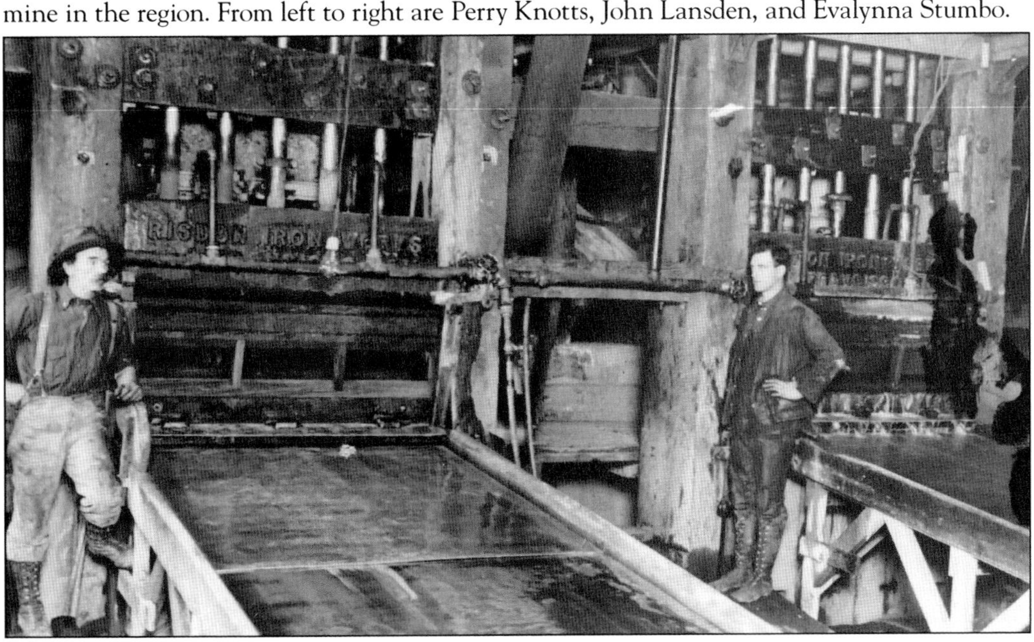

Flotation tables at the Braden Mine's stamp mill separated the gold, black sand, and other minerals from finely crushed ore; the waste material, or mud, flowed into collecting ponds. Although the mine eventually played out, it is estimated that by 1917 the Braden Mine produced $300,000 in gold (millions at today's gold prices). The workers in this 1910 photograph are identified as Perry Knotts (left) and Merton Coffman (right). (SOHS.)

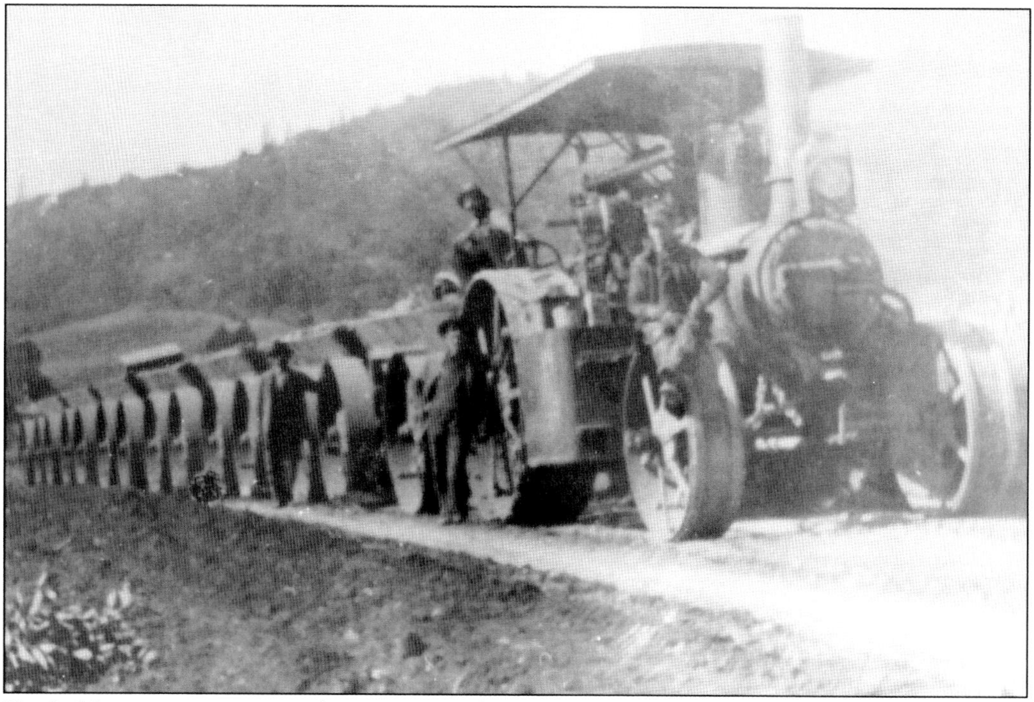

Hauled by a steam tractor, this 1900s Braden Mine ore train carried gold-bearing ore over Foley Lane to the ten-stamp mill close to town. The Braden Mine was at a 1,350-foot elevation, 2 miles south of Gold Hill on Kane Creek. It operated for over 30 years. More than 3,000 feet of tunnels were dug, and numerous different operations were around, as the basin itself was said to be fully 1,000 feet wide.

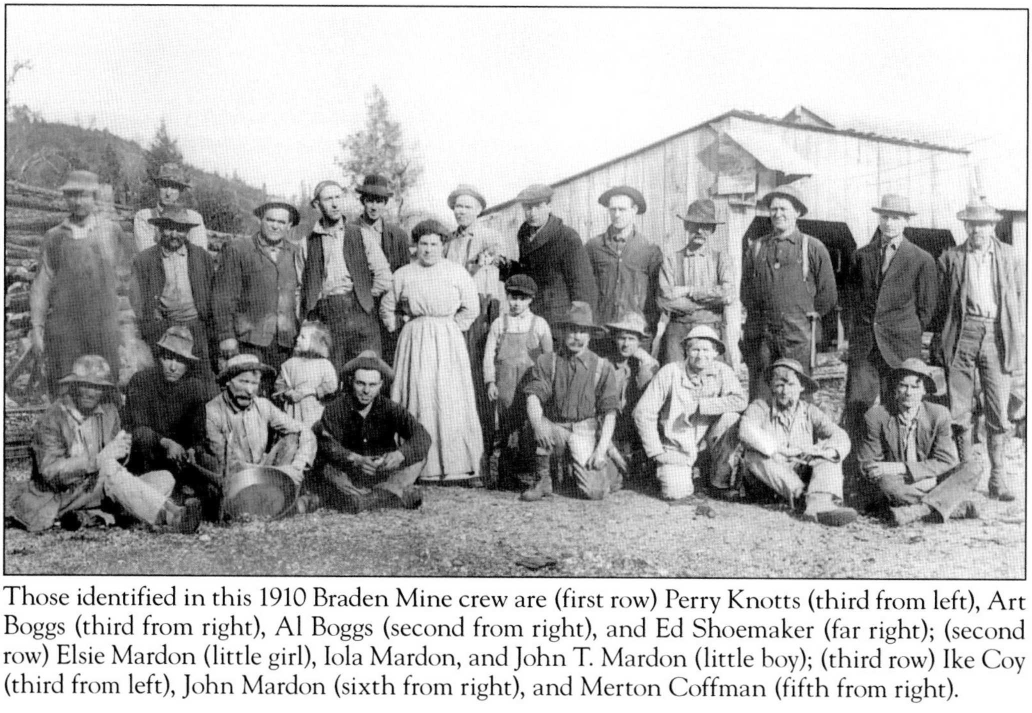

Those identified in this 1910 Braden Mine crew are (first row) Perry Knotts (third from left), Art Boggs (third from right), Al Boggs (second from right), and Ed Shoemaker (far right); (second row) Elsie Mardon (little girl), Iola Mardon, and John T. Mardon (little boy); (third row) Ike Coy (third from left), John Mardon (sixth from right), and Merton Coffman (fifth from right).

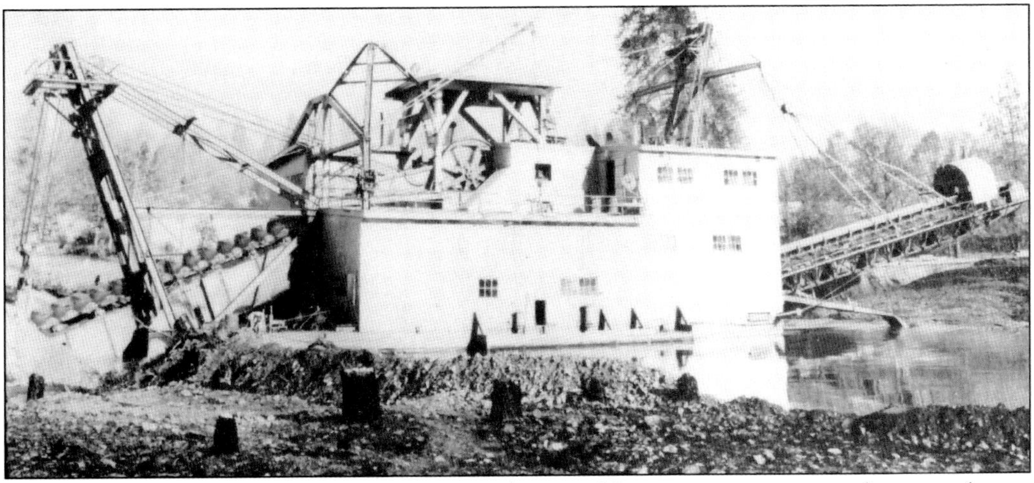

Owned by the Champlin Dredging Company, this wood-burning, steam-powered monster began operating on Foots Creek in 1903. It had 36 eight-foot buckets that moved 2,000 yards of gravel daily. The hull of the "boat" was 122.5 feet long with an 80-foot ladder or digging beam. Two large locomotive boilers provided the steam for powering the digging; when electricity came from Gold Ray Dam, the efficiency greatly increased. Optioning 2 miles of land up Foots Creek from the Rogue, the company had 1,200 total acres to work on. The buckets dropped the gravel into a hopper that shook up the rocks; after aggressive sluicing and water baths, the gold eventually separated from the lighter sediment. Different companies operated dredges on other tributaries such as Kane Creek, and operations continued up until World War II. The creek beds are overgrown now with trees and shrubbery, hiding the mining effects.

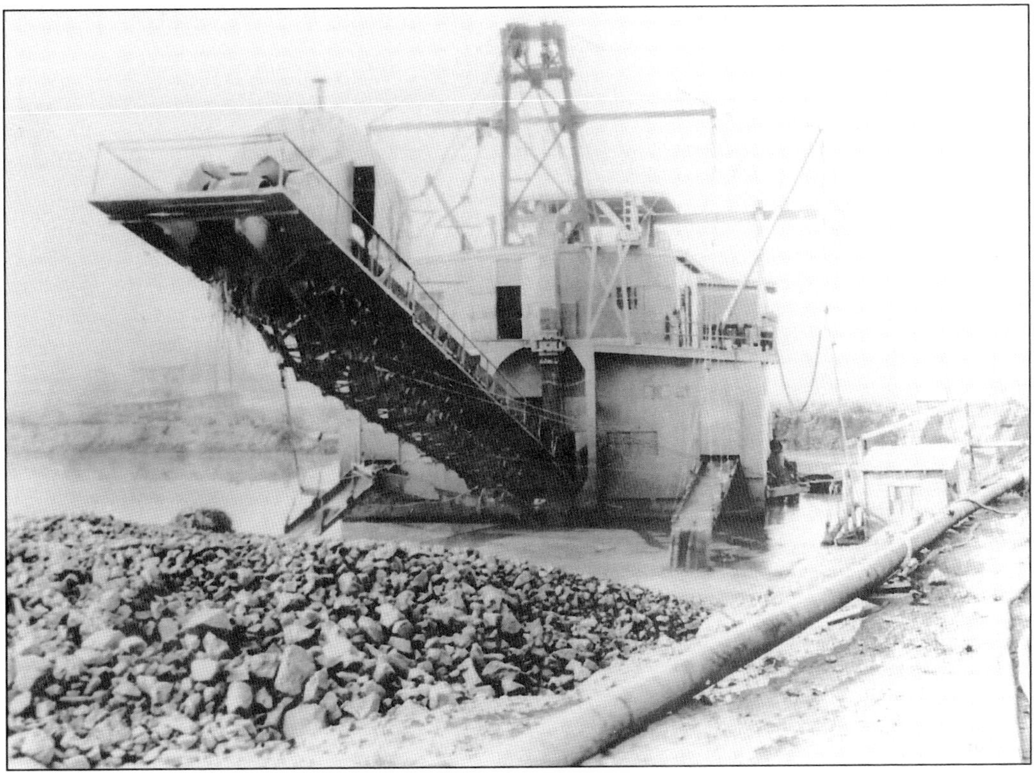

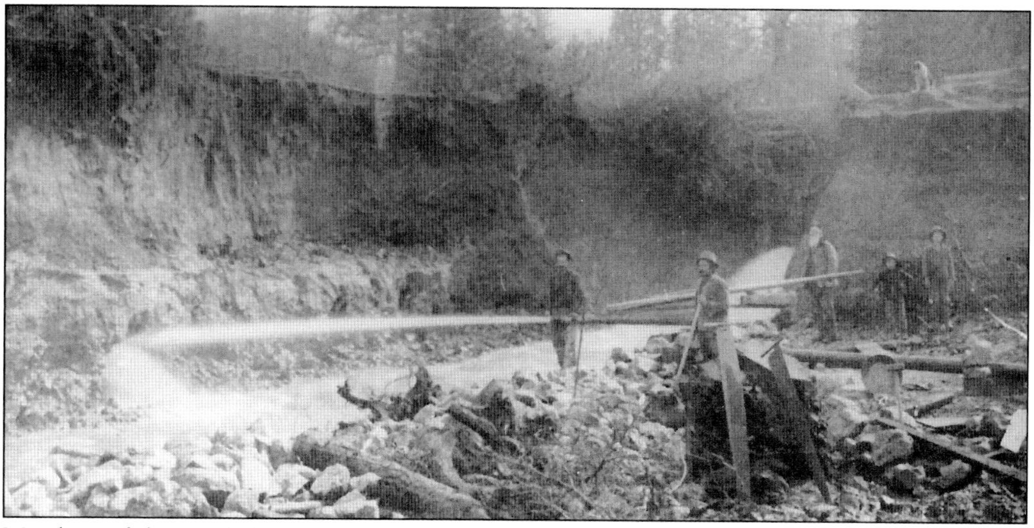

Members of the Cook family were running this hydraulic mining operation in December 1898 on Foots Creek. The high-pressure water cannon flushes away the overburden to uncover the underlying rocks with gold deposits down to bedrock. This is then sluiced or panned for the golden nuggets. Numbers of families would farm from spring to early autumn, then mine when winter rains brought sufficiently high water to work with.

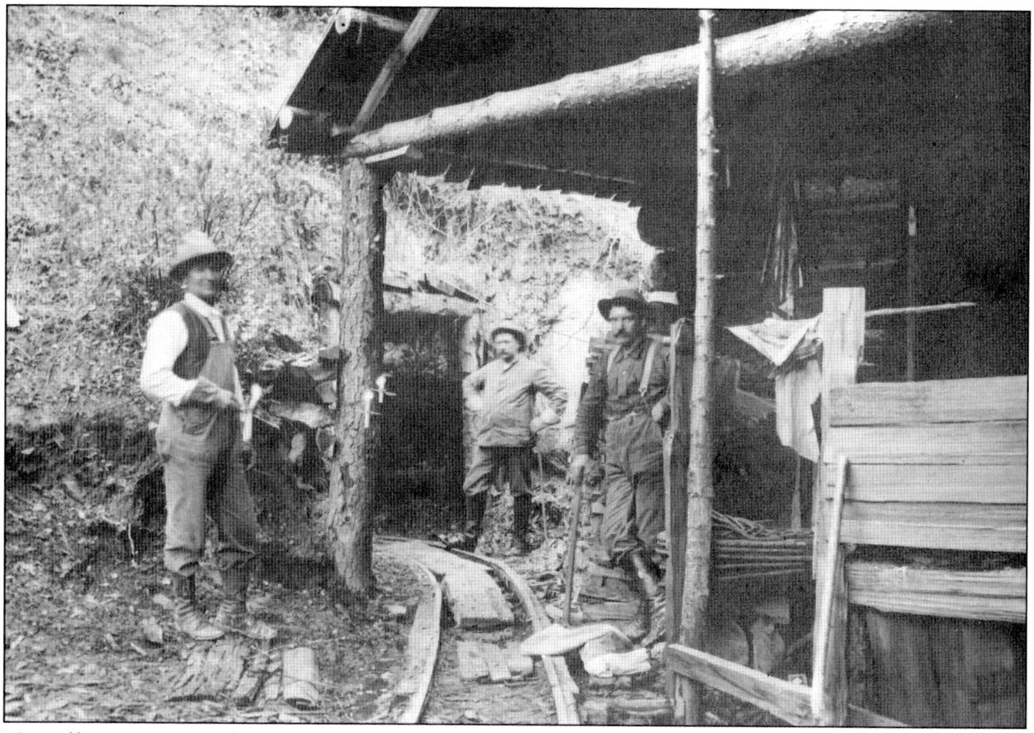

Not all mines were for gold. This 1906 photograph of the Blue Ledge Mine shows William Thompson (left), an unidentified man (center), and Mr. Waley, all in working gear. Over $2 million was spent developing the property, and two daily stages from Medford hauled out crushed copper ore, destined eventually for a smelter in Tacoma. The four mining camps were terraced and had a hotel, dance hall, machine shops, bunkhouse, and homes.

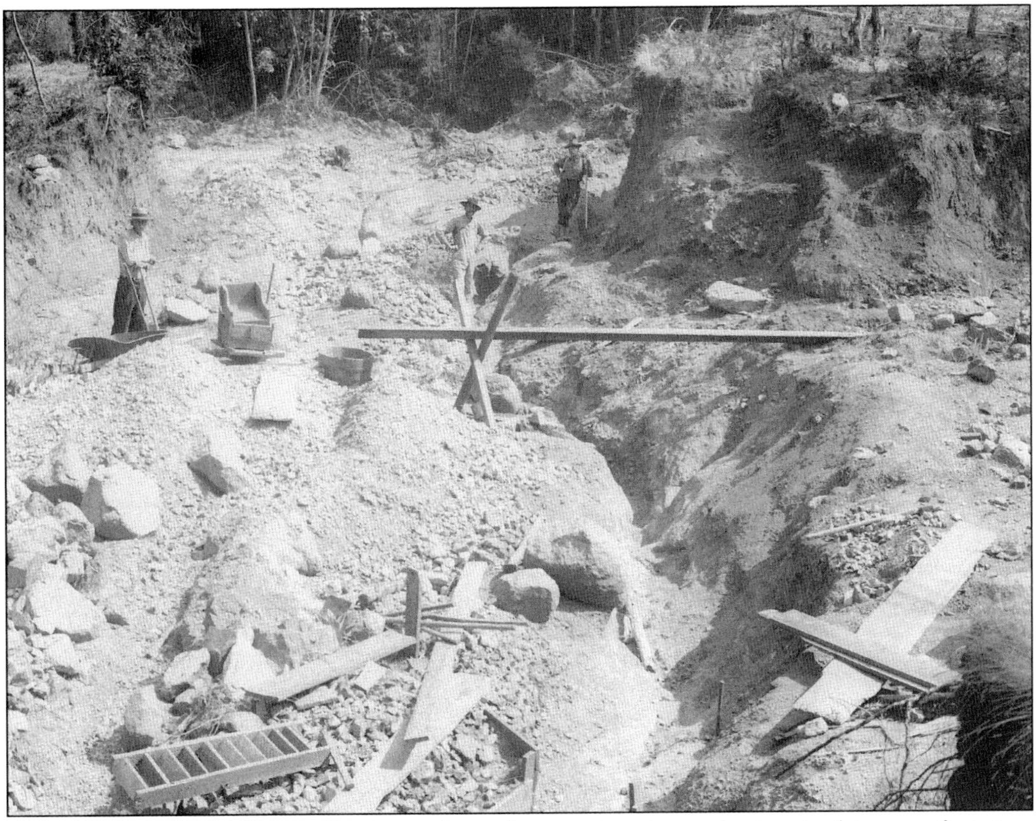

This photograph of a placer mine shows the surface erosion that took place in this type of mining. Except for wider spots in the nearly dried-out creeks during the summer, all of these operations are now nearly undetectable, overgrown with large trees and shrubs. Today, residents and tourists alike drive by, admiring the scenery. This placer is probably the Cherokee, dating from 1915 to 1920, showing Lloyd or Lee Cook.

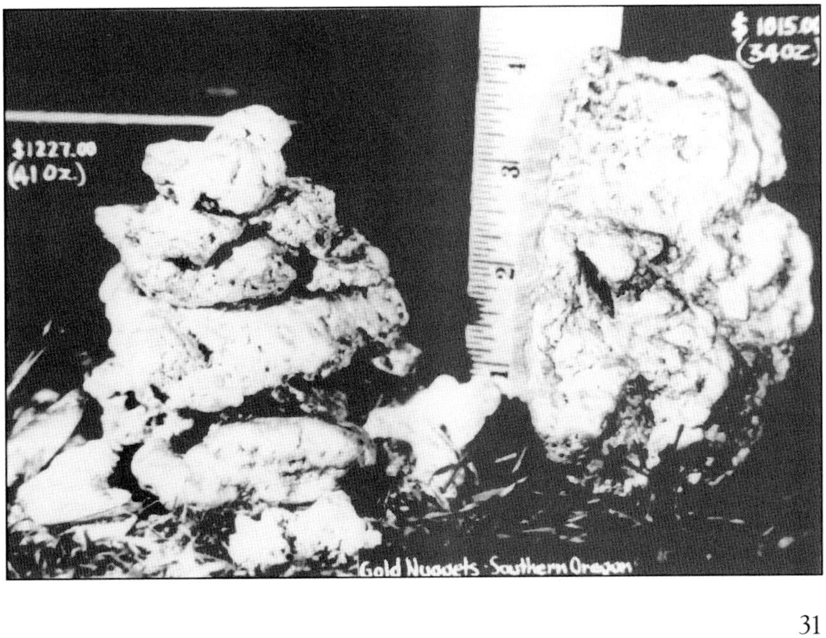

When a rich strike was found, the money rolled in. At today's prices, a 4-inch-high gold nugget would be worth a huge sum. However, this was always the exception.

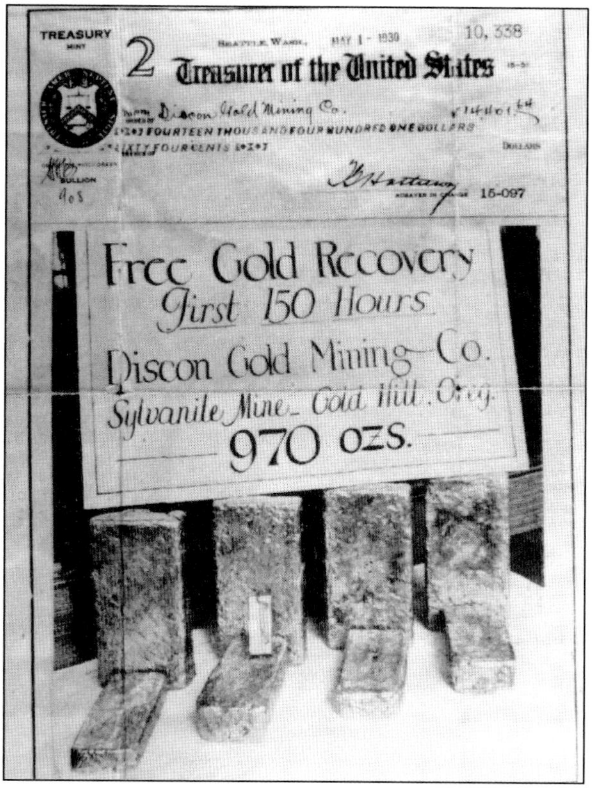

Discovered in 1890, the main shaft of the rich Sylvanite mine went down 900 feet before the vein turned toward the river. The lead was still strong when the tunnel flooded, and this ore shoot reportedly yielded $700,000 in total over time, or $75 million in today's dollars. The main workings of the Sylvanite were on 80 acres of patented land 3 miles northeast of Gold Hill.

Deep-rock mining companies also raised money for their operations by selling stock to the public or private investors. The Sylvanite Mining Company issued this certificate for 100 shares, paid for by services or money. The capital stock that could be issued was up to $1.5 million—a huge amount in those days.

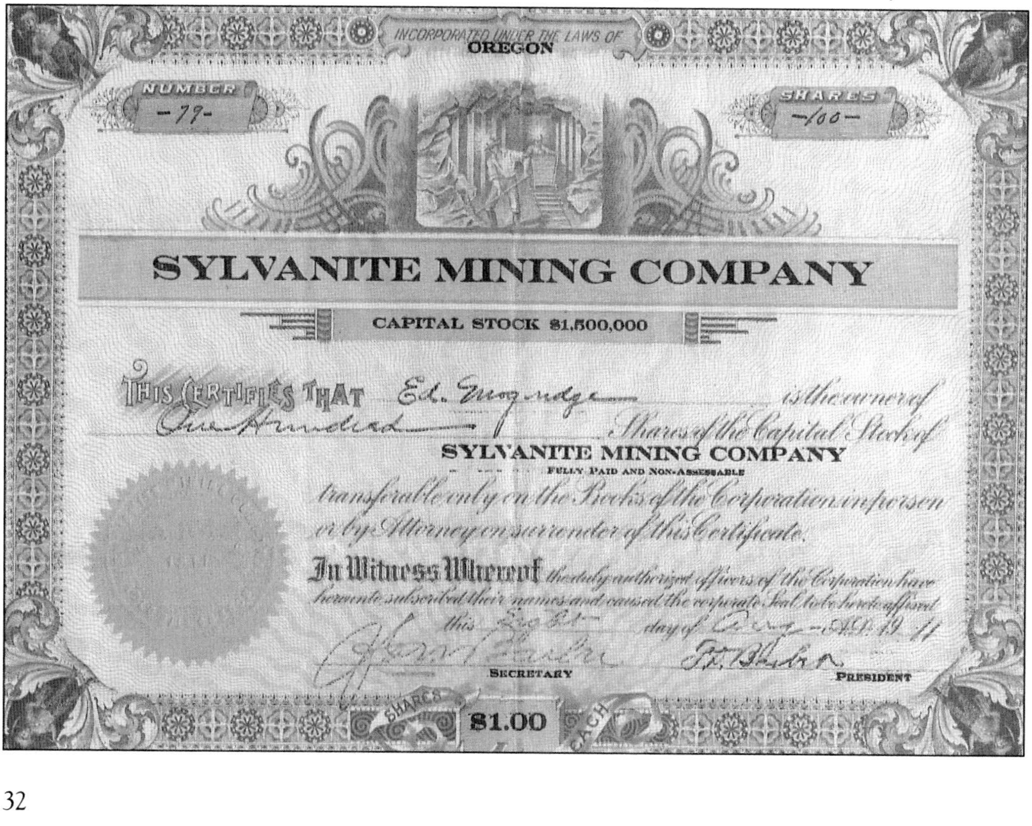

In this 1923 photograph, George Hall is pointing to where he took out a gold pocket at his Centennial Mine, one of the numerous ones on Kane Creek. Over time, miners continue to search for gold there and elsewhere, but large operations are not possible now due to environmental restrictions.

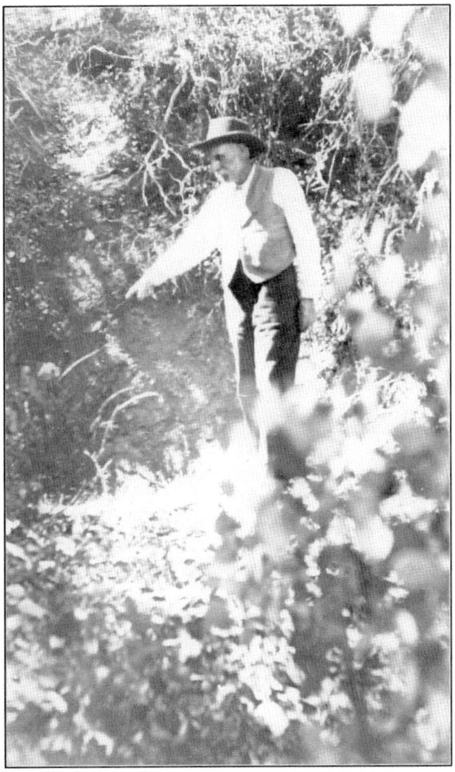

The death blow to area gold mining came during World War II. The War Production Board ordered all gold mining operations to shut down and shift to mining metals that were strategic to the war effort. This remained in effect until July 1, 1945. Scant operations started up again afterward. The search for the Gold Hill Pocket vein, however, continued, such as this 1950 effort by Stearns and Owens. In this image are Ralph Strickling (left) and Harold Drysdale. With the original pocket on the hill to the left, this and all subsequent efforts were not successful.

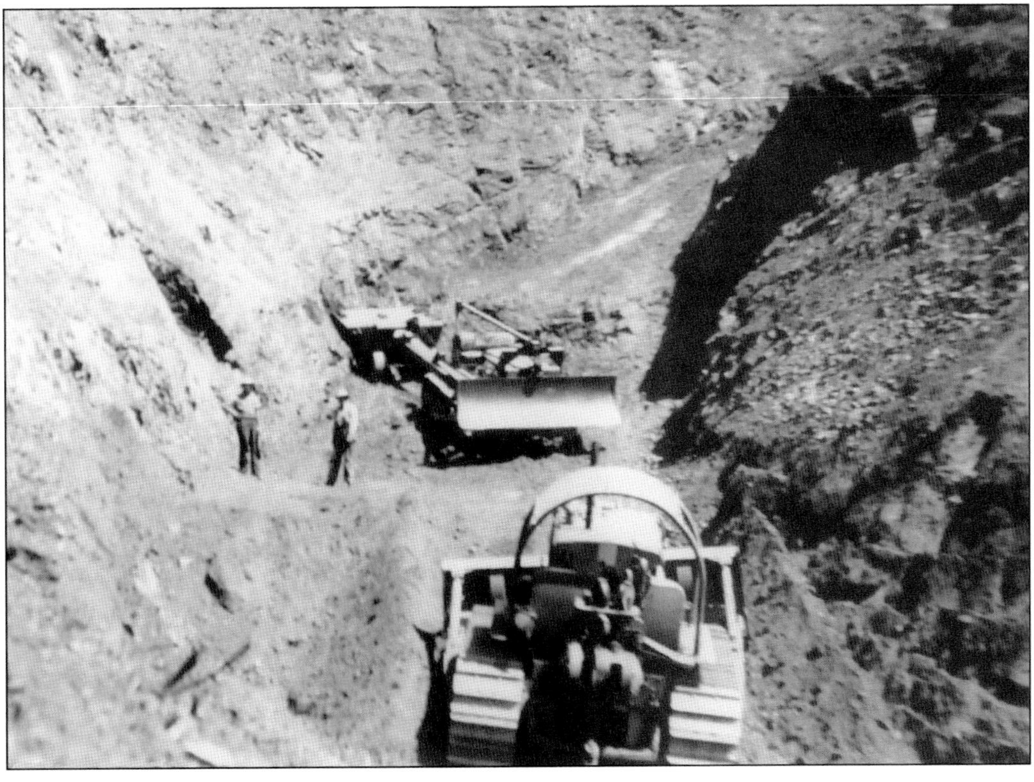

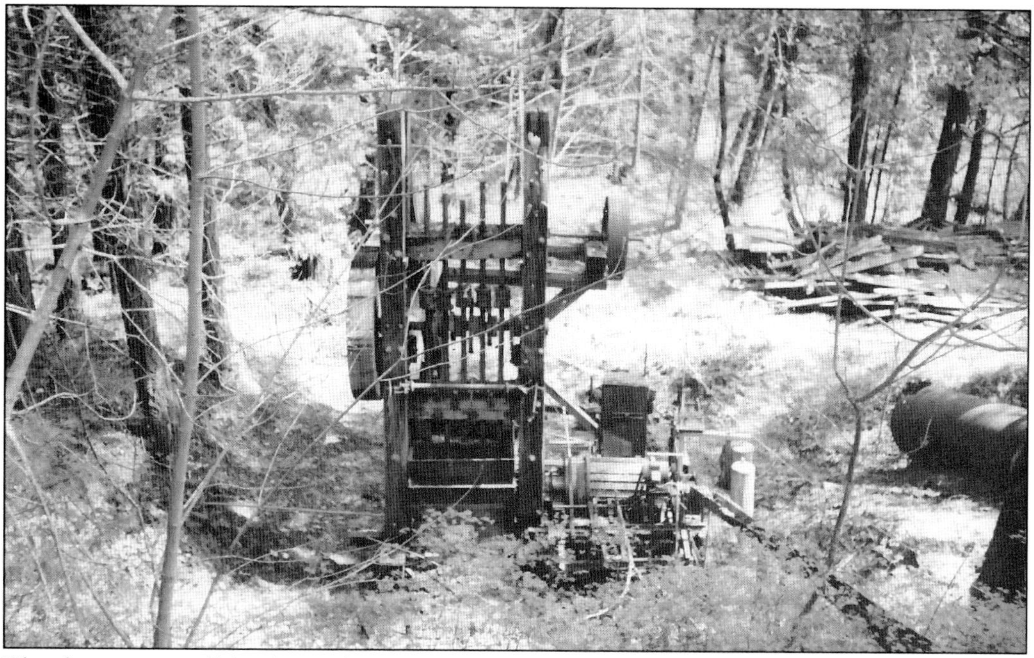

This five-stamp mill for the Lucky-Bart Mine on Sardine Creek in 1894 was the only large mill recognized then, as 22 gold ledges were being mined within a radius of 20 miles. By 1905, the area stamp mills had grown to over 100 with the increased operations. As seen in this 1993 picture, the three-story stamp mill was in disrepair. It was dismantled, moved, and rebuilt to stand tall in the backyard of the Gold Hill Historical Society's Beeman-Martin house.

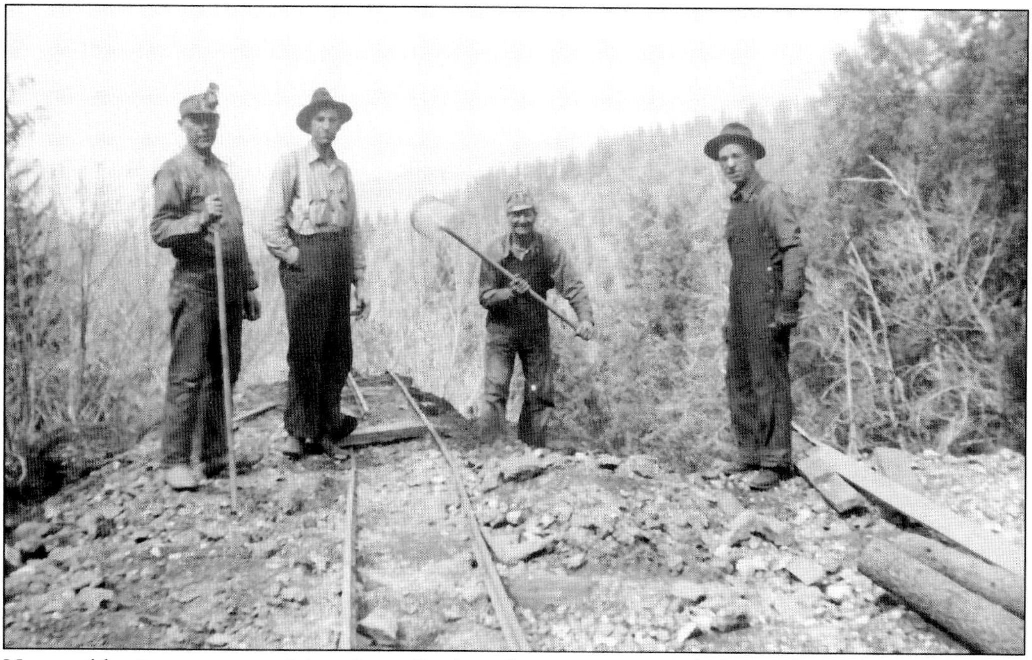

Here gold miners are repairing the rails that the ore cart traveled over from the mine to the outside. All of the mining work was hard and risky and wages were low. Until the gold played out, this was a driving economic force in the area.

Three

The Growth of a Town and Its Townsfolk

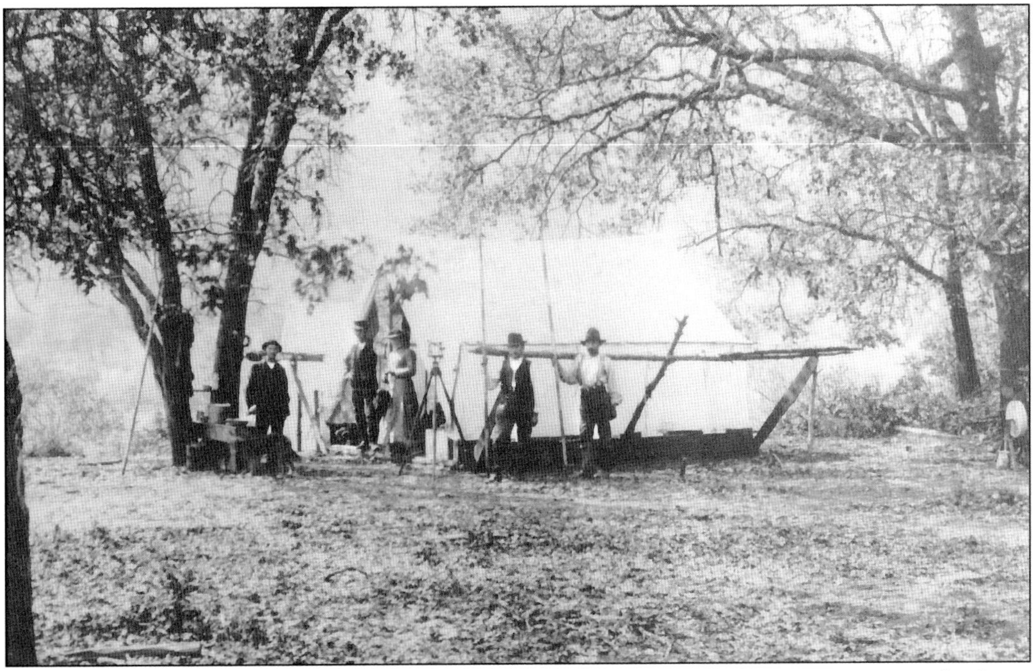

The Oregon Central Railroad Company reached the Rogue Valley in 1884. Due to the line's financial problems, Southern Pacific took it over in May 1887 and completed the rails to the California border by that December. William Newton (second from right) and Curtis Miller (far right) from Sardine Creek are shown resurveying the Gold Hill area for the railroad in this 1886 photograph, along with Charles Strong (far left).

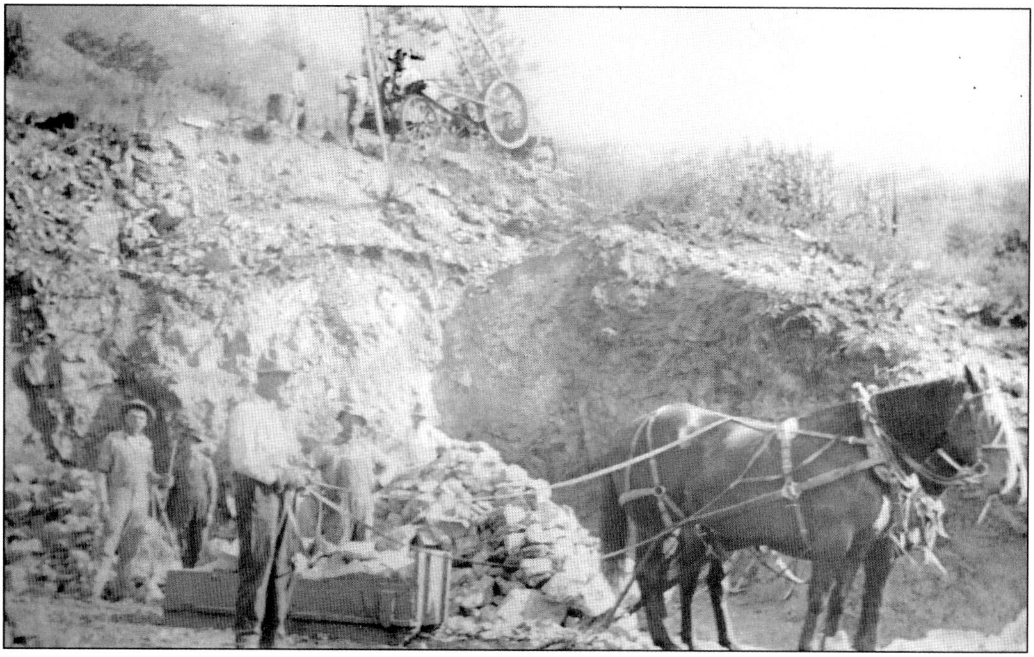

The excavation and building of the railroad tracks and right-of-way were difficult work, using a combination of laborers, horses, and steam shovels. In the picture above, Ted Fleming and his horse Blaze are using the scarifier for track excavation. In the image below, a track-mounted shovel is being used in 1884 to construct the rails past Gold Hill, near the town of Tolo where Gold Ray Dam was to be built.

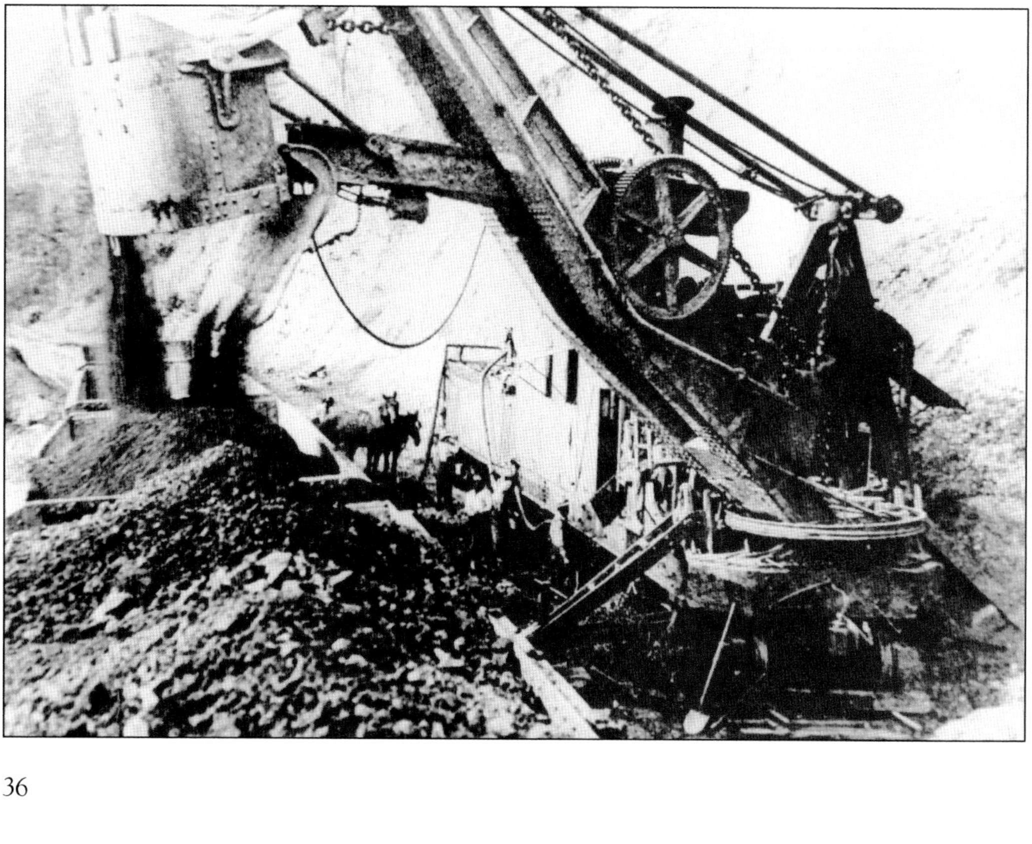

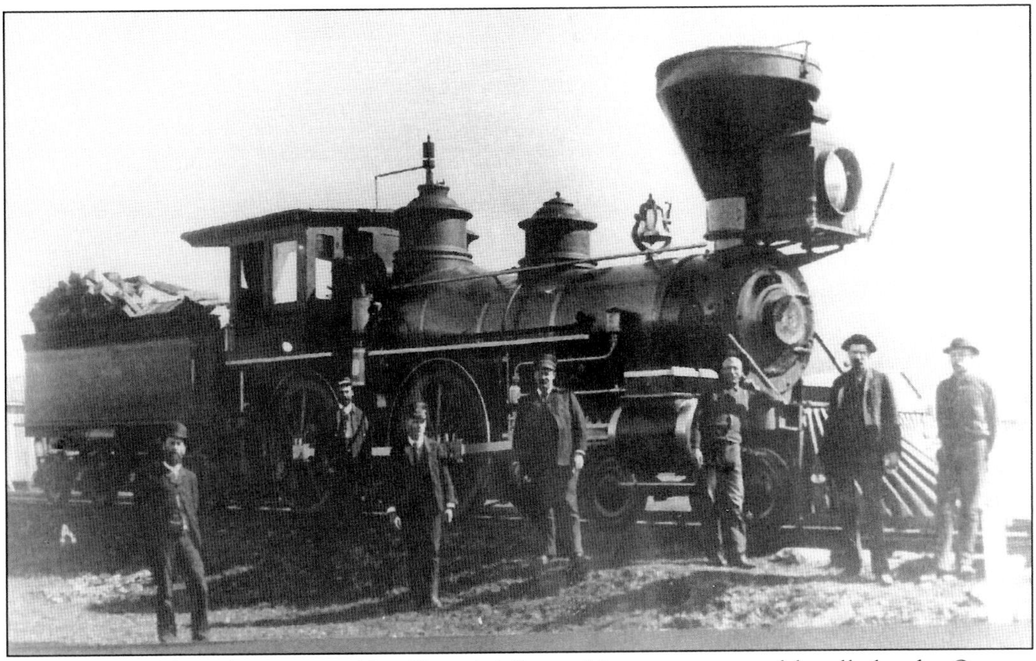

This 1880 Baldwin locomotive No. 22, a 4-4-0 wood burner, was used locally by the Oregon and California Railroad in the early 1890s; the crew is not identified. The impact of the railroad choosing one town like Gold Hill over another for its depot was substantial. A depot town became a hub for everything needing to be shipped, plus warehousing.

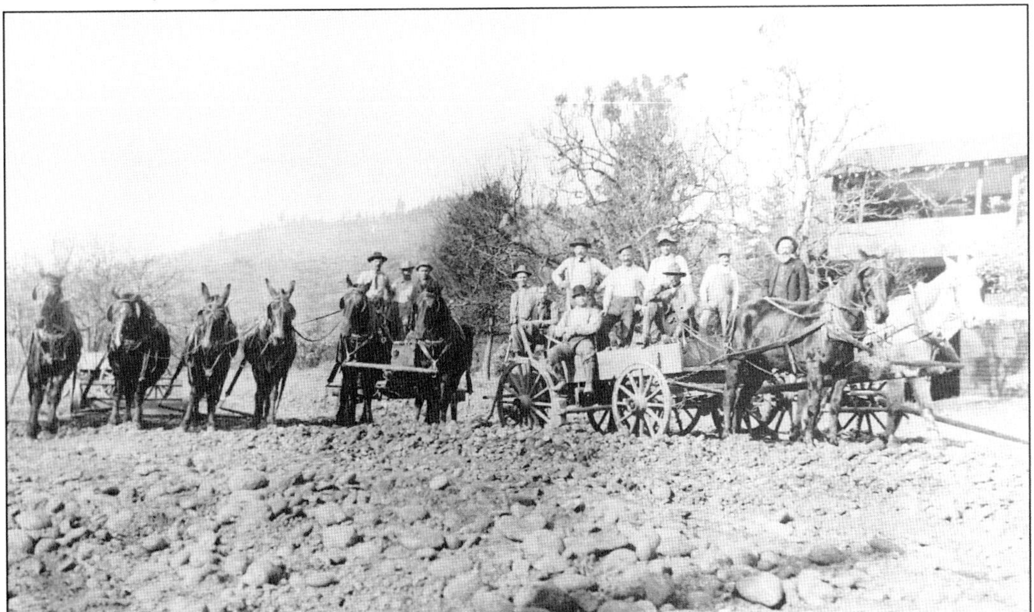

As there were no city road departments to work on the streets in the early days, local citizens did the work. Number 8, Section 2 of Gold Hill's ordinances required that all male residents over the age of 21 and under 50 had to work on the streets; the wealthier farmers and men, however, paid others to do their obligatory roadwork. Bill Hays is the older looking man with a flowing beard in the back of the wagon.

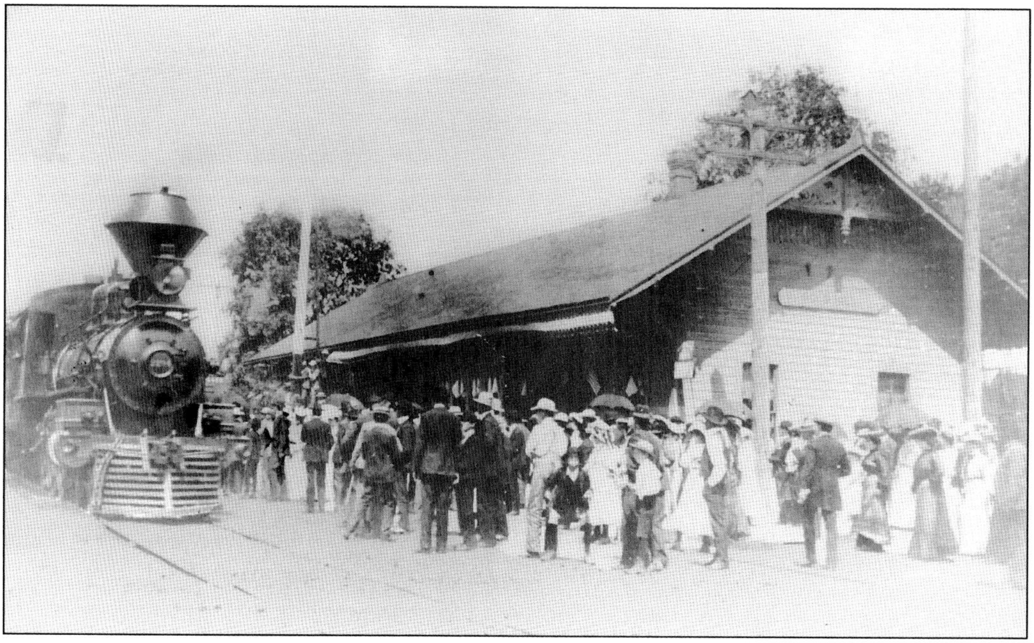

An 1890 Baldwin 2-2-0 locomotive is pulling train 15 at the dedication of the new Gold Hill Depot in 1900, as attested by the formal, flowing dresses of the women and the attire of the men. The first Gold Hill train depot had been built in 1883 and was torn down for this one.

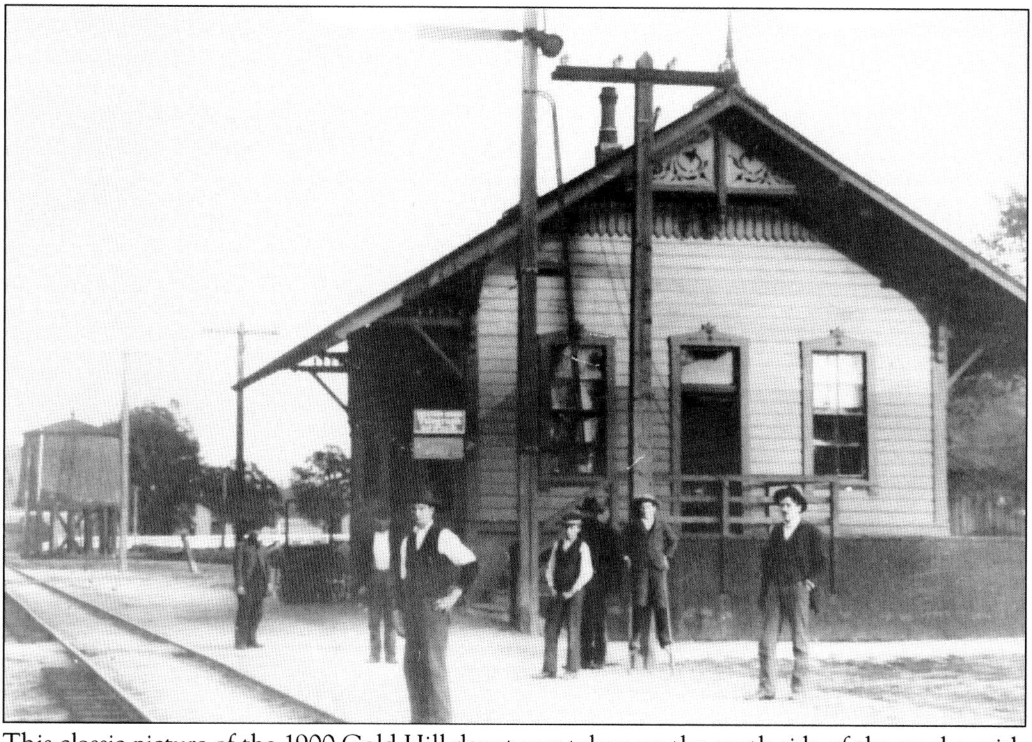

This classic picture of the 1900 Gold Hill depot was taken on the south side of the tracks, with the huge water tower for the railroad engines in the background. The trains hauled lumber, gold, quartz, fruit, grains, livestock, and passengers to and from the thriving town.

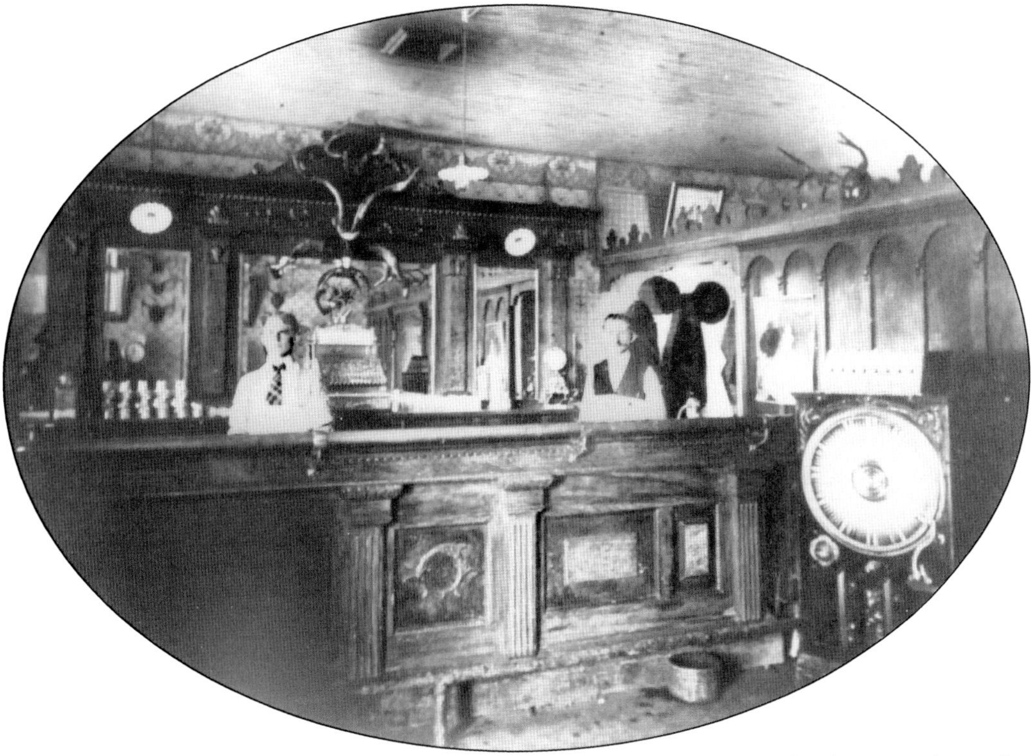

The bartenders in the Gold Hill Miners Home Saloon were ready for another big Saturday night. Miners from the different operations would soon descend on the town with gold dust and dry throats; buying grub and supplies would be a distant second task. This picture was found inside a bar gaming device.

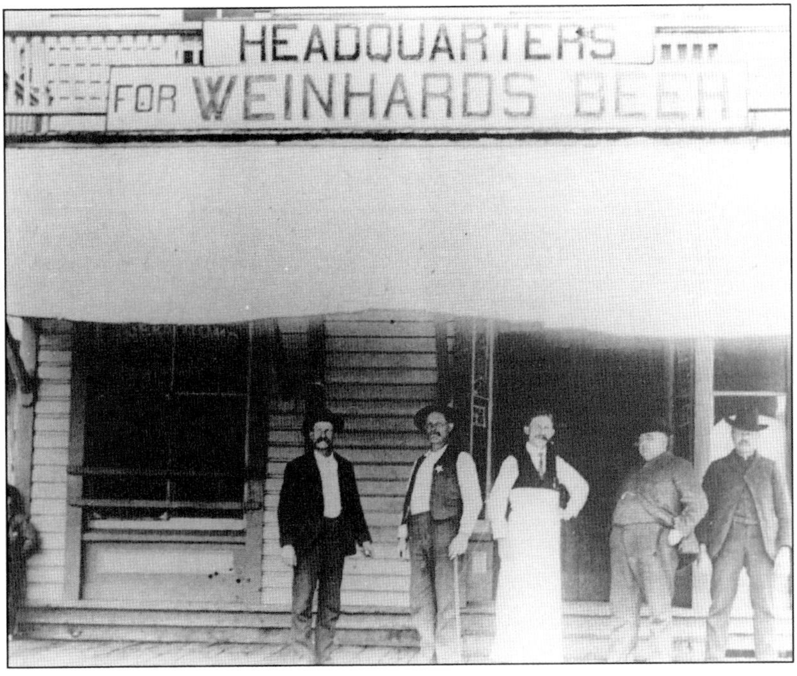

The sheriff, bartender, and a few steady customers are seen in front of the late 1800s Miners Home Saloon, "Headquarters for Weinhards Beer," on Fourth Avenue. Many a miner washed the grime from his throat and spent the gold dust from his poke at this place.

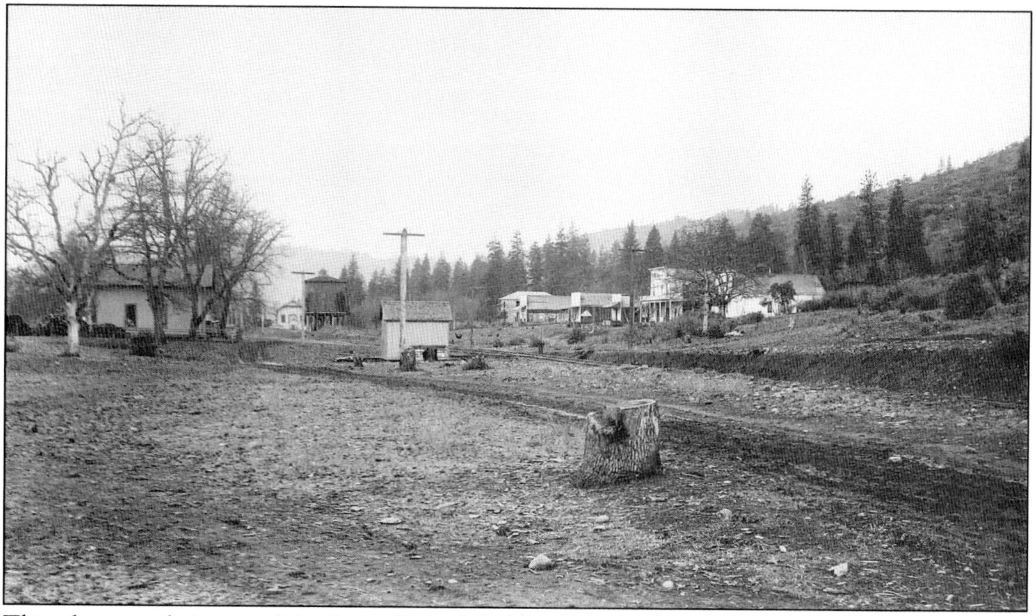

This photograph is one of the first taken of Gold Hill and dates to 1887. The photographer was looking over the railroad tracks toward the Fourth Avenue business district. The railroad depot is in the background with residences to the left. Telegraph poles follow the railroad tracks. It would not be until 1895 that the Rogue River Telephone Company would build telephone lines and install a system.

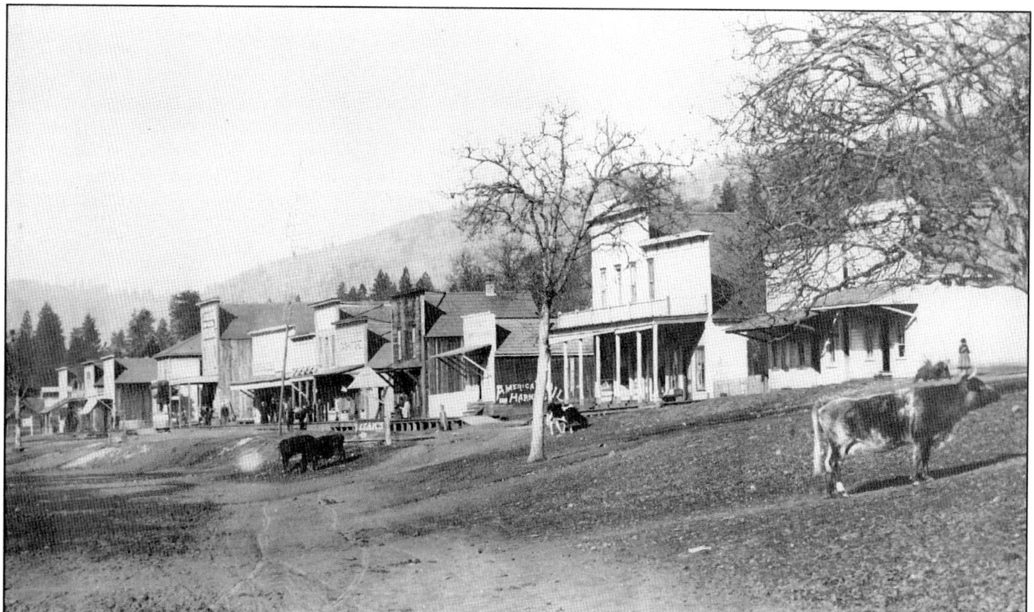

In 1890, sheep and cattle grazed at will in Gold Hill. Unfortunately, they also ate everything in sight and left a mess, with a few ranging cows killed by passing trains. The town ladies called a meeting and free-range grazing was banned. This image shows Fourth Avenue with its saloons, offices, cafés, drugstore, grocery store, and other businesses. The railroad is below.

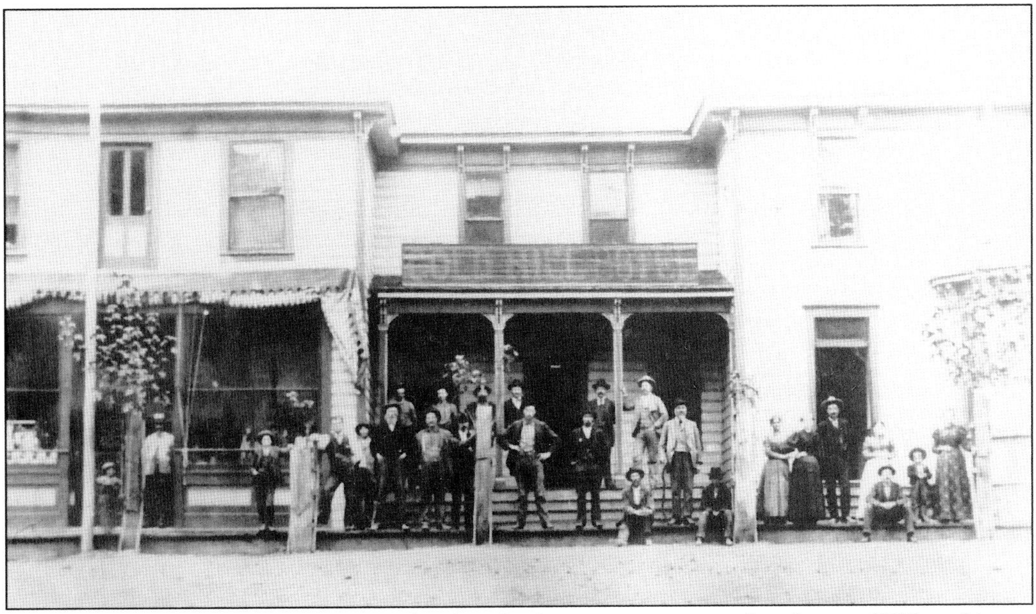

The Gold Hill Hotel was a prominent landmark. Construction started in August 1887, and it was originally called the Barlow House. The March 23, 1888, issue of the *Democratic Times* wrote, "The Barlow House at Gold Hill is now opened for the reception of guests. It is a fine large hotel, its rooms being hard-finished and comfortably fitted up, and it will be conducted in first-class style. Mr. and Mrs. Barlow will spare no pains to please the public."

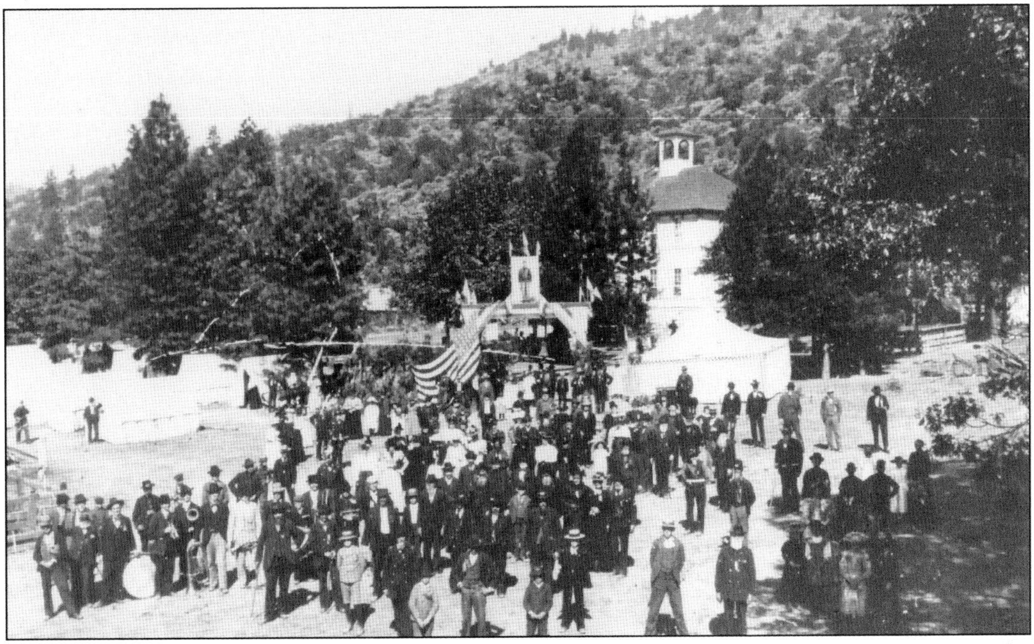

This image of a Grand Army of the Republic (GAR) encampment in Gold Hill dates to the late 1800s. The GAR was composed of Civil War veterans who had served in the Union army. By 1890, membership in this association was nearing 500,000. The annual encampments were elaborate multiday events, which often included camping out, formal dinners, and memorial programs. These events were held every year until 1949.

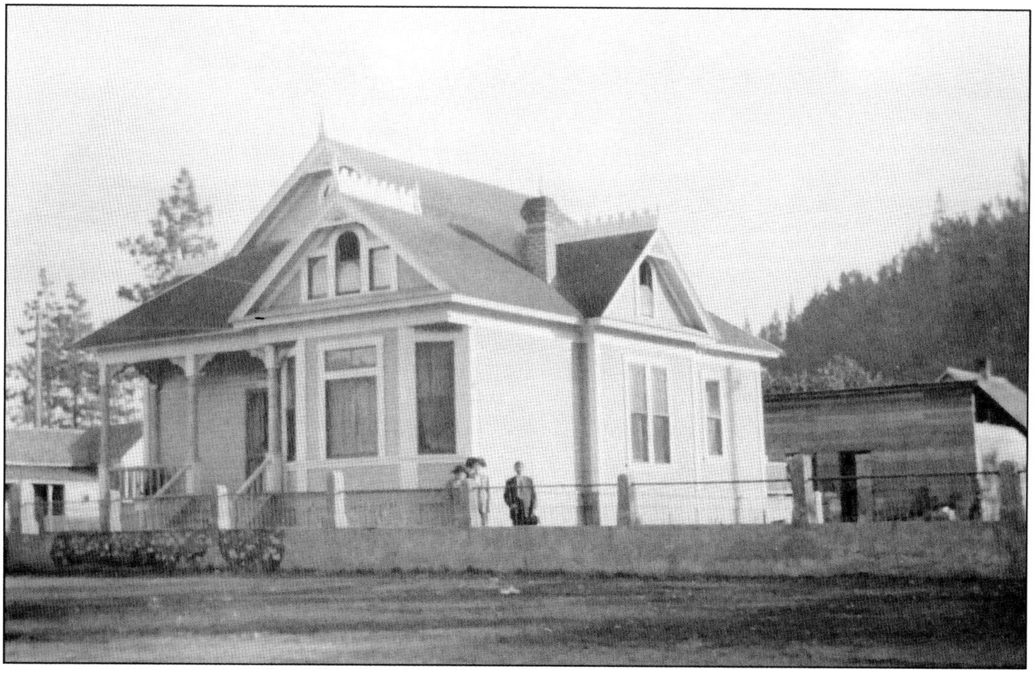

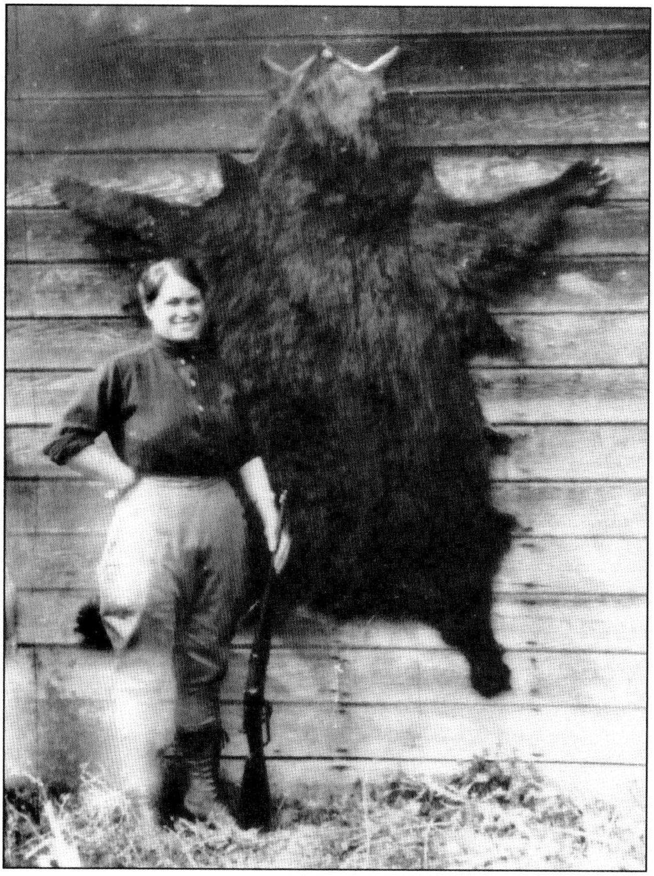

One of Bill Hay's daughters, Hattie, married Josiah Beeman, whose Lucky Bart Mine revenues built this fine Gold Hill home in 1901. Josiah, Hattie, and their children lived there for years. The Gold Hill Historical Society acquired the exquisite Beeman-Martin house in 1993 and is housed there. Volunteers spent months refurbishing this historic building to its present fine condition. This picture dates from around 1910.

This early 1900s image shows Hattie Beeman with the hide of a bear that she shot. While her husband Josiah was running his mining operations, Hattie was not one to shy away from taking care of marauding bears. The gun is either a Model 99 Savage or an 1873 Winchester. Hattie was an expert shot.

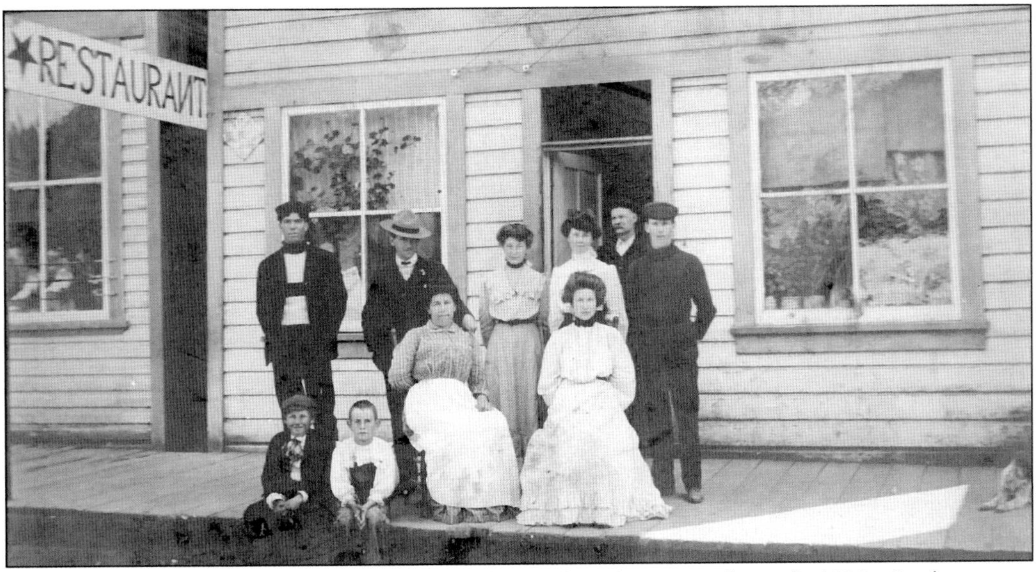

Molly and Dick Walker owned this boardinghouse for 15 years in the early 1900s. In this image are, from left to right, (first row) Alva Walker, Clint Walker, Molly (Perry) Walker, and Della (Walker) Evans; (second row) unidentified, Fritz Snider, unidentified, Nina Dusenberry, and two unidentified men.

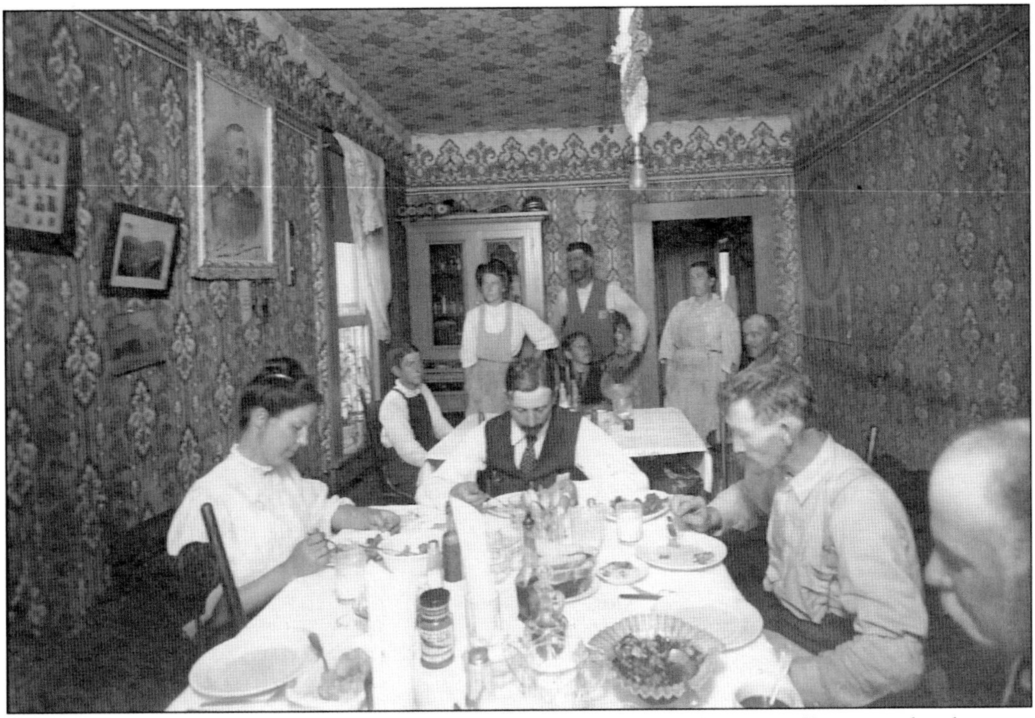

Customers are in the formal dining room of Walker's boardinghouse. Folks came for showers, partying, sleeping, and being civilized until they headed out again to the gold fields. Sitting at the back table are, from left to right, Clint Walker, Alva Walker, and Floyd Sutton. Standing behind them are, from left to right, Della, Dick, and Molly Walker. Della was the waitress, Molly was the cook, and Dick also ran a livery stable as a blacksmith.

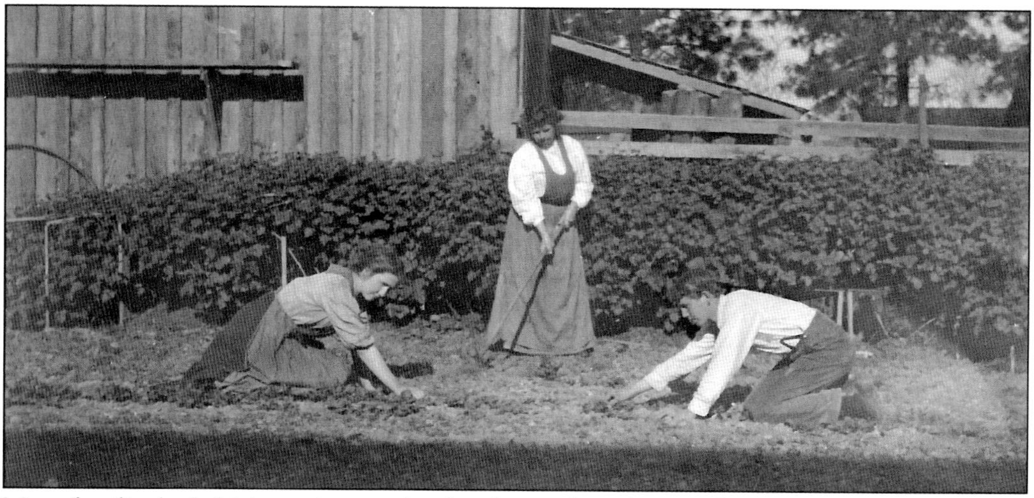

Many families had chickens along with a family cow furnishing milk and butter. They tended to their own gardens, with different fruit trees. The Walker Boarding House also had boarders to feed. Alcohol was not served there, except at Christmas and on special occasions with a special homemade Elderberry wine. Shown here behind the boardinghouse on Second Avenue are, from left to right, Della Walker, her mother Molly, and Alva, Della's brother.

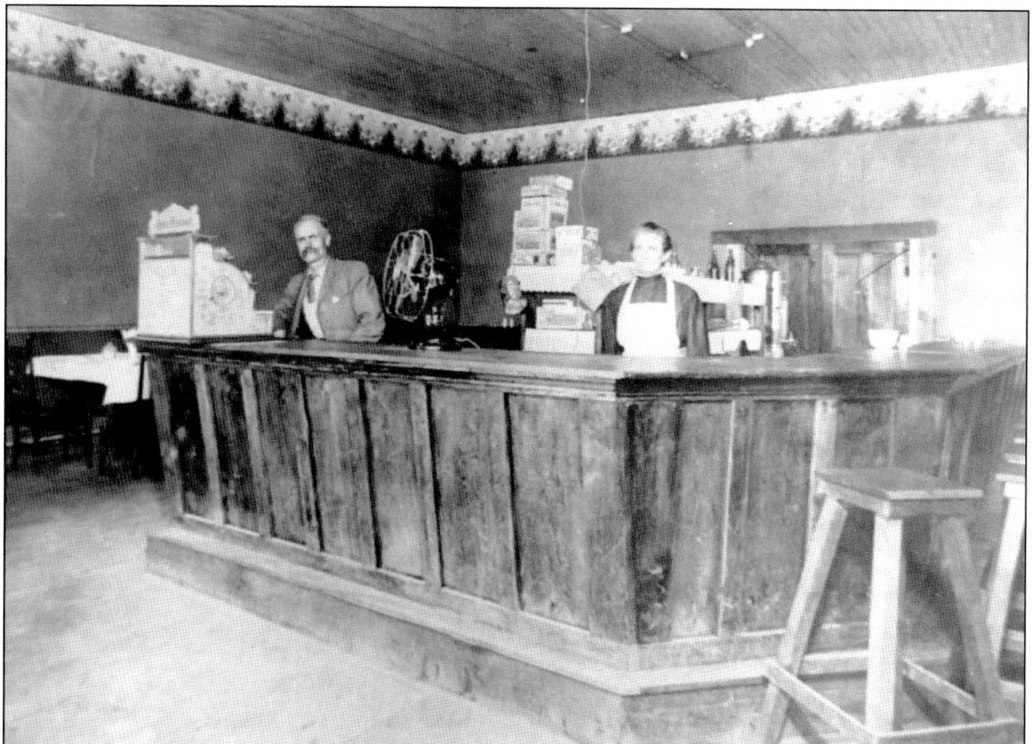

Shown in this 1913 image are Wesley and Cora Truax, the owners of the Gold Hill Café. Cora was the first woman elected to public office in Jackson County on April 7, 1913, when she became Gold Hill's first councilwoman. This restaurant was located on Fourth Avenue between Third and Fourth Streets, facing the railroad tracks. It was a popular place to eat, with a home atmosphere and wooden stools.

Wesley W. Truax is seen here in front of his restaurant, the Gold Hill Café on Fourth Avenue, in 1910. Truax was a prominent businessman in those early years, with several business ventures in progress, from real estate to merchandising and restaurant operations.

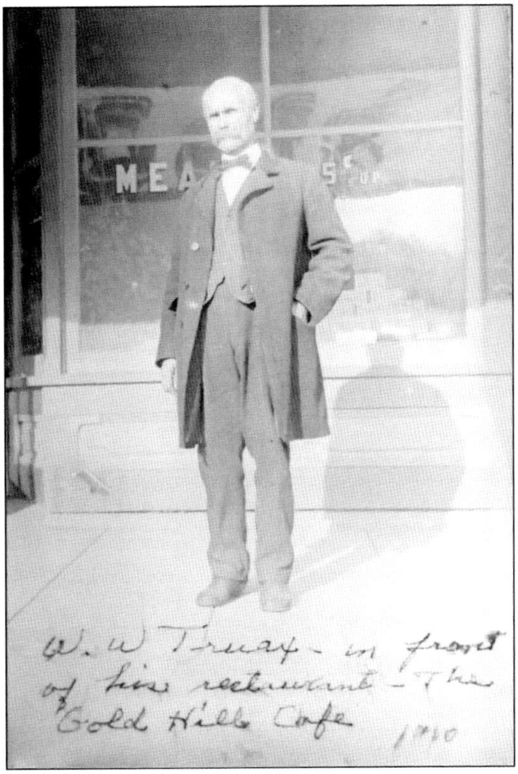

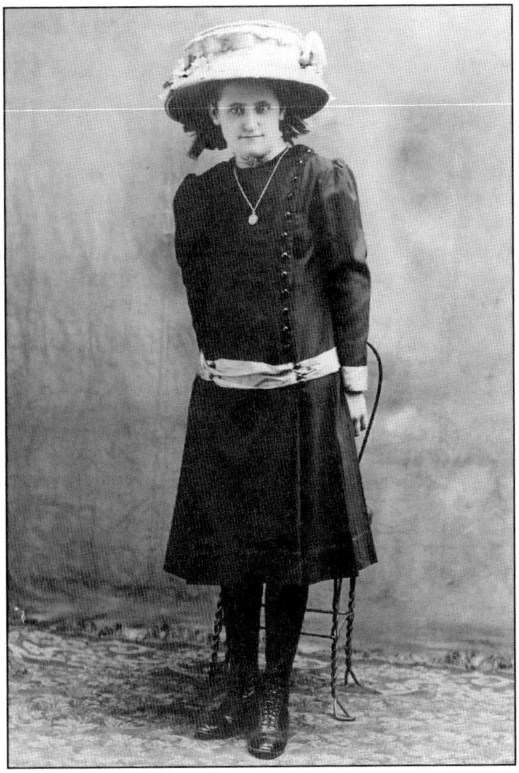

The inscription on this photograph of Mary Truax Hendricks reads, "The newest in Easter hats. Made by a Gold Hill milliner, 1909." Mary rode her bike up the hill to feed the chickens and gather the eggs for the family restaurant. On weekends, she baked pies at her parent's Gold Hill Café, where everything was home grown. She also waitressed during her time off from school.

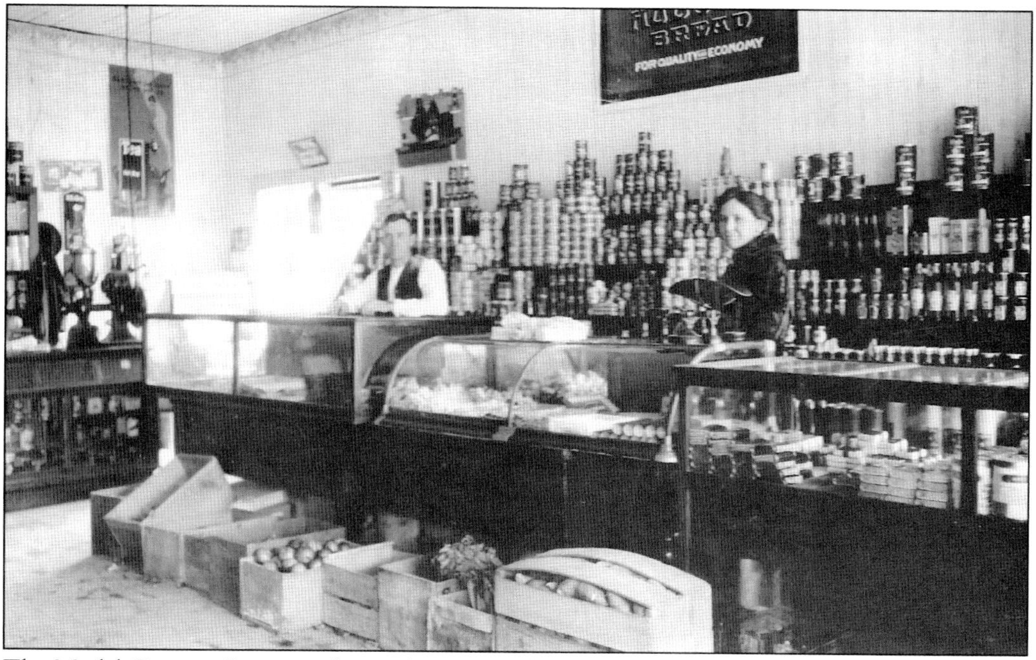

The Model Grocery Store was located on Second Avenue. W. H. and Della Miller, seen in this 1910 image, operated the store and lived on the same street. Of note are the boxes of fruit and a vintage coffee grinder.

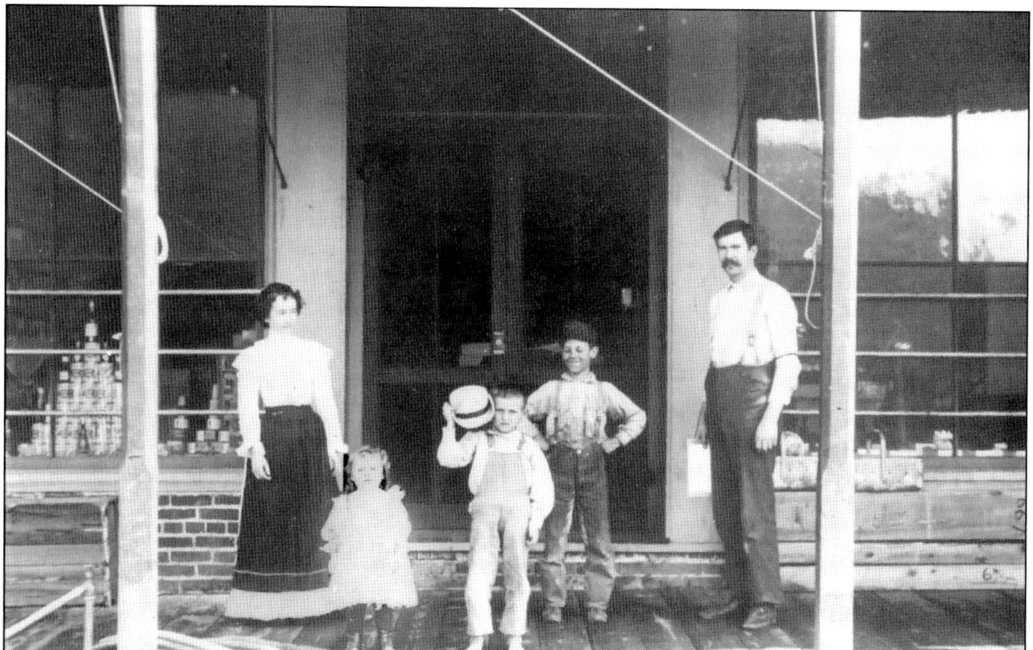

This general merchandise store was owned by Oris Crawford and William Carter in the early 1900s. Pictured are, from left to right, Amy Crawford (Otis's wife), daughter Juanita Crawford Butler, two unidentified boys, and Oris Crawford.

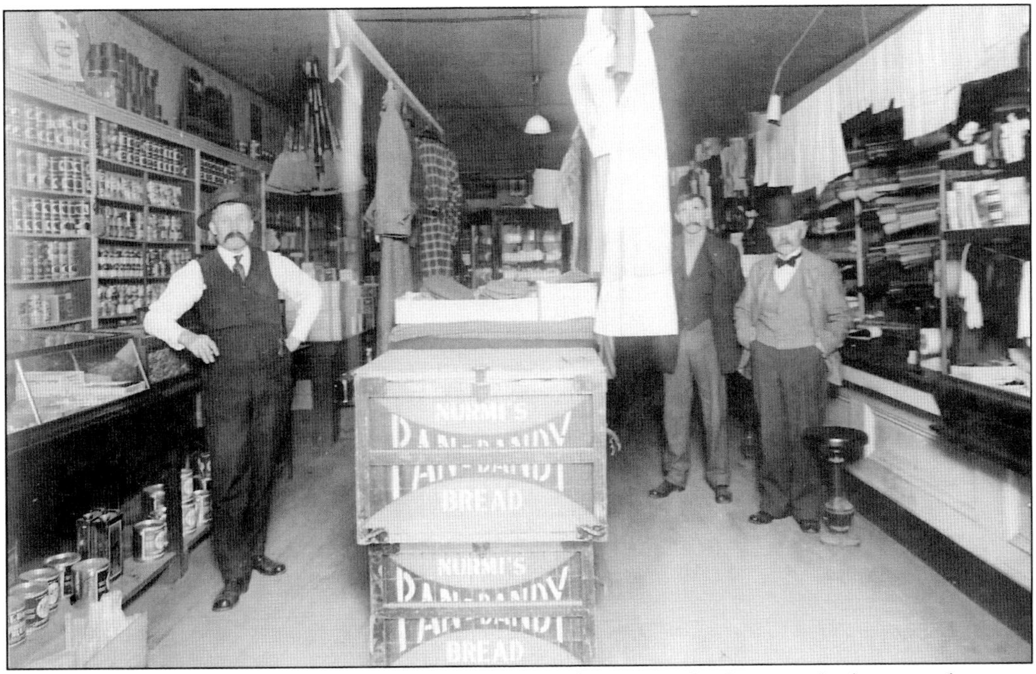

August Schuerman's store in Gold Hill was a typical mercantile. It carried whatever the store felt it could sell, whether this was bread, canned goods, bolts of cloth, or clothing. In this 1908 image there are boxes of bread, unlike today's individually wrapped loaves.

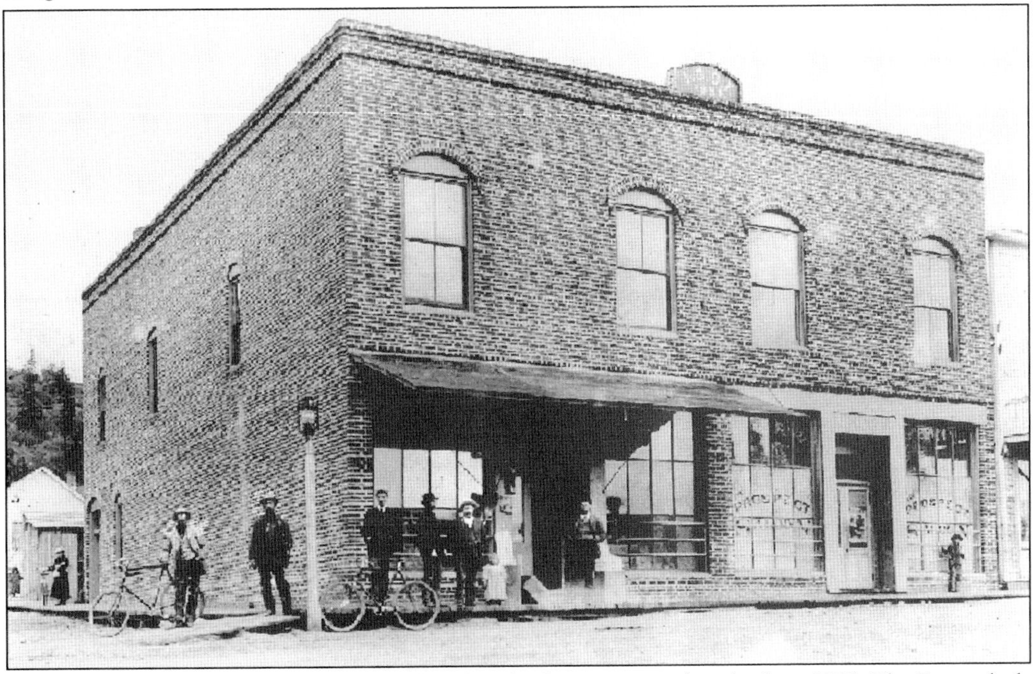

The Independent Order of Odd Fellows building had two stories when built in 1895. The Rosenthals had a mercantile store on the first floor. In January 1963, the upper story was removed, so that the building is now one story, but the original bricks from the old structure were reused. This picture was taken in 1899, and the Prospect Saloon was doing "great" business.

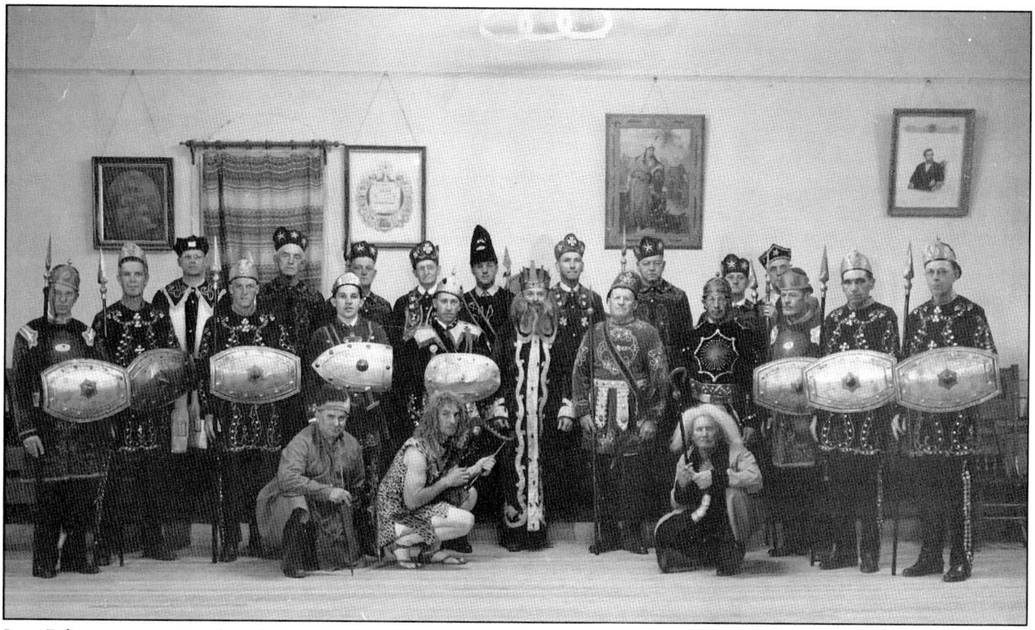

In 17th-century England, it was considered odd for people to organize for the purpose of giving aid to those in need and pursuing projects for the benefit of all mankind. Those who belonged to such an organization were called "odd fellows." The charitable Independent Order of Odd Fellows continues today, both internationally and in Gold Hill. On the reverse side of this image is inscribed, "Odd Fellows, 1rst Degree Ceremony, Gold hill. IOOF.129."

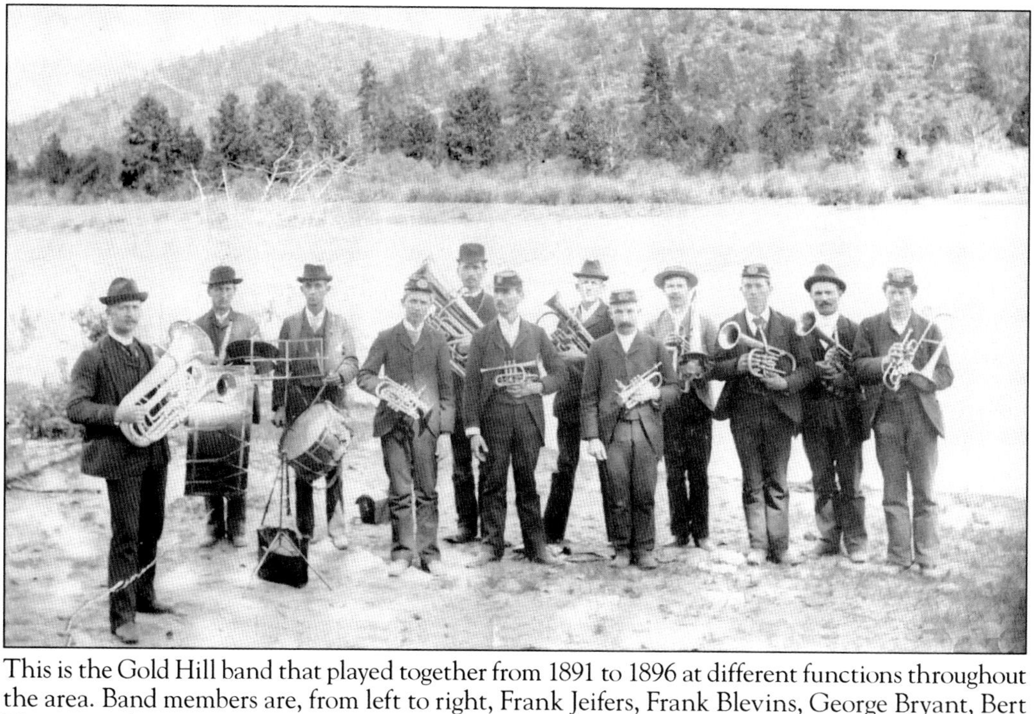

This is the Gold Hill band that played together from 1891 to 1896 at different functions throughout the area. Band members are, from left to right, Frank Jeifers, Frank Blevins, George Bryant, Bert Thomas, Alex Carter, Arthur Fitzgerald, Jerome Fitzgerald, J. E. DeBoy, Oris Crawford, W. A. Carter, Tom Hammersley, and Robert M. Cook.

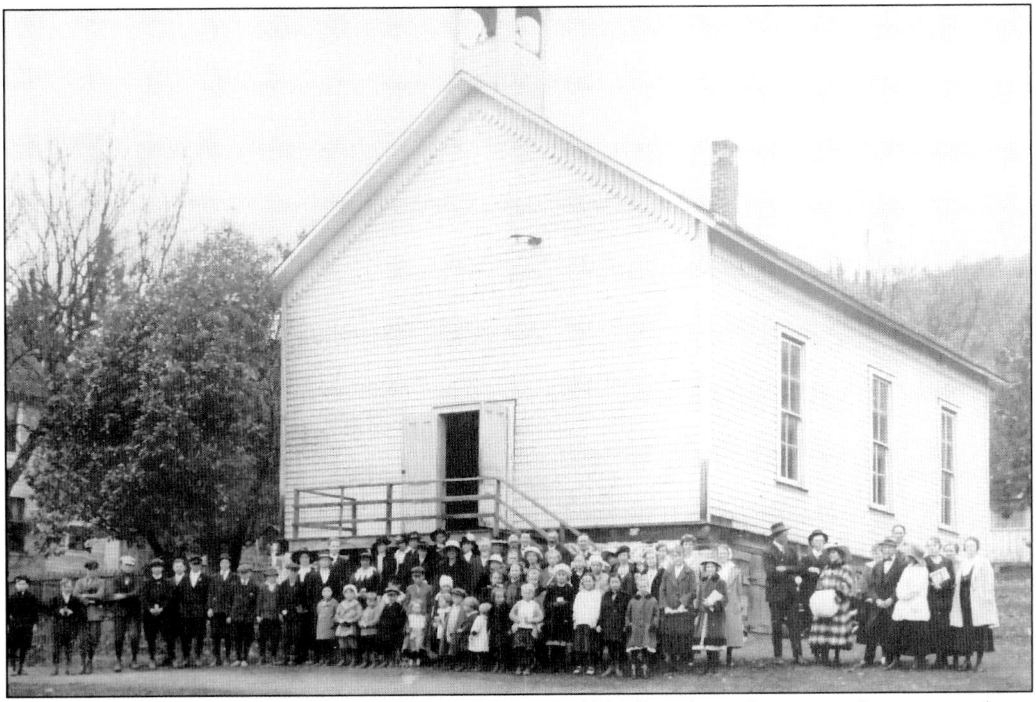

Religion was an important element of early life in Gold Hill and nearly every other city in those times. This picture of the Methodist church was taken in 1914; it was located at Fifth Avenue and Seventh Street (now Gustaf Street). C. E. Wharton was the pastor then.

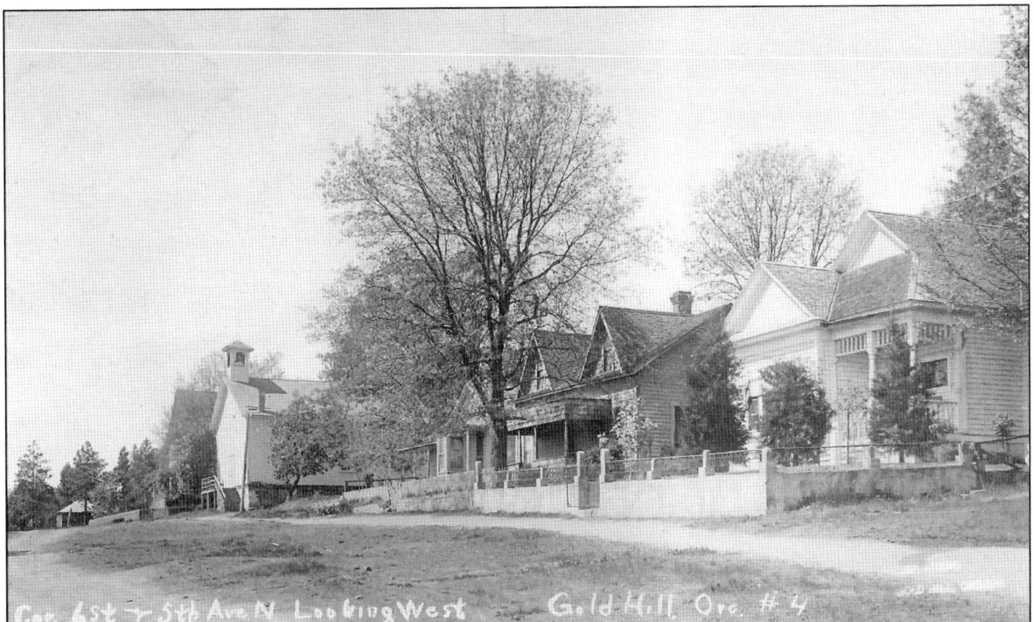

The houses in Gold Hill used to be primarily above the business district and railroad tracks. This image from Sixth Street looking toward Fifth Avenue around 1910 shows a long stretch of homes, but no sidewalks or paved streets.

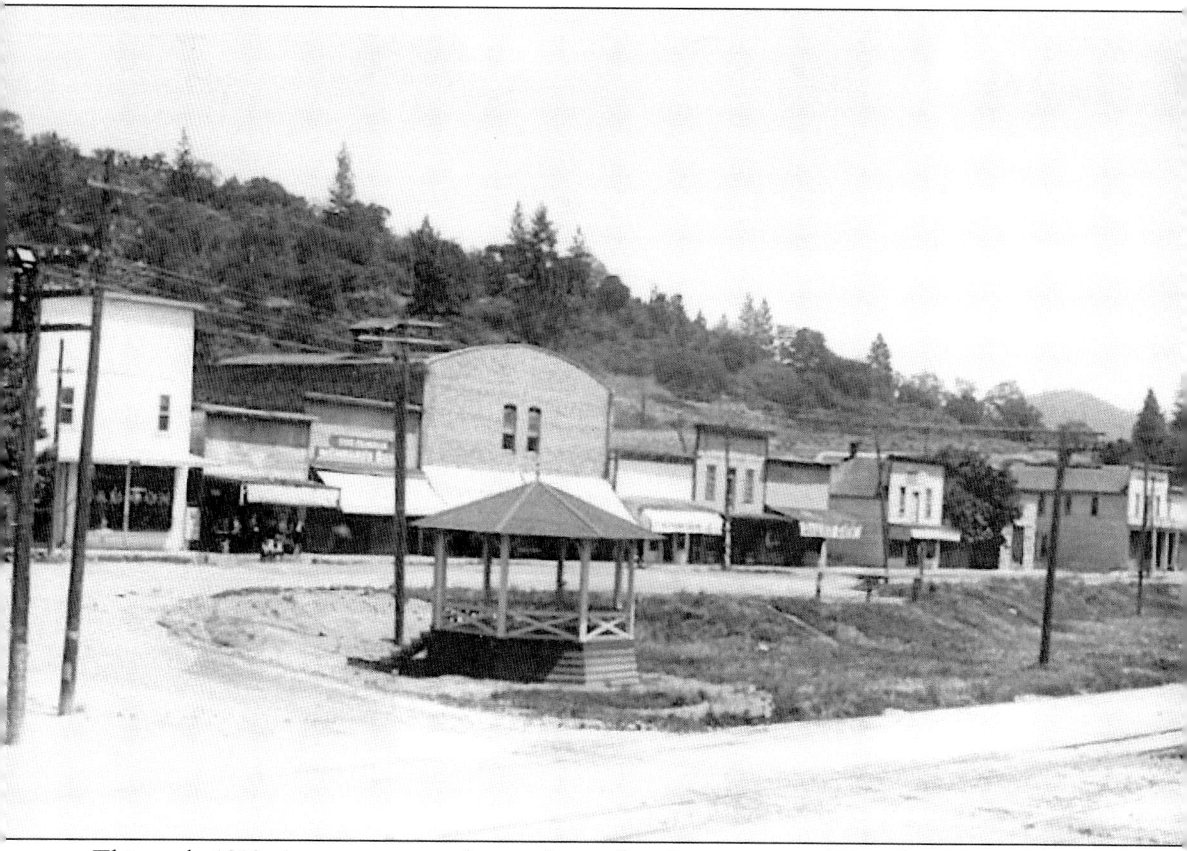

This early 1910s image captures the gazebo, railroad crossing, and Fourth Avenue from the northeast. As Mary Truax Hendricks observed, "The main street in those days (1911–1915) was Fourth Avenue where the Gold Hill Hotel was. Across Fourth Street (now Dardanelles) from the hotel were a saloon, Johnny Reed's Bon Bon store, another saloon, Lance's dry goods store with the opera house above (the elliptical brick building where the top floor also served as a dance hall and skating rink), meat market, telephone office, the Gold Hill Café, bakery, and Mrs. Hutson's rooming house. On the hotel's other side to the north were the Gold Hill Bank, a barber shop, Turner's candy store, bookstore, drug store, and a merchandise store at the end of the block." The town had a weekly newspaper, the *Gold Hill News*, as well as a Western Union telegraph office and a hospital. Across the railroad tracks on Second Avenue were livery stables, blacksmith shops, and even a huge pavilion where dances, basketball games, and county fairs were held.

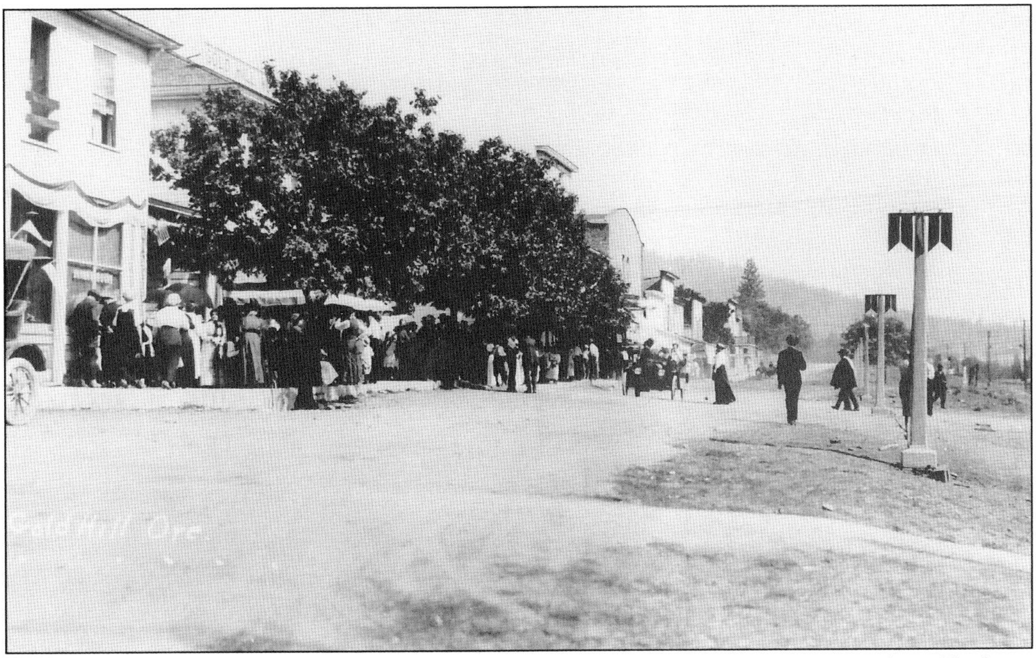

Fourth Avenue was bustling on this day in 1915. Gold Hill was wet at that time, and Medford was dry—as to alcohol. On Saturday, the saloons were full with folks from all over. During the summer months, the two open-air dance pavilions were filled, and dances were held every Saturday night at the opera house. The outdoor pavilions were within blocks of one another.

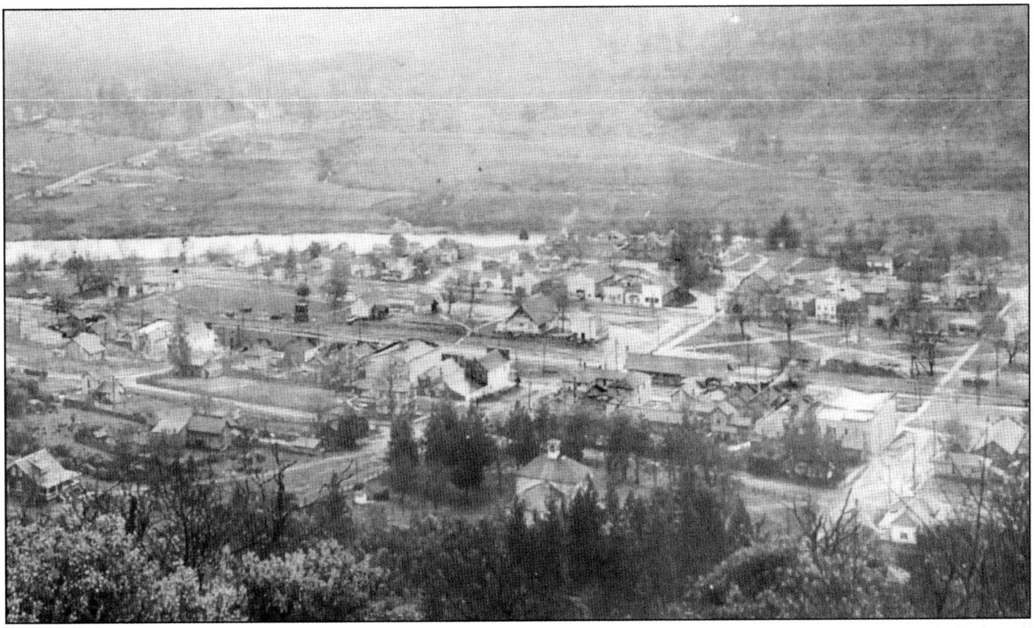

This early 1900s image shows the Gold Hill Public School, or second school, in the park behind Fourth Avenue. The Gold Hill Hotel is on the corner in front of the railroad depot; two streets down and toward the Rogue River is Second Avenue with its Darling and Hodges livery stable (fourth building to the left of the intersection, with the odd roofline). Across the river, I-5 now cuts straight through the plains. The Dardanelles is to the left.

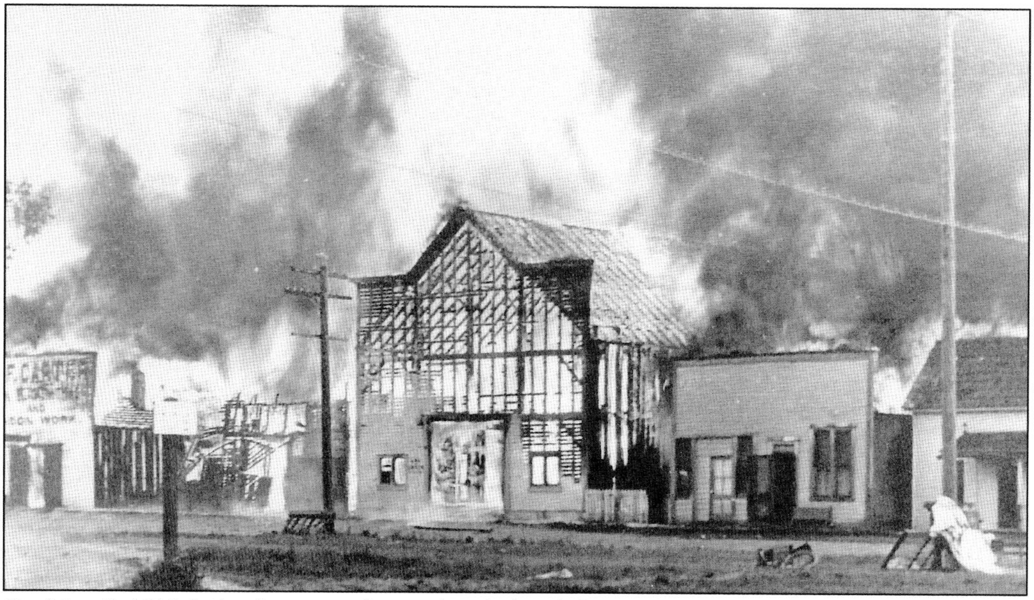

On May 5, 1915, kids playing with matches behind the Darling and Hodges livery stable (the middle building) on Second Avenue started a deadly fire. Fanned by winds, the conflagration quickly spread to the adjoining wooden houses, barns, and shops before firemen arrived. Luckily, the gaps between buildings allowed the firefighters—even with antiquated fire apparatus and hand-operated pumps—to keep the fire from destroying the entire town. Ben Hur Lampman, owner of the *Gold Hill News*, wrote, "The community interest displayed in fighting the fire was heroic, as everybody worked like 'Trojans': the fire boys, the high school students, with quick initiative and intelligent action made a rush for the high school fire equipment, and with a record making dash, were soon on the scene with cart and hose and did splendid service in staying the flames, and the citizens too formed a fire brigade to be proud of."

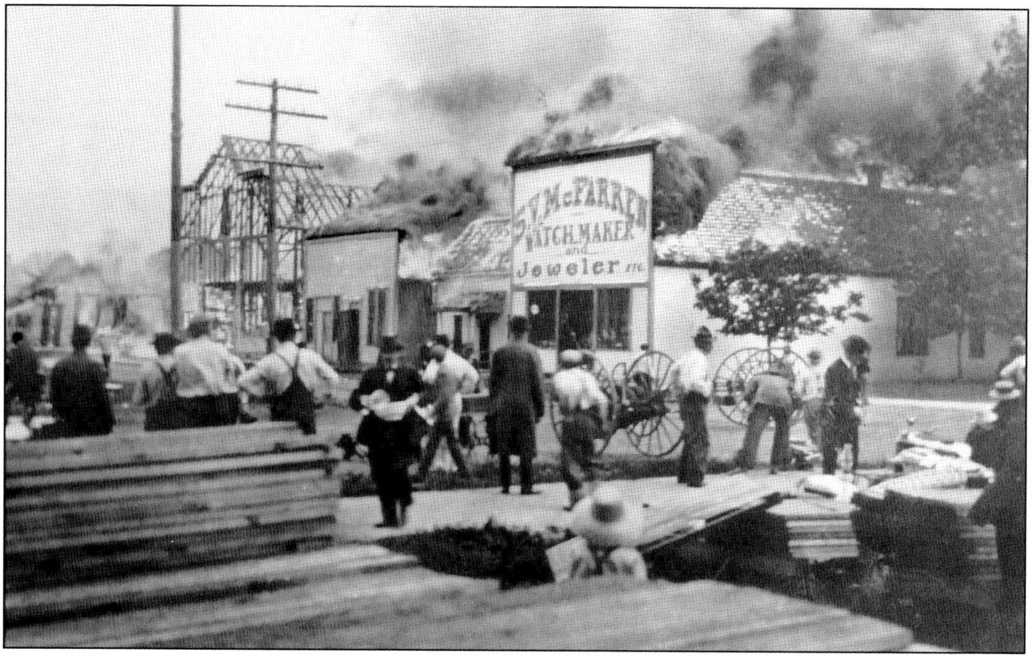

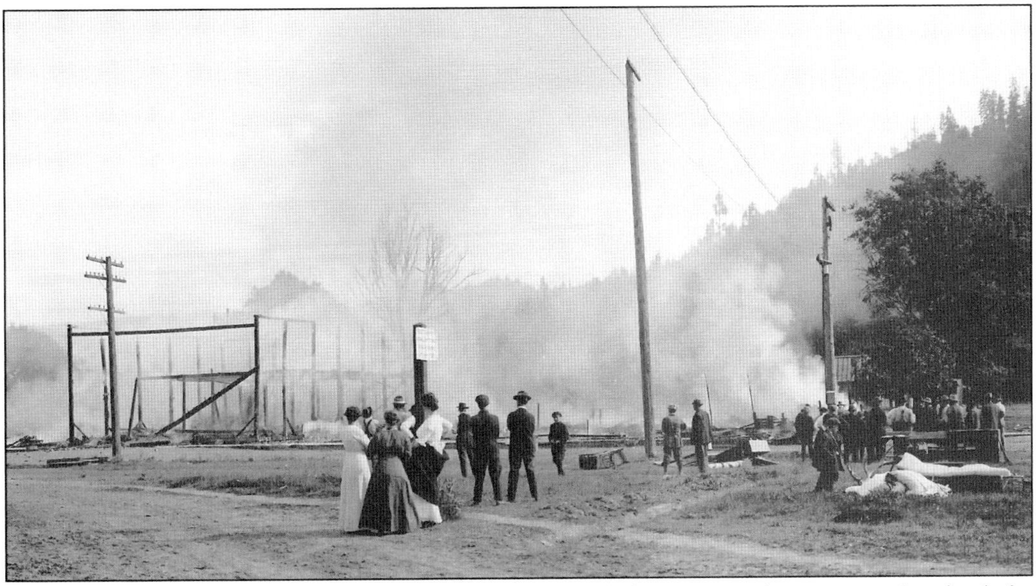

The fire smoldered for days after being contained, and the catastrophe was a real setback for many businesses that had no or inadequate insurance. The losses entailed the livery stable, S. V. McFarren Jewelry, the blacksmith, and other shops, homes, trees, gardens, horses, and livestock. The fire burned for over a block to the present Gold Hill Market at the corner of Second Avenue and Dardanelles Street. The town rebuilt.

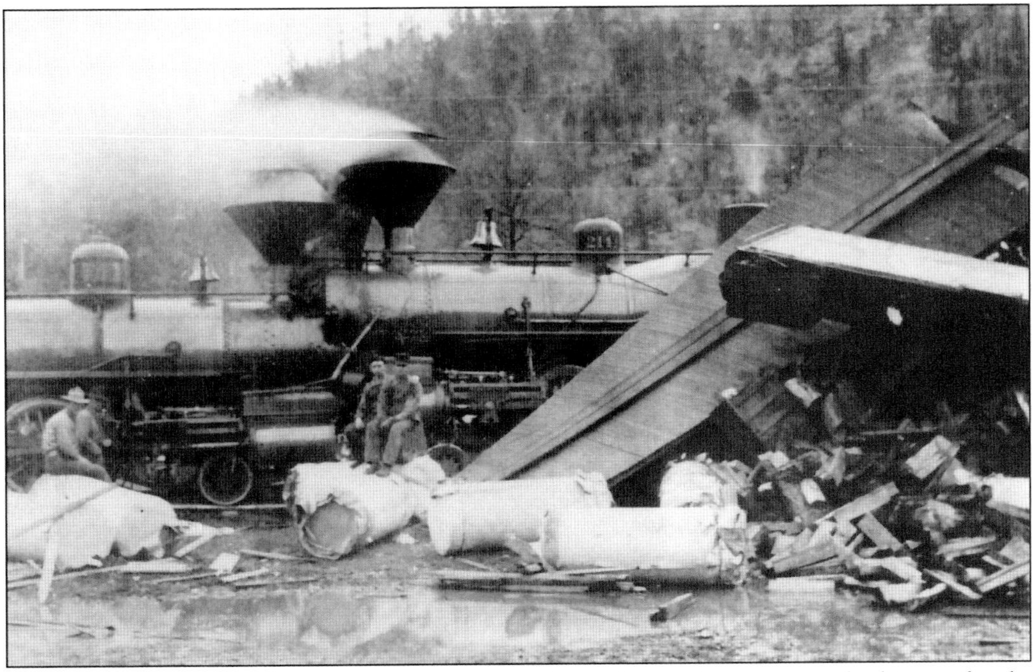

In May 1903, an approaching wood-burning ten-wheeler lost its brakes. It crashed into a freight train, both smoke boxes telescoping, with freight cars literally exploding. Their contents were thrown around the wreck, including that of one car loaded with huge rolls of newsprint. Although two cars laden with explosives split open and dynamite was tossed all around the track, none exploded and no loss of life took place.

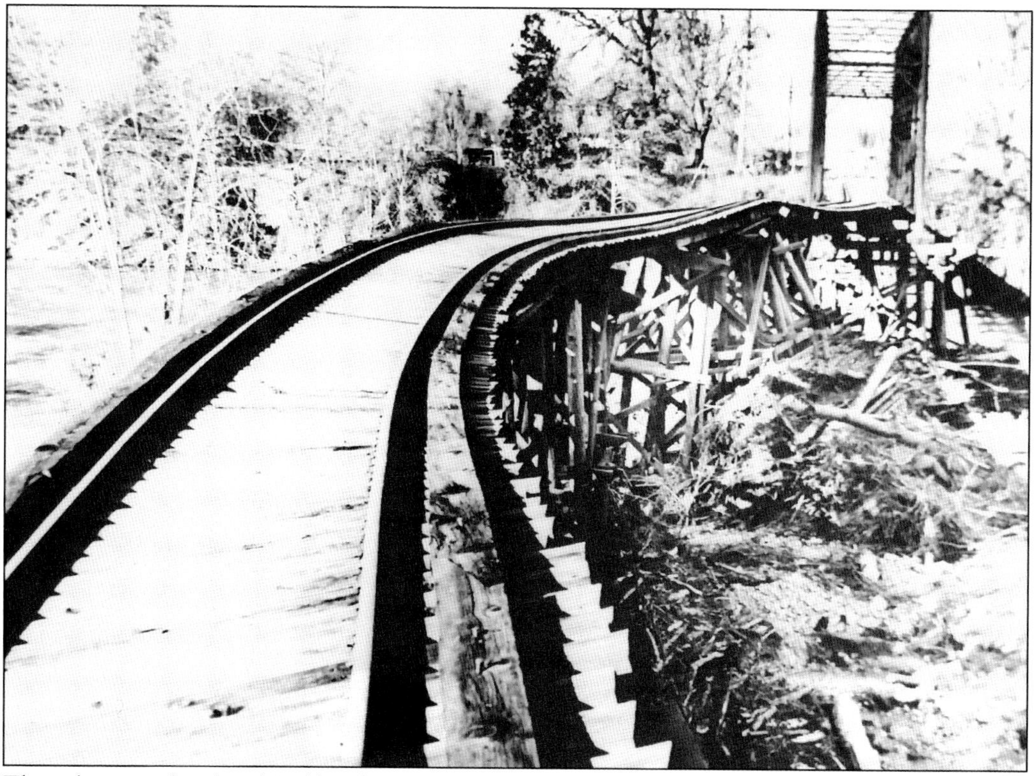

The calamities that faced Gold Hill, as with other communities, also included floods and extensive damage to railroad bridges. This bridge crossed the Rogue River at Grants Pass on Marble Mountain, a spur line of Southern Pacific that was leased by the Beaver Portland Cement Company. This particular flood occurred in 1953.

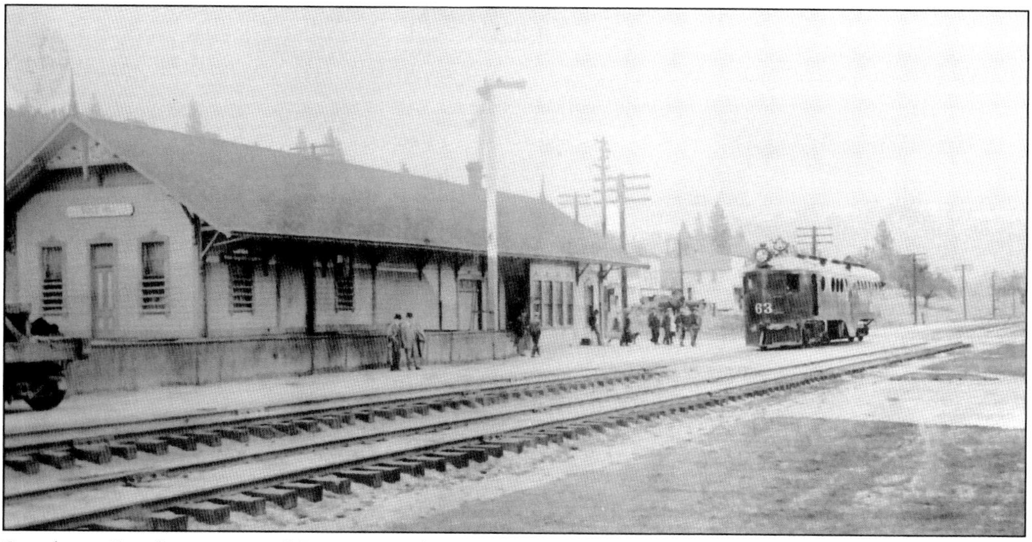

Southern Pacific motorcar No. 63—with a McKean gas engine—ran the line later through Gold Hill. This rail-mounted passenger bus and others operated through the town for over 70 years, ending its service at the Gold Hill railroad depot on July 31, 1956. The depot was then shut down and ultimately removed.

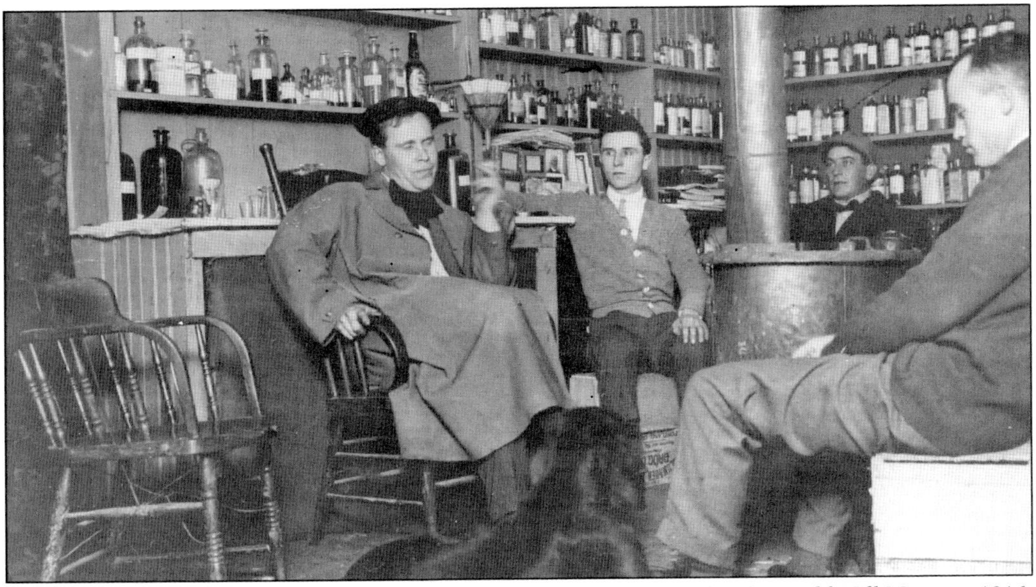

Ben Hur Lampman was not only a reporter and four-year editor for the *Gold Hill News* to 1916, he later was a longtime editor at *The Oregonian* in Portland and poet laureate of Oregon. A renowned essayist, short story writer, poet, and avid fisherman, he returned for years to Gold Hill. He is seen to the left in this 1915 image in the Gold Hill Pharmacy with Gordon Stout (center, left of stove).

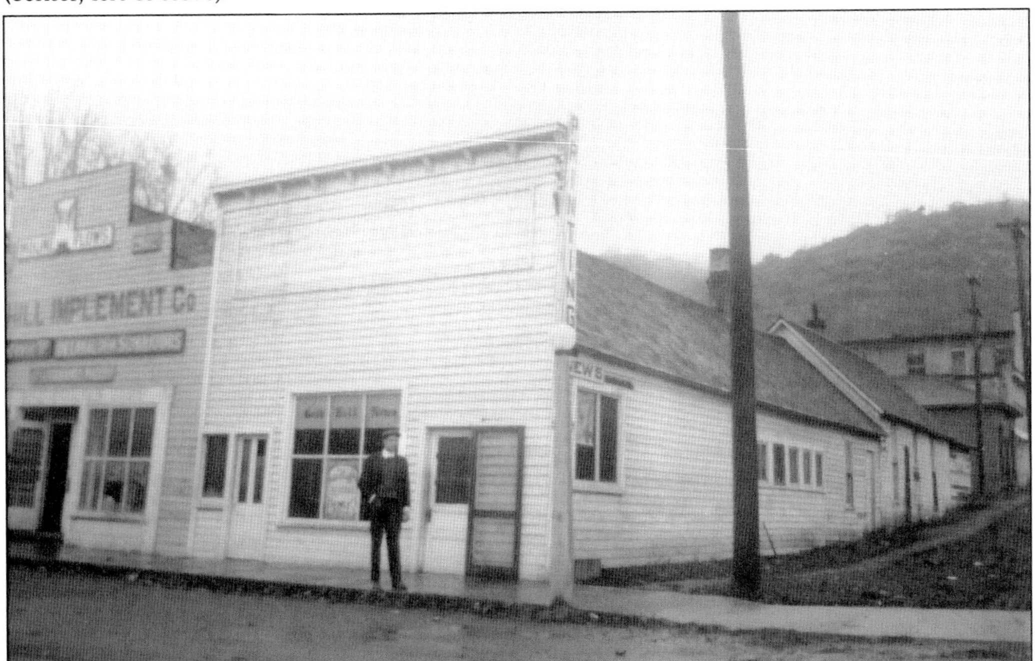

Editor and publisher Howard Wharton is shown after buying the newspaper. Wharton was also the dealer for Geary trucks, and the entire business was sold in 1926 to C. J. Shorb. This structure was across Fourth Avenue and Fifth Street from the Odd Fellows Hall. Kelsey's Hospital is in the background to the far right, and the lamppost in front creates the illusion of an oversized storefront.

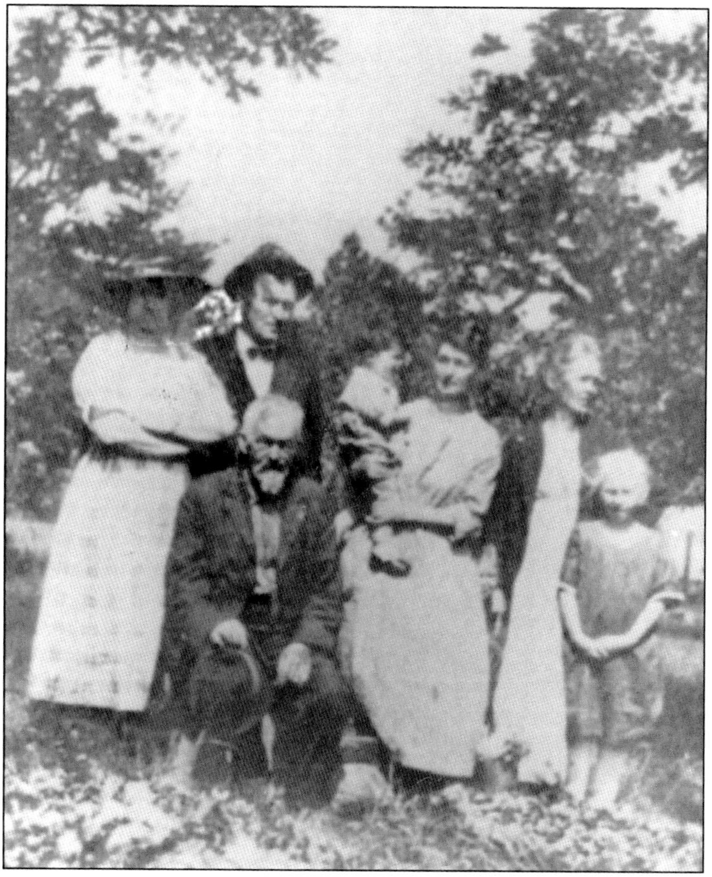

In Hay's Cemetery, from left to right, are Hattie Beeman, Bill Hay (seated), Josiah Beeman, Jack Martin (Josiah's grandson and Virgie's son), Virginia (Virgie) Beeman-Martin, and an unidenfitied woman and child. Bill Hay is buried in Hay's Cemetery, now owned and maintained by the GHHS and once part of his ranch that overlooked the Rogue River. Older members of the historical society insist today that Hays's friendly ghost resides in the Beeman-Martin House, and they have nicknamed him "Willie."

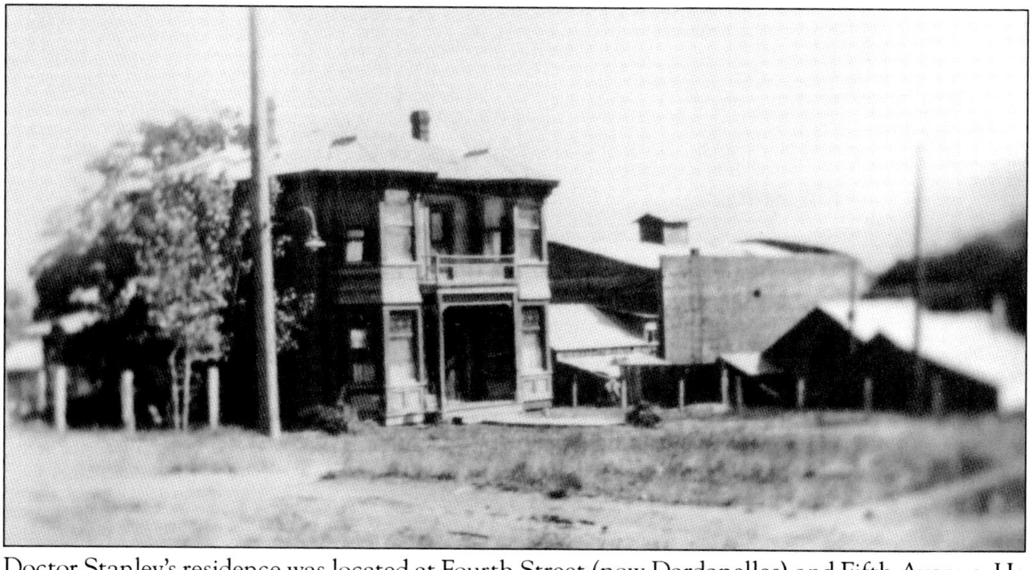

Doctor Stanley's residence was located at Fourth Street (now Dardanelles) and Fifth Avenue. He was a 1900s doctor, treated patients in his home, and used the bottom floor as a hospital, while he lived upstairs. Moving from Tolo to Gold Hill in 1892, Dr. Stanley served as president of the city council for numerous years.

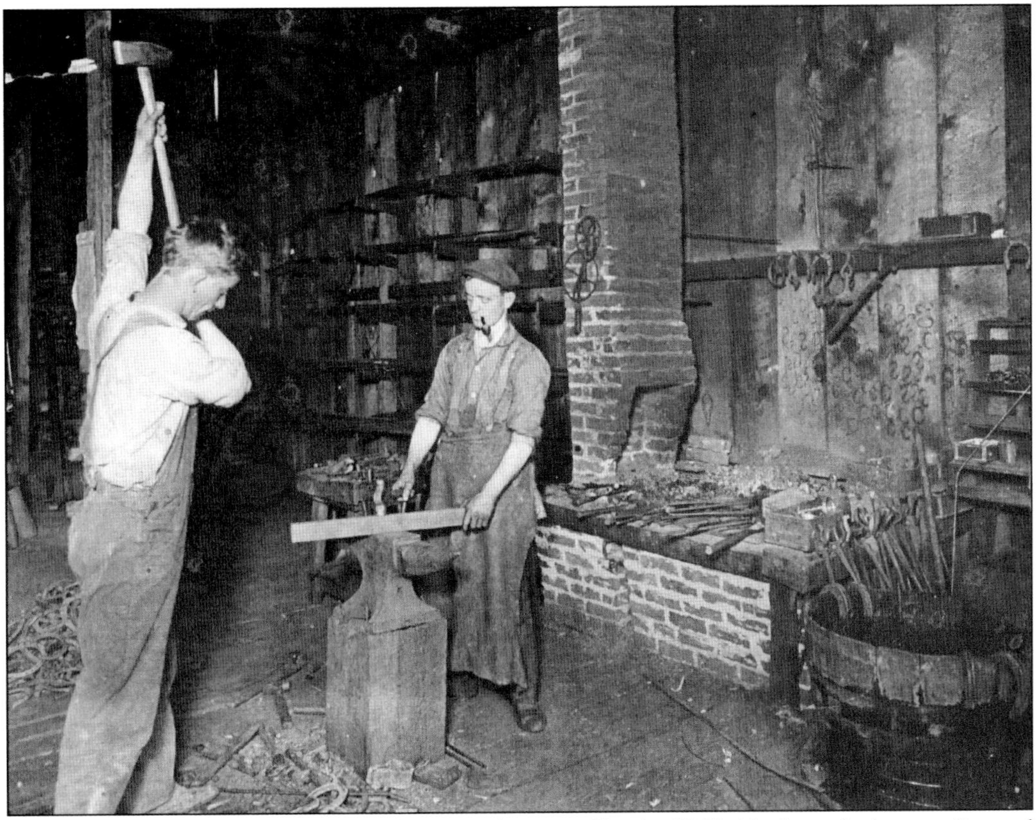

Fred Eddings is slamming his sledgehammer down at Charles Kell's blacksmith shop on Second Avenue in the 1900s. Kell saw the trend to horseless buggies and later switched to car repair. In 1920, Kell (below) is in the machine shop area in Kell's Garage, down the block from his onetime blacksmith shop. Delos Walker's station was in front; Kell's Garage was in the back. A gasoline station is still being operated there.

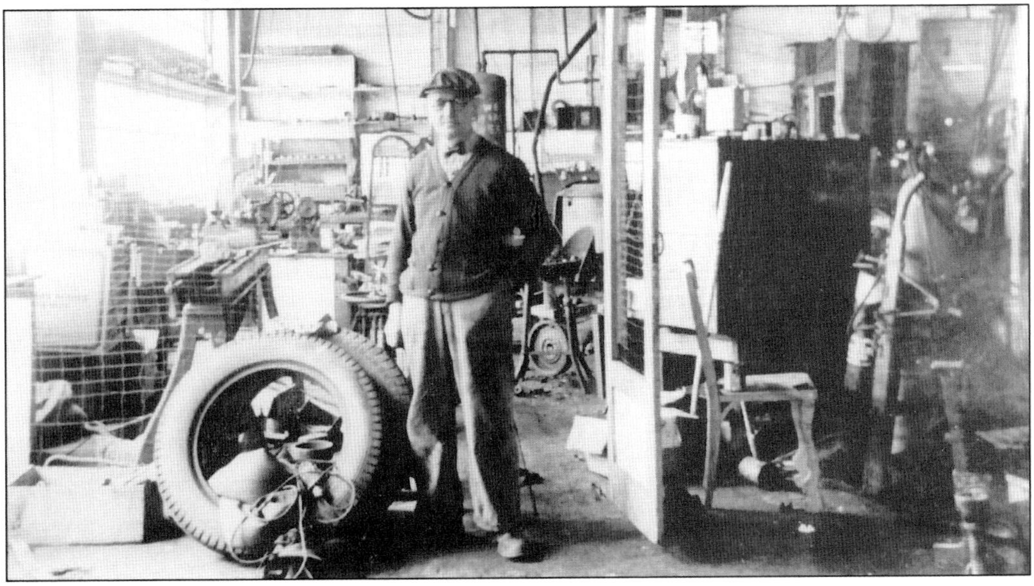

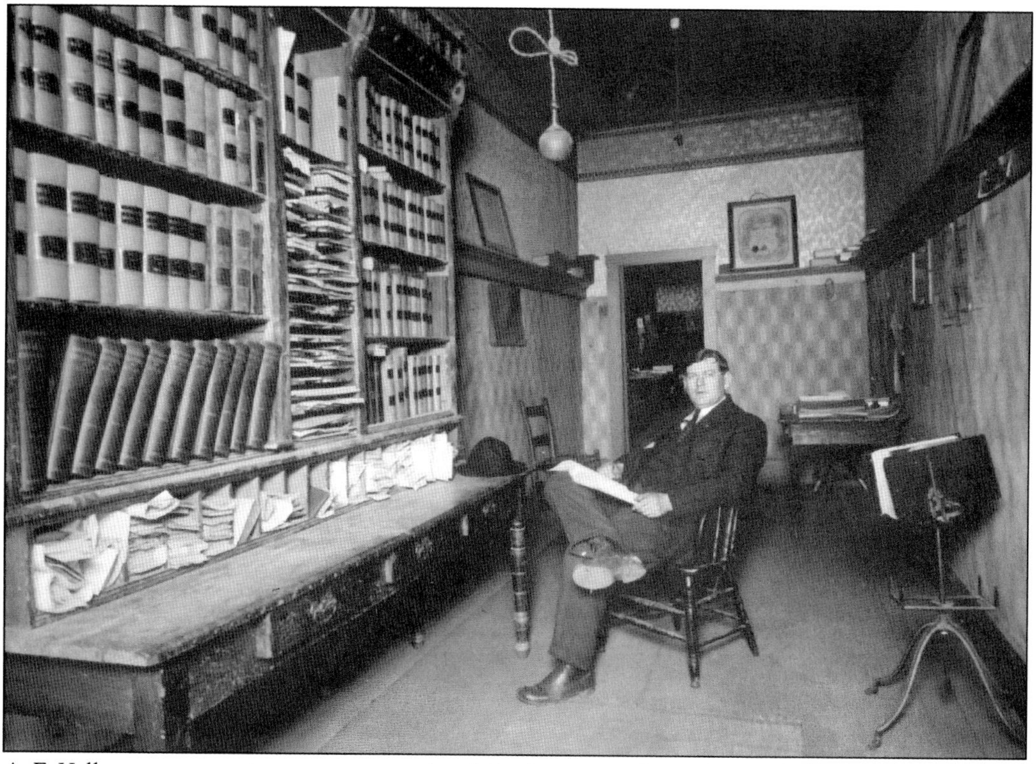

A. E. Kellogg was a prominent attorney and early businessman, shown here in his law office and library above the post office in the early 1900s. He was also at various times the county coroner, a mine owner, mining journal writer, and a livery stable owner. A street is named after him in Gold Hill.

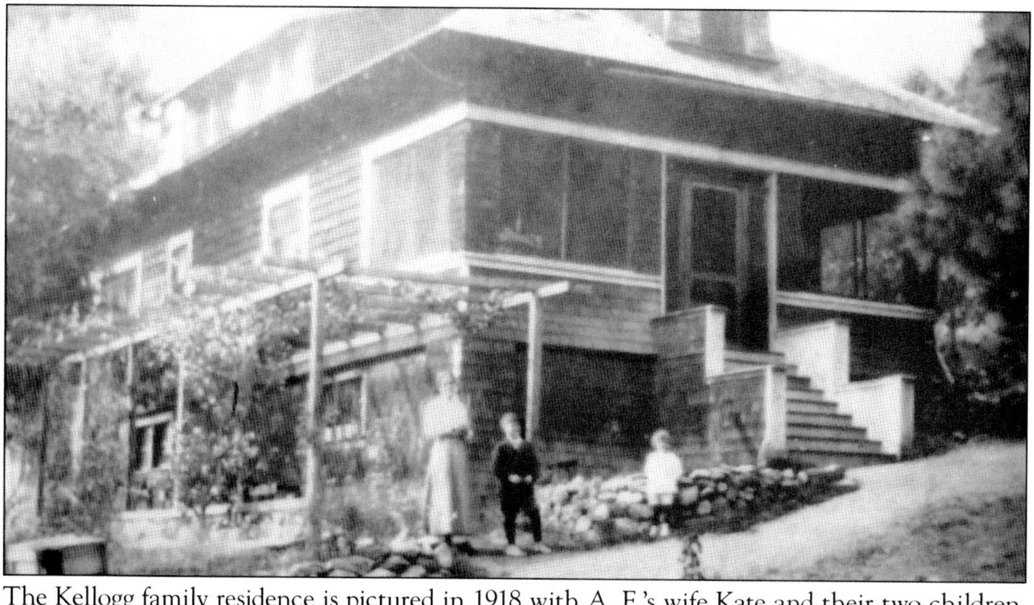

The Kellogg family residence is pictured in 1918 with A. E.'s wife Kate and their two children, Boyce and Noah. Kate was a nurse practitioner as well as a very accomplished seamstress and singer. The three-story structure shows the type of home that successful merchants and mine operators in town could afford. It was located above the business district in the hills.

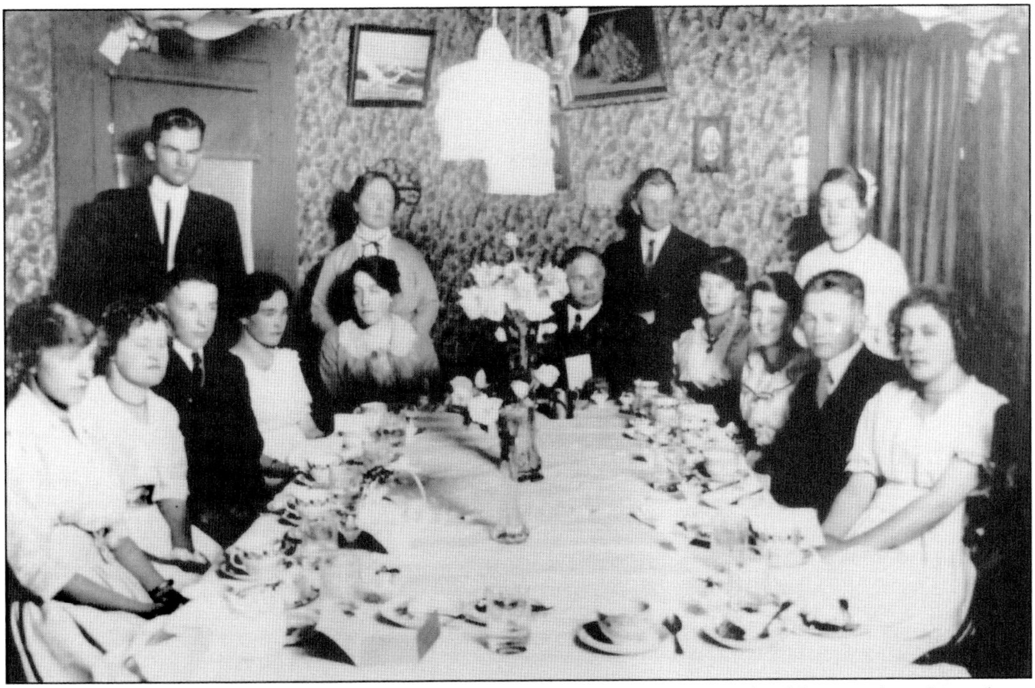

The Milam boardinghouse was one of the places—in lieu of apartment buildings or hotels—where people could stay long term, especially if they preferred a more informal and homelike environment. These dressed-up folks are celebrating in 1919, although the reason is unknown. Ida Starns met Howard Wharton at the boardinghouse and later married him; their son Ted was born there. They are not pictured here.

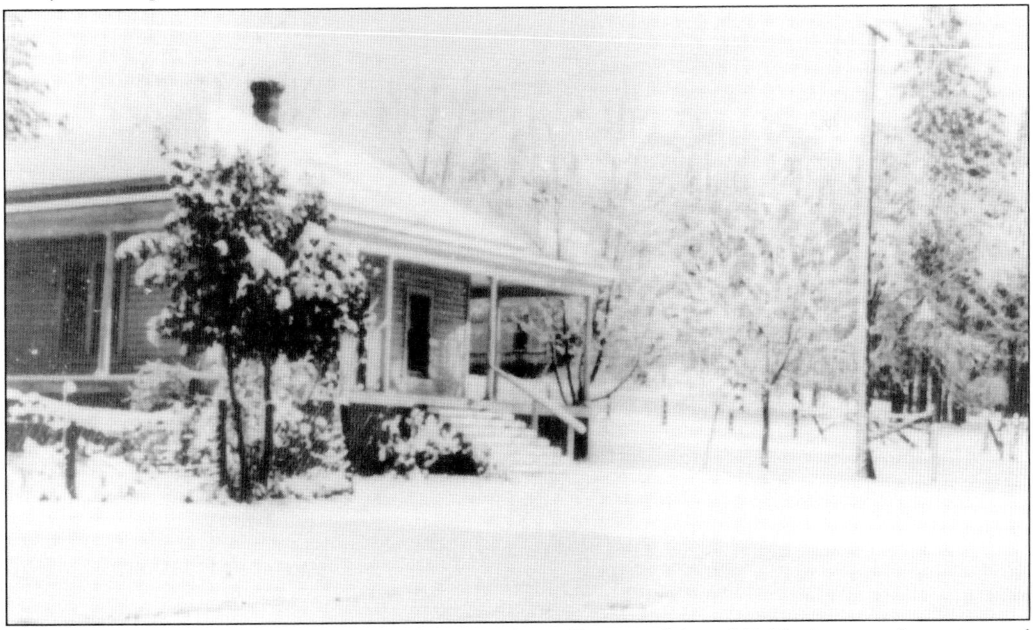

The boardinghouse was located at Fifth Street (now Estremado) and Fifth Avenue. It is pictured here in December 1919 during a particularly brutal winter when temperatures reached 10 degrees below zero.

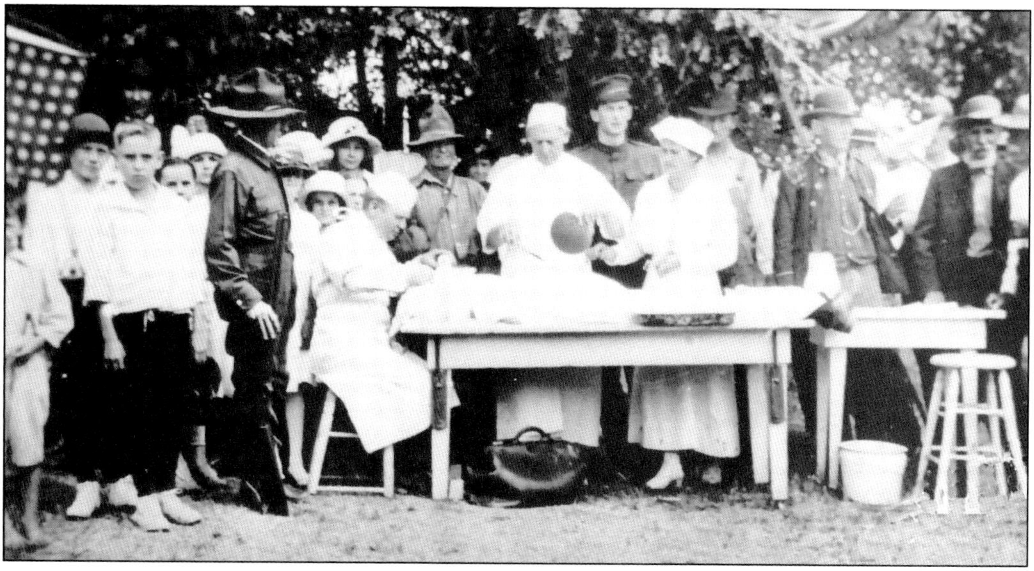

In 1918, "Doc" Kelsey (center), a physician who owned his own hospital, is operating on the kaiser to remove his gall bladder in this skit during World War I. C. C. McClendon is to the far right, with the flowing beard, and Howard Wharton, the *Gold Hill News* editor and owner, is wearing the officer's cap in the middle.

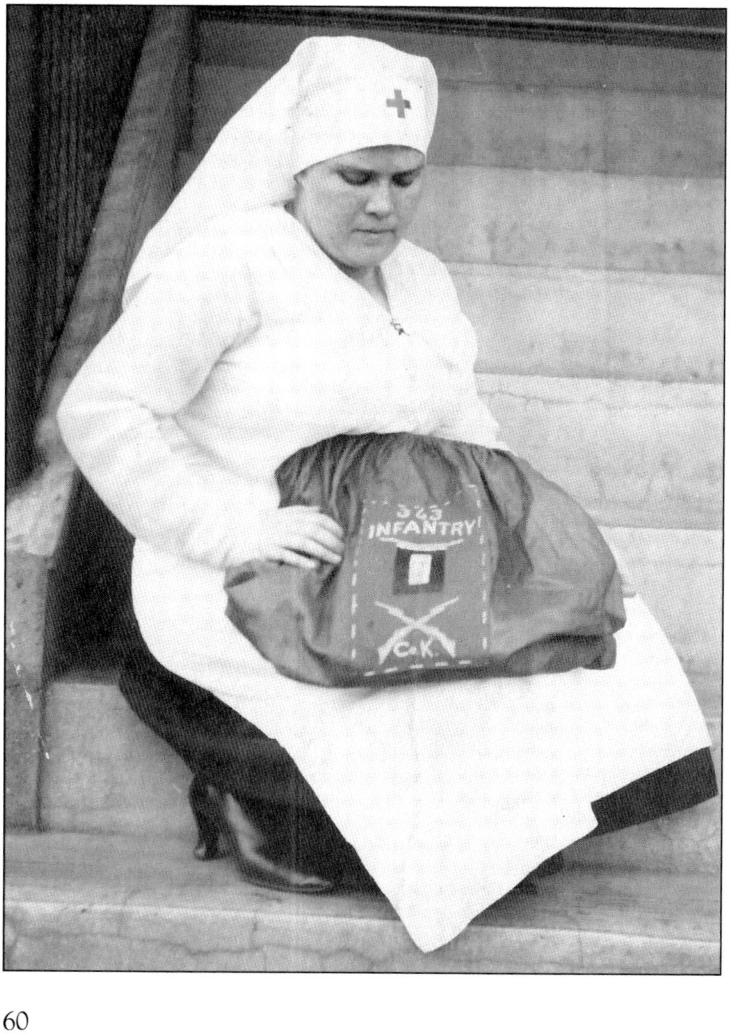

Mrs. E. O. Billings, a Red Cross medical worker, is holding a bag marked "323 Infantry C. K." The *Gold Hill News* ran this picture on November 2, 1918, with the caption, "Mrs. Billings, nee Rosy Lewis, has received word that her husband, Ernest Billings, was killed in action in France."

Four

Schools and Education

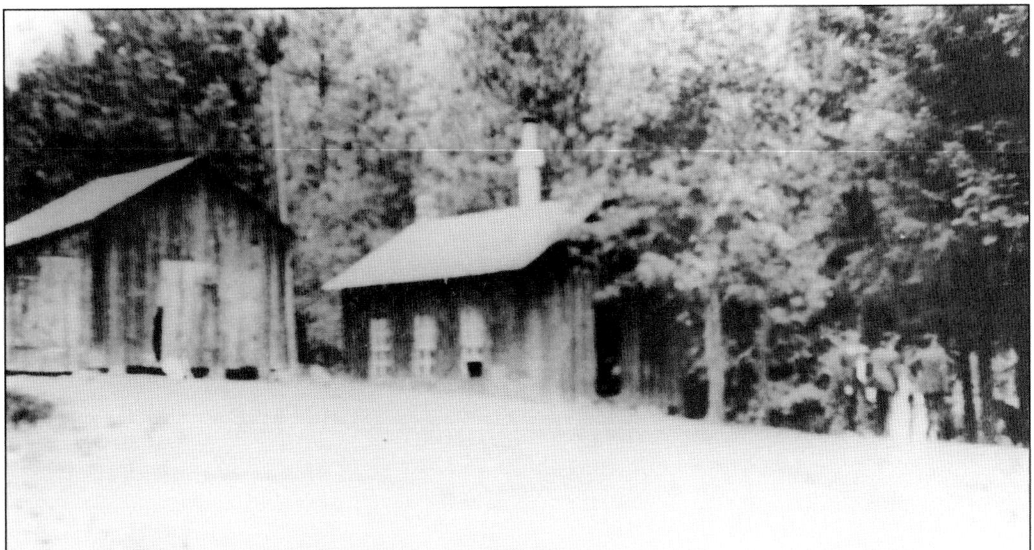

Students had to walk miles to school every day, and if they were lucky, they might hitch a wagon ride. From the creeks to Gold Hill and Sams Valley, schoolhouses were scattered about in various locations. These typically one-room schools included all grades, and the teacher was usually a young woman who lived with another family or in a small house built by locals. Because of the oil lamps used, fires were a constant danger. This was the first Sardine Creek School, constructed in 1906.

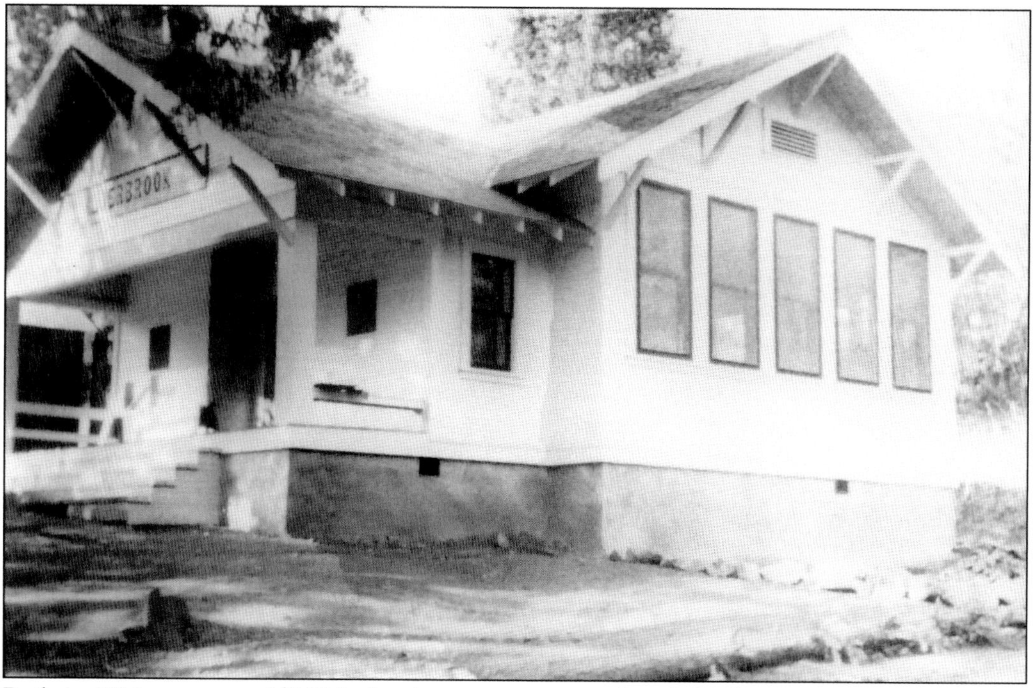

Built in 1915 at a cost of $1,200, this larger structure replaced the first Sardine Creek School. Named Alderbrook, the school was annexed to Gold Hill District No. 57 in 1939 and subsequently closed when students were bused to Gold Hill schools.

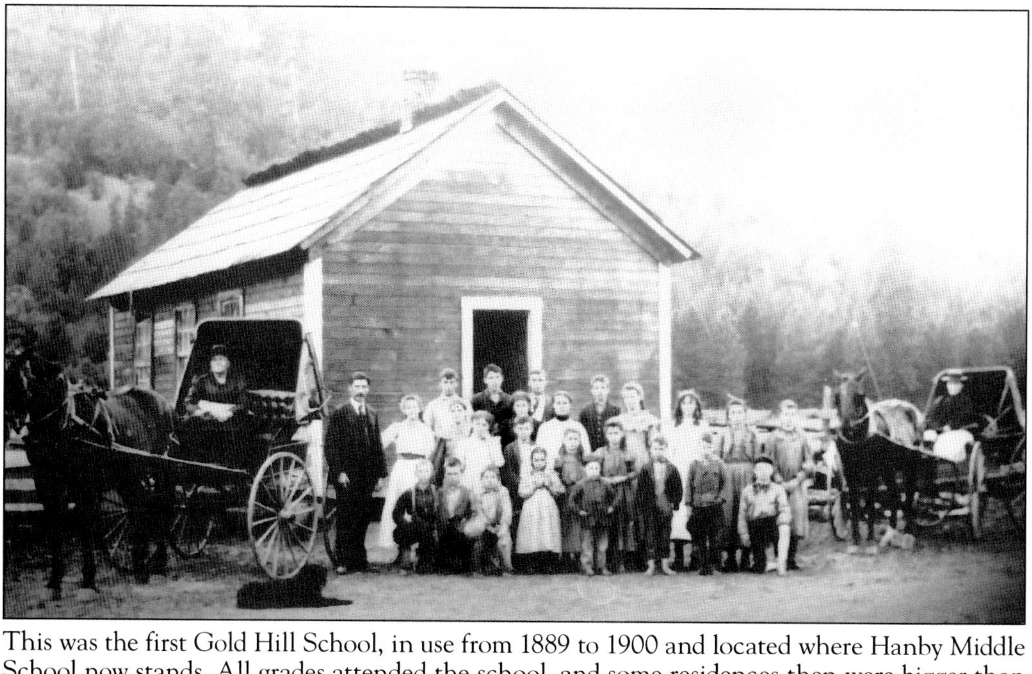

This was the first Gold Hill School, in use from 1889 to 1900 and located where Hanby Middle School now stands. All grades attended the school, and some residences then were bigger than this cabin. Prior to this structure, one-room subscription schools existed, where local residents paid the teacher directly.

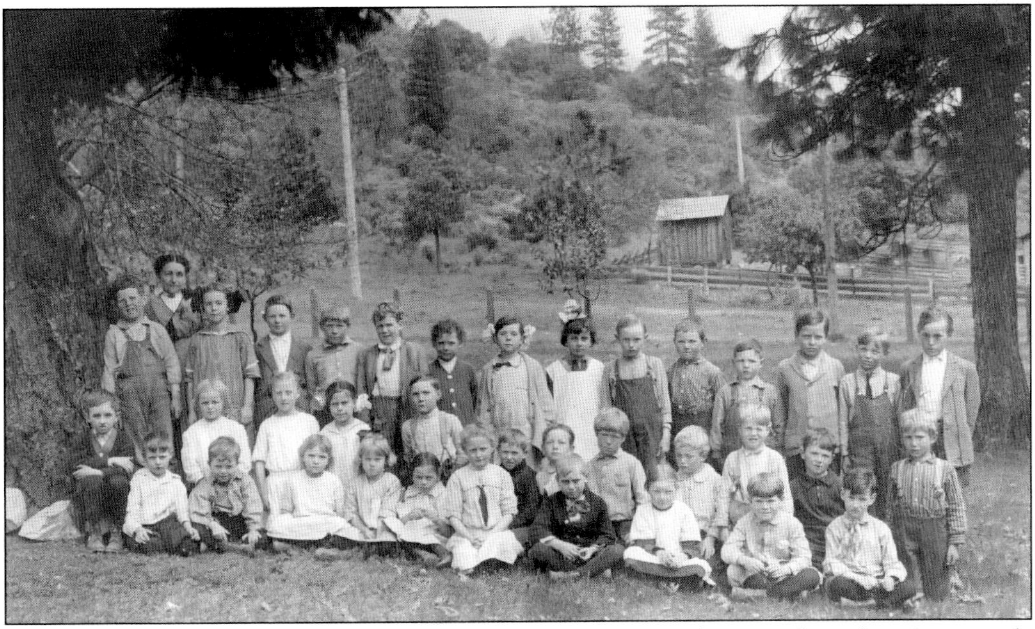

The young children in the Gold Hill Public School's lower grades were dressed up for an early 1900s school picture. The wilderness surrounding them is striking when contrasted with today. Despite all grades attending, class pictures were important.

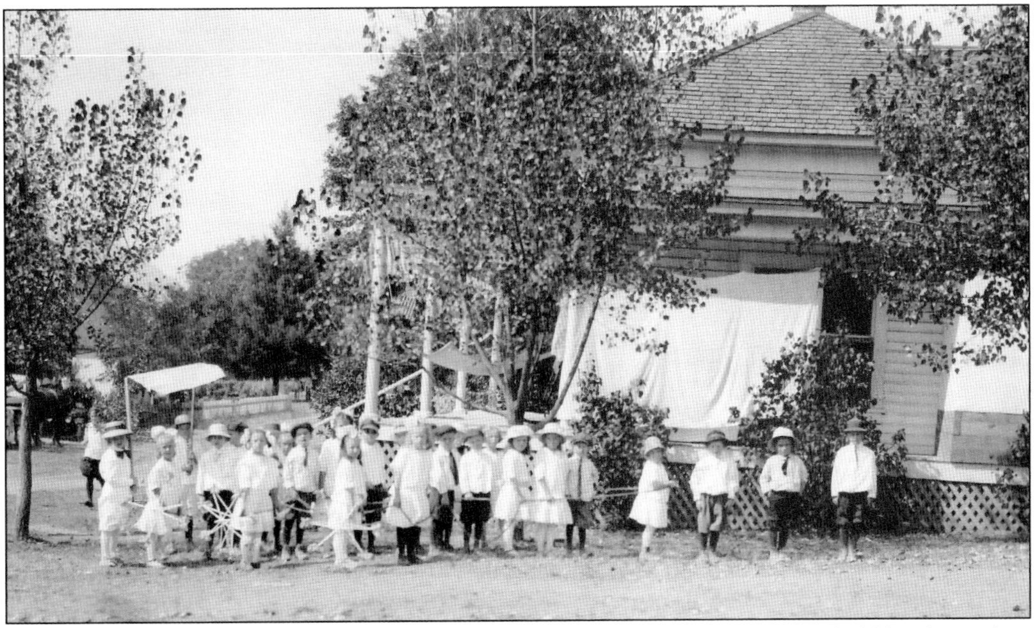

Around 1900, these school children were at their primary grade school fair, held by the Milam boardinghouse. All are dressed up, the girls in white dresses and hats, the boys generally in white shirts with ties.

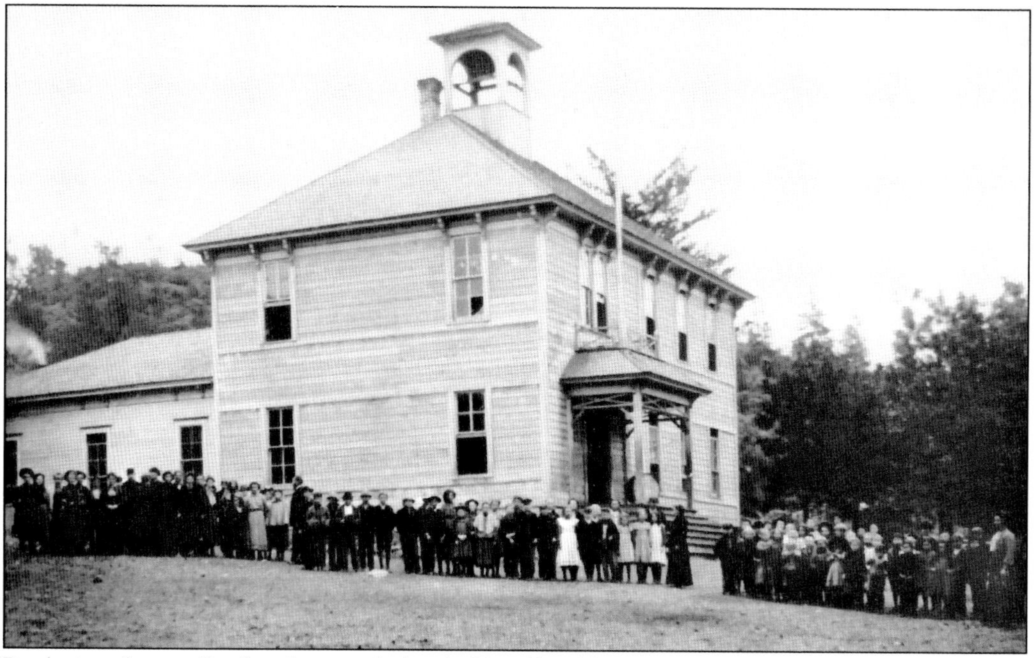

Replacing the small cabin first used, the Gold Hill Public School, or second school, became the school for ten years starting in 1901. Located at Third Street and Sixth Avenue, it covered all grades until the new Hanby Public High School was constructed in 1910. After being used for secondary education, then as the city hall and library, this structure was finally razed to make way for the present-day city hall complex.

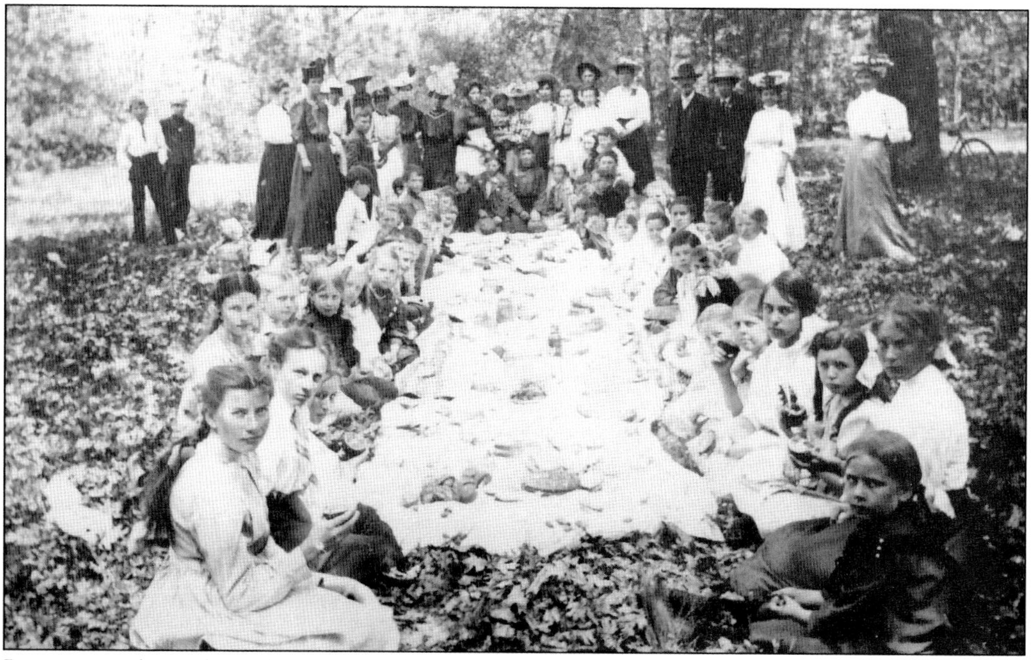

Primary-grade students from Gold Hill are enjoying a box lunch social near the Dardanelles schoolhouse around 1905. This place was referred to as Chavner's Grove and was located where the present Laurel Hill Golf Course is now, off the Interstate 5 exit.

This June 10, 1897 photograph shows Andrew Jackson (A. J.) Hanby, an early Gold Hill schoolteacher and principal for whom Hanby School is named. Hanby taught in the area for a total of 42 years. He was an ordained Christian minister and vice president of the First Federal Savings and Loan Association of Medford from 1937 until his death in 1957.

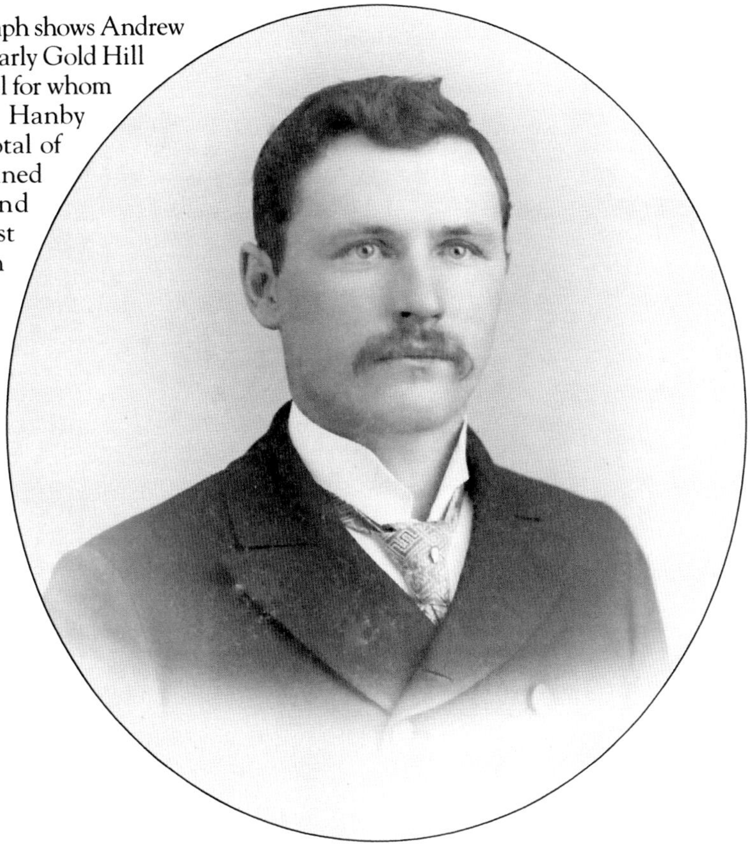

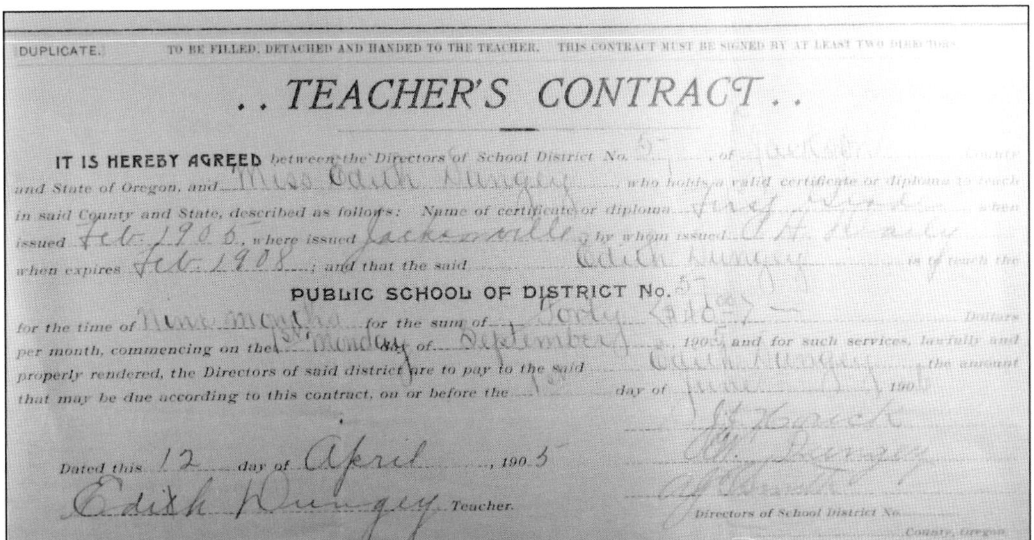

DUPLICATE. TO BE FILLED, DETACHED AND HANDED TO THE TEACHER. THIS CONTRACT MUST BE SIGNED BY AT LEAST TWO DIRECTORS

..TEACHER'S CONTRACT..

IT IS HEREBY AGREED between the Directors of School District No. 57, of [illegible] County and State of Oregon, and Miss Edith Dungey who holds a valid certificate or diploma to teach in said County and State, described as follows: Name of certificate or diploma First Grade when issued Feb. 1905, where issued Jacksonville by whom issued [illegible] when expires Feb. 1908; and that the said Edith Dungey is to teach the

PUBLIC SCHOOL OF DISTRICT No. 57

for the time of Nine months for the sum of Forty ($40.00) Dollars per month, commencing on the 1st Monday of September 1905 and for such services, lawfully and properly rendered, the Directors of said district are to pay to the said Edith Dungey the amount that may be due according to this contract, on or before the 1st day of June 1906

Dated this 12 day of April, 1905

Edith Dungey Teacher.

[illegible]

Directors of School District No.

County, Oregon.

This 1905 teacher's contract for Edith Dungey is dated April 12, 1905, and was to last nine months from September 1905 to June 1906 at $40 per month. It states that Dungey held a valid certificate to teach first grade, issued in Jacksonville in February 1905, and valid for three years. District 57 was the Gold Hill district, where she would be employed.

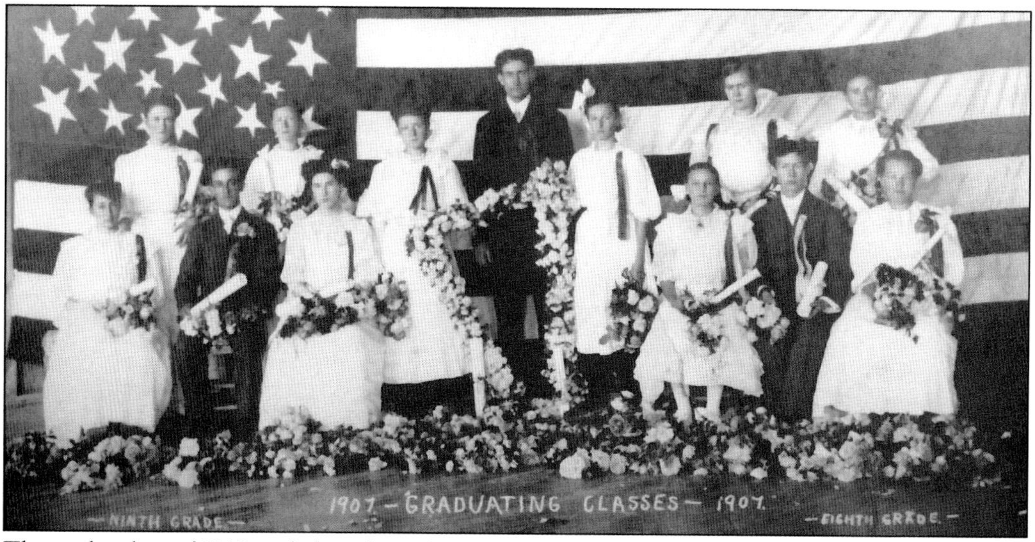

This is the class of 1907, eighth and ninth grade graduates of Gold Hill Public School. A. O. Freel was the principal. Since students then might not graduate from high school—having to work on their family farms—junior high school graduations were also important.

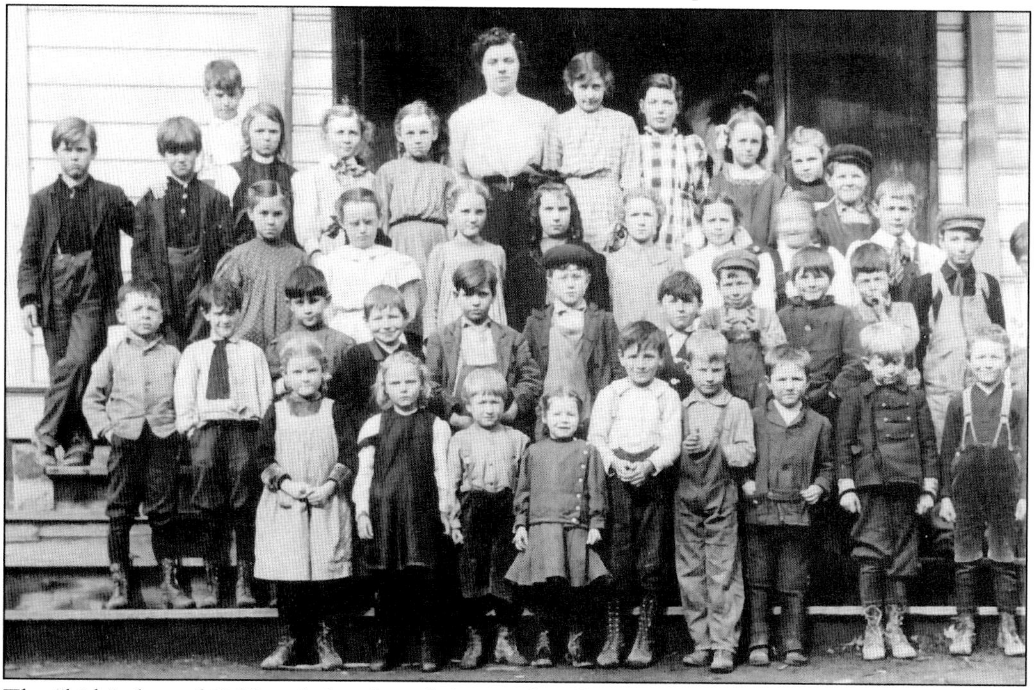

The "kids" class of 1909 includes, from left to right, (first row) Susan Starns, Bertha Coy, Tom Chisholm, Eleanor Huntington, unidentified, Lyle Olsen, unidentified, Vernon Fleming, and Jim Chisholm; (second row) Kenneth Davidson, Joe Lewis, Cleo Gilchrist, Frank Carter, Floyd Jarvis, unidentified, James Huntington, unidentified, Lucious Huntington, unidentified, John McClendon, and Antone Olsen; (third row) Edna Sutton, Leda Harvey, Evagene Starns, Hazel Knotts, Margaret Chisholm, Vineta Flemming, Lizzie Horn, and unidentified; (fourth row) Lete Pratt, Otis Olsen, unidentified, Maude Coy, Ada Lewis, Gladys Childers, teacher May Smith, Sara Horn, Ritha Horn, Euna Roberts, and Floyd Darling.

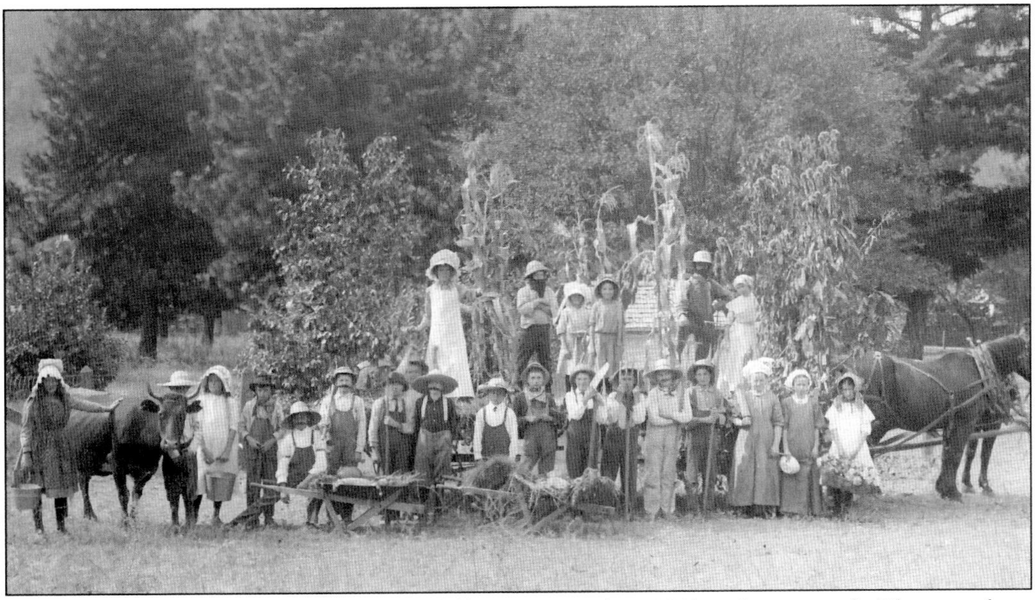

These fifth and sixth graders are in their fall costume garb in 1913 at the city park. They are, from left to right, Katherine Cook, Vernon Fleming, Susan Starns, Willard Britt, John McClendon, Cecil Johnson, Jim Chisholm, Nester Anderson, Gerald Owen, Floyd Darling, Harry Hicks, Melvin Ballard, Abram Meyers, Joe Lewis, Frank Carter, Leda Harvey, Veneta Fleming, Linwood Blakely, Dolores Kelsey, Otis Olsen, Leona Stoall, Alice Johnson, Myron Anderson, and Evagene Starns.

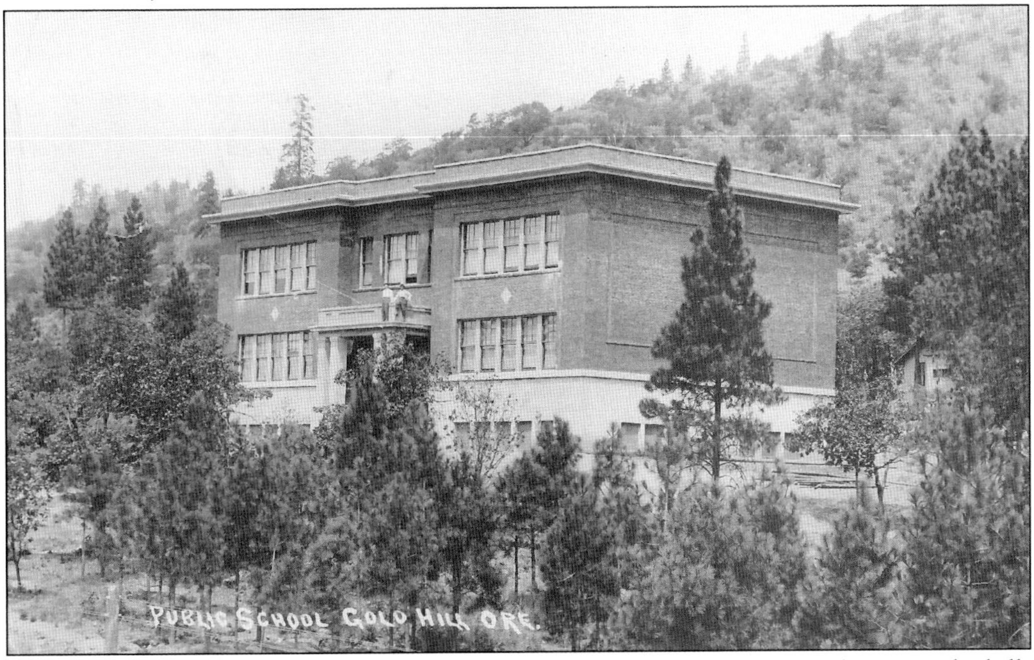

In 1910, this sturdy brick building was constructed above the town's business district in the hills between Fifth and Sixth Avenues. Serving all grades until 1950, the school became a middle school and was named Hanby in 1956 in honor of longtime respected educator A. J. Hanby. Still in use for school administration purposes in the current school complex, it was listed in 1991 on the National Register of Historic Places and celebrated its centennial in 2010.

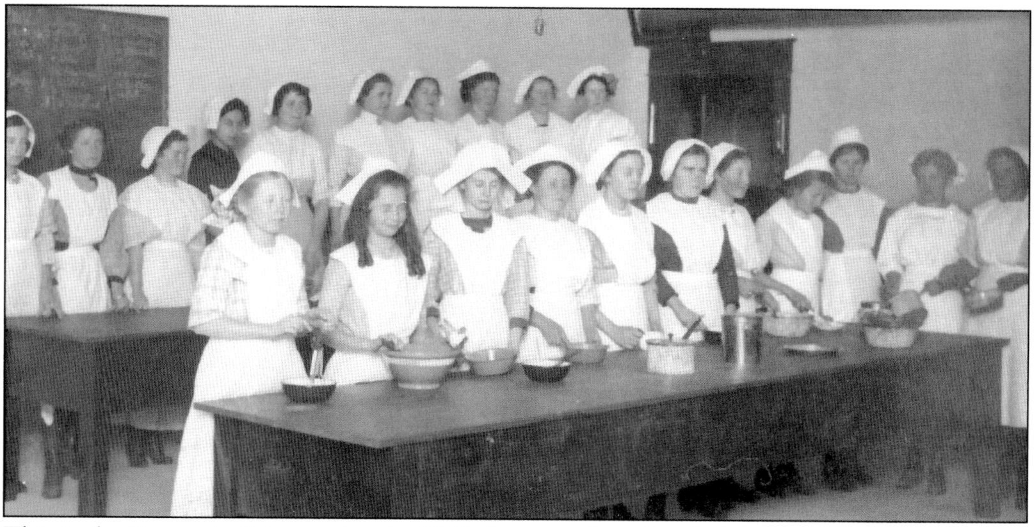

This is the Domestic Science class in 1912, for seventh and eighth graders at the new school. Pictured in this image, in no particular order, are Hattie Hodges, Pearl Collins, Mary Truax, Thelma Davidson, Dorothy Smith, Ethel Lawrence, Gladys Haymond, Ida Starns, Mildred Myers, Ethel Davidson, Letsy Hodges, and Mary Newton, among others.

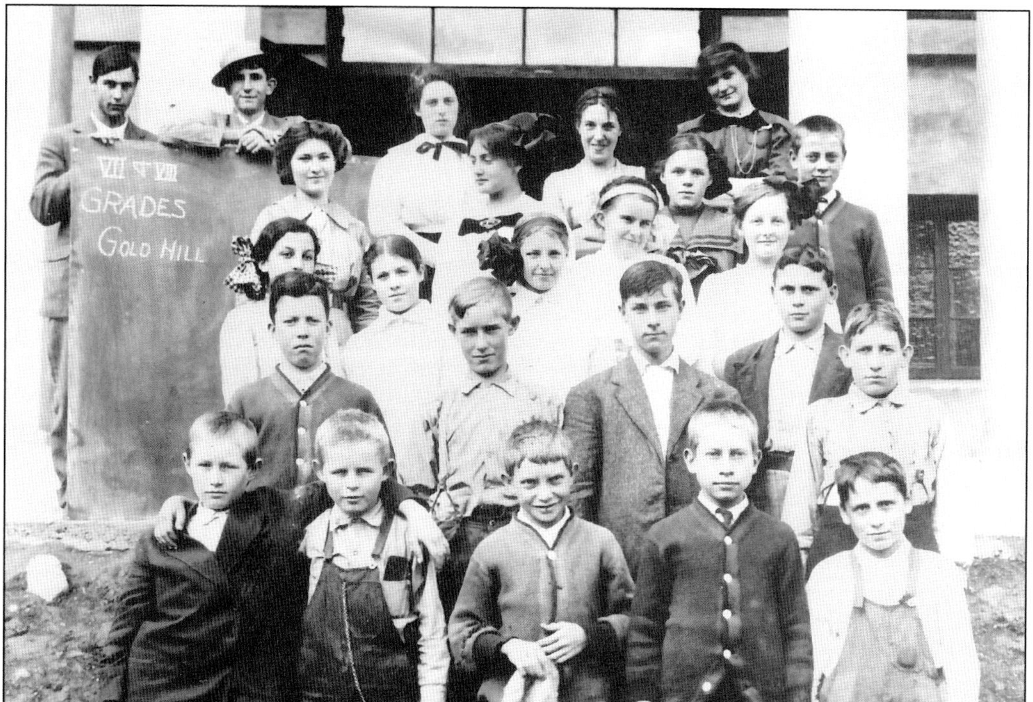

The seventh and eighth grades for the 1914–1915 school year are, from left to right, (first row) J. Horton Beeman, Donald Avery, Theron Pankey, Frank Reidel, and Leroy Dungey; (second row) Floyd Lance, Eugene Bowman, Clarence Van Houten, Elmer Dungey, and Warren Coppock; (third row) Agnes Dietrich, Letsy Hodges, Pearl Knowles, Mildred Myers, and Lily Starns; (fourth row) Earl Van Houten, Clint Walker, Icie Bailey, unidentified, Margaret Hoffman, Thelma Hammersly, Mary Newton, Pearl Collins, and Frank Reidel.

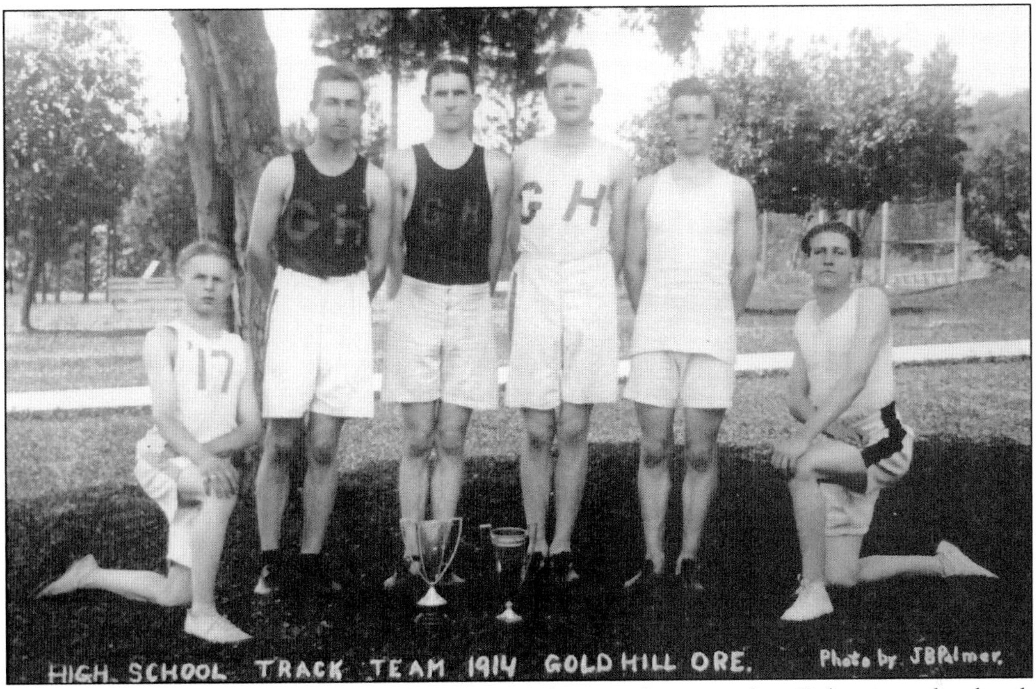

The 1914 Gold Hill High School track team won the area championship. Balancing schoolwork and athletic activities with the required chores on family farms or businesses made their lives very busy! The members of the team are, from left to right, Don Avery, Bill Kelsey, Clinton Walker, Ernest Lyman, Lloyd Miller, and Warren Coppock.

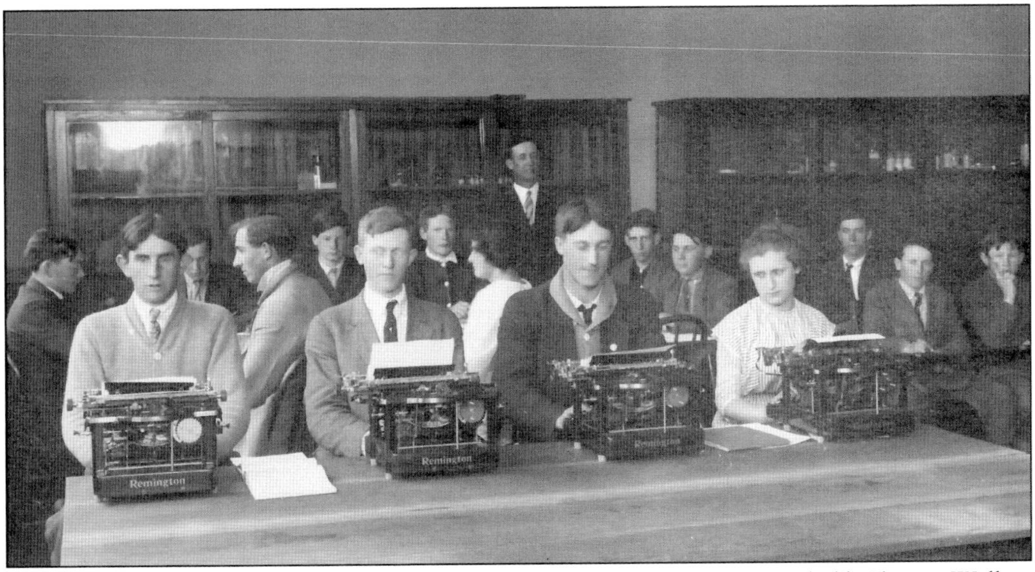

Pictured in this 1915 typing class are, from left to right: (first row, at typing desk) Clinton Walker, Benjamin Haymond, student body president John Kelsey, and Mary Truax; second row (facing left) William Kelsey and Pearl Collins; (third row) Richard Morelock (facing right), Elmer Dungey, Alton Dungey, Ernest Lyman, teacher/principal B. G. Harding (standing), William Foley, J. Horton Beeman, Lloyd Miller, Warren Coppock, and Clarence Van Houton.

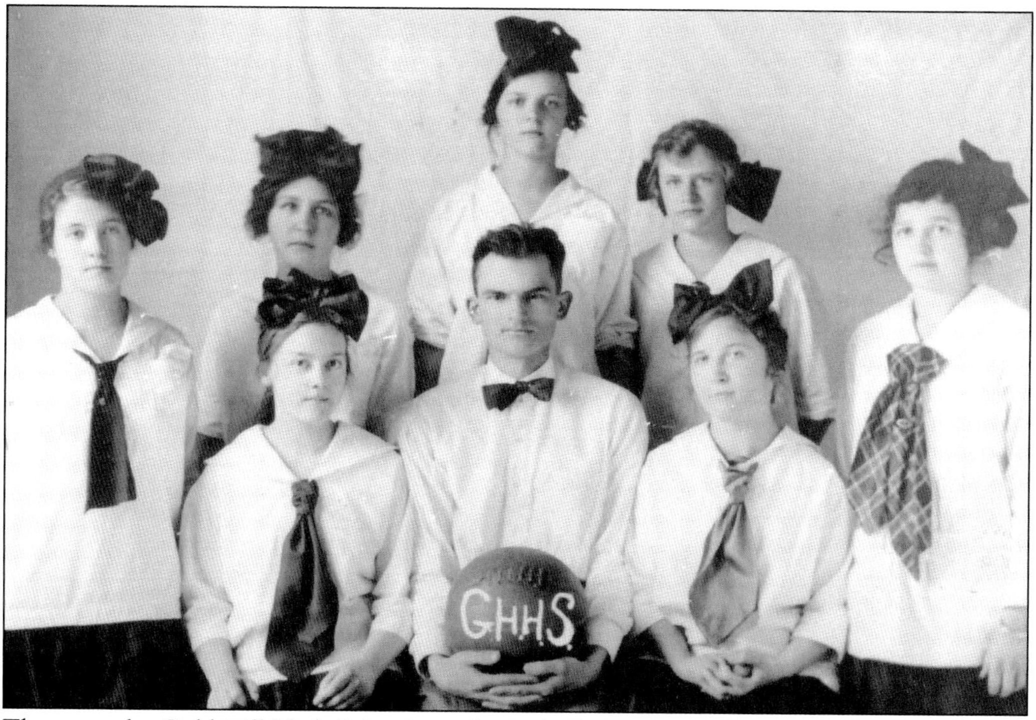

These are the Gold Hill High School area basketball champions for 1916. They are, from left to right, (first row) guard Ida Starns, coach Victor Flint, and forward Ada Lewis; (second row) captain Letsy Hodges, center Loleta Hougham, substitute Maude Coy, guard Marguriete Wharton, and forward Ida Johnson.

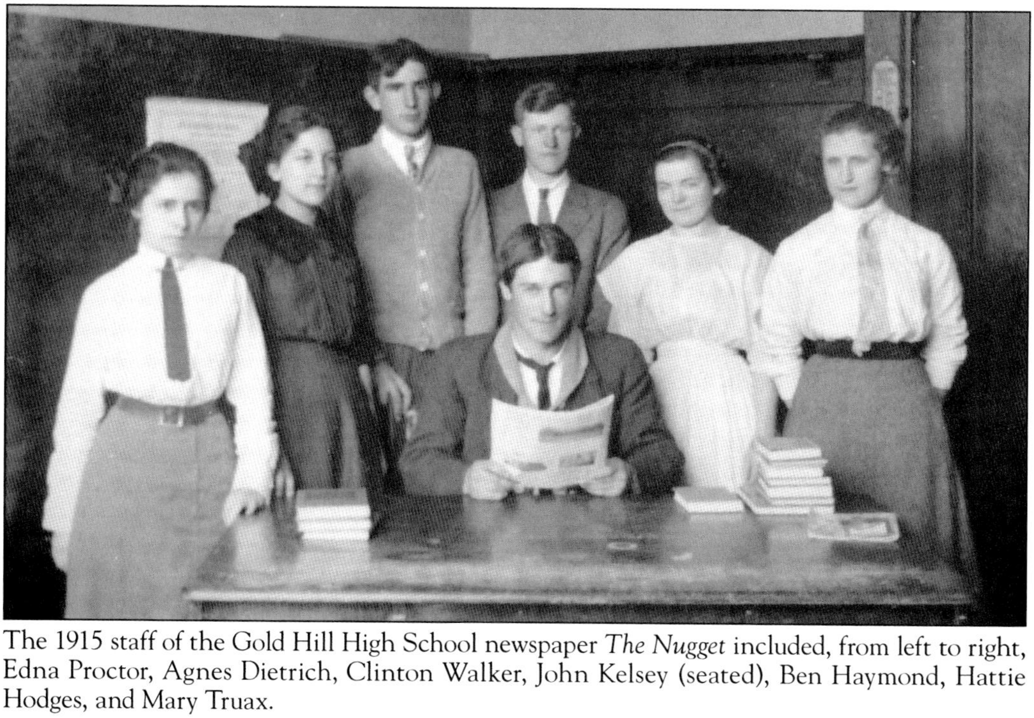
The 1915 staff of the Gold Hill High School newspaper *The Nugget* included, from left to right, Edna Proctor, Agnes Dietrich, Clinton Walker, John Kelsey (seated), Ben Haymond, Hattie Hodges, and Mary Truax.

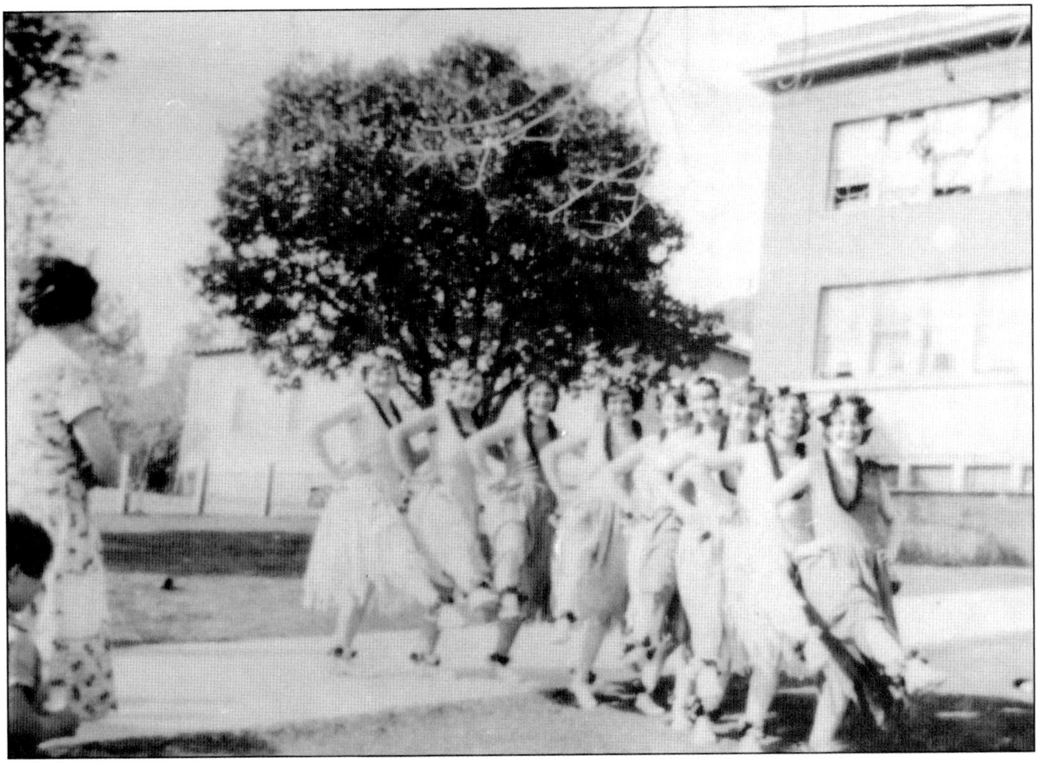

These students of the Roaring Twenties were the cast in a Gold Hill High School play in 1929, with a very definite Hawaiian theme.

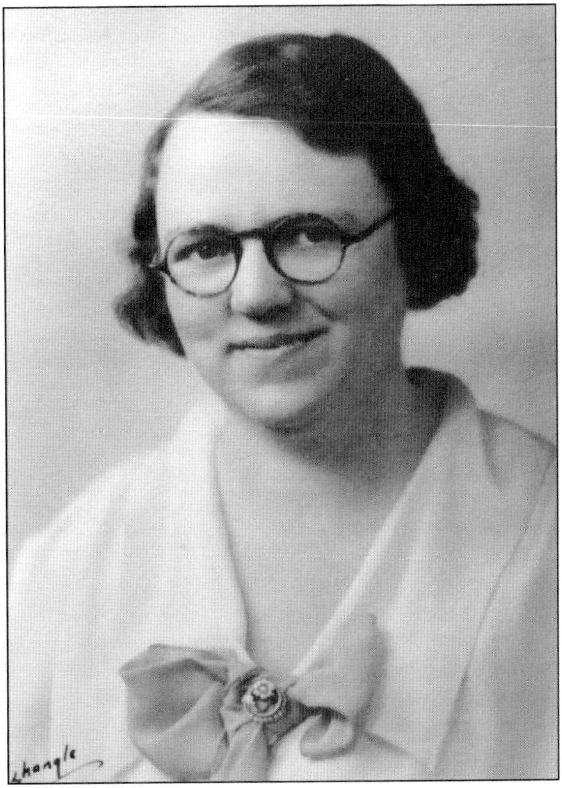

Maude Coy Robinson, a longtime, well-liked educator, is pictured in 1935. Not only a graduate of Gold Hill Public School, Maude taught there from 1921 to 1932 and later retired as principal of Medford's Griffin Creek School. She was an officer and quite active in the Oregon State Teachers Association.

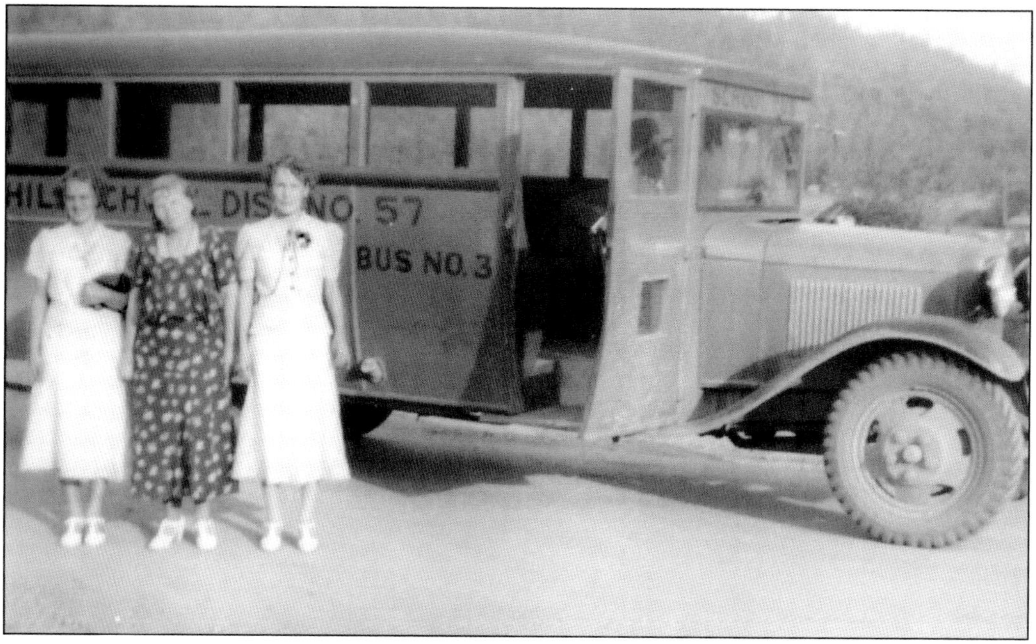

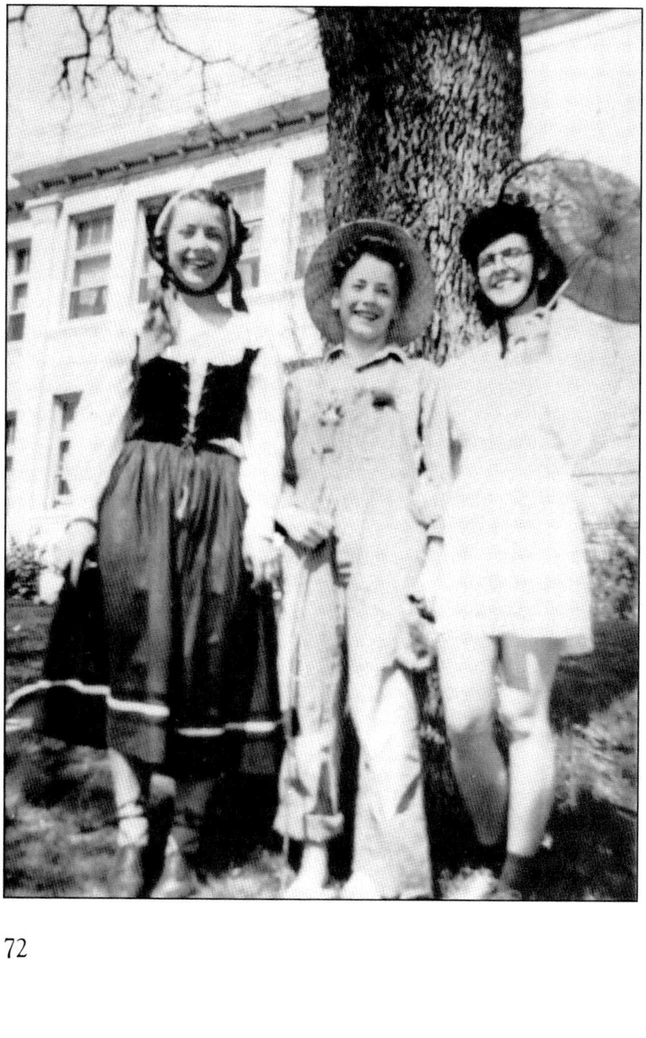

The old school bus No. 3 was a 1933 Ford that Carl Routh drove in 1936 when this picture was taken. From left to right are June Robbins, Mary Shoemaker, and Beth Paulson.

For the 1939 senior dress-up day, three girls are in costume. They are, from left to right, Alice Annernst, Arlene Jean Campbell, and Charlotte Walker.

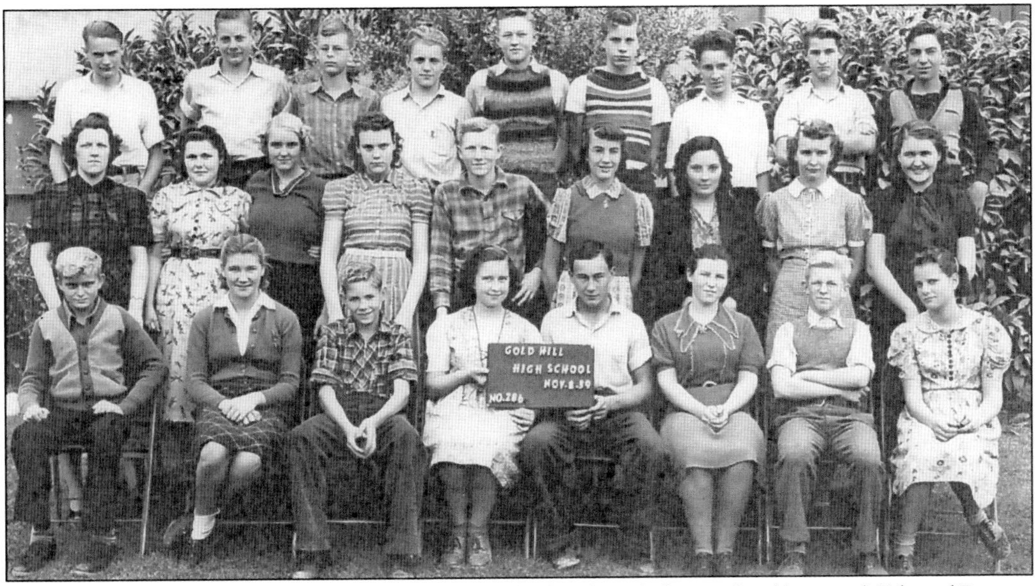

The high school freshman class of 1939–1940 includes, from left to right, (first row) Edward Prauss, LaVerne Parkhurst, Alvis Winn, Norma Lee Ward, Jim Martin, Dorothy Ray, Donald Bowers, and Thelma St. Germaine; (second row) teacher Miss Evans, Maxine Cook, Lenore Clement, Marjorie Smith, Lee Marsden, Evalyn Christensen, Della Prefontaine, Geraldine Parker, and Rae Clement; (third row) Jim Spencer, Charles Rosecrans, Wilson Flick, Stanley Robbins, Kenneth Herrin, Harold Wilson, George Kile, Harlow Banry, and Joe Smith.

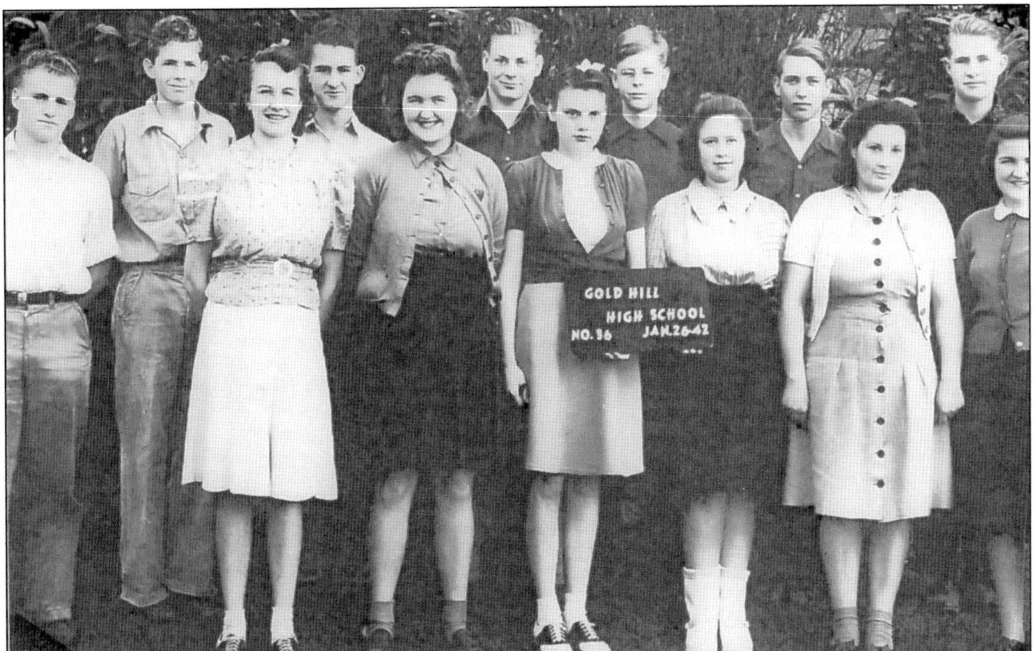

The 1941–1942 Gold Hill High School junior class includes, from left to right, (first row) Evalyn Christensen, Rae Clement, Marjorie Smith, Norma Lee Ward, Della Prefontaine, and teacher Miss Burket; (second row) Stanley Robbins, Alvis Winn, Harlow Banry, Charles Rosecrans, Wilson Flick, Leroy Carter, and Warren Albright.

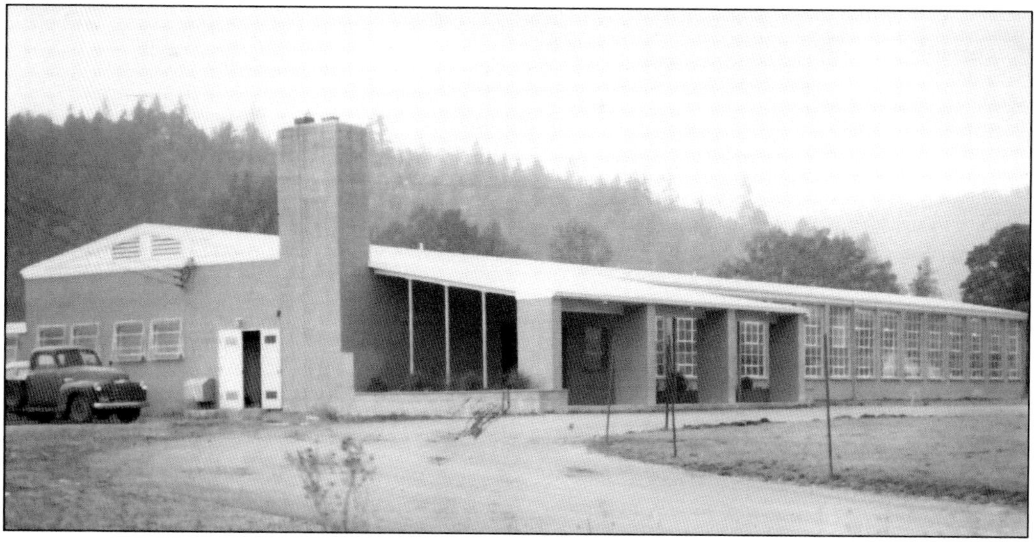

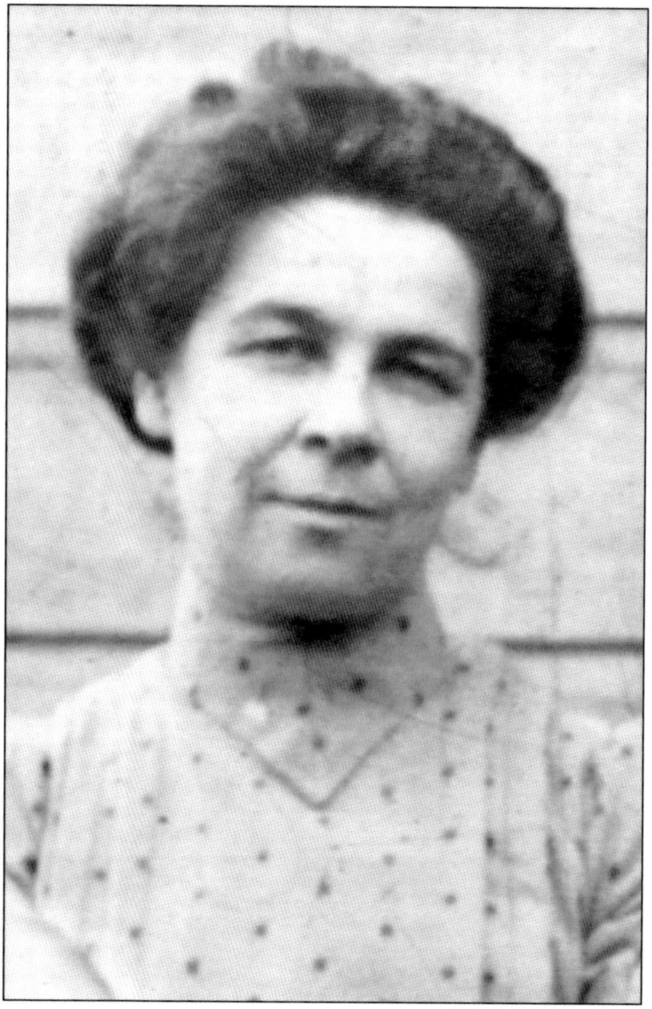

Patrick Elementary School (above) was named after longtime teacher Margaret Griffiths Patrick when built in 1956 to relieve the load on Hanby. Gilbert Mack was the long-serving principal, and his Chevrolet truck is at the left. Known as Aunt Peggie, Margaret Patrick (left) taught school in Gold Hill for the better part of 50 years. She started her teaching career when she was 17 in 1882 in a one-room schoolhouse in Rock Point. In 1904, at the relatively late age of 39, she married orchardist George Patrick, and they lived on his farm in Gold Hill, where she returned to teaching school upon her husband's death. Patrick Elementary School in Gold Hill was not only named in her honor but also stands in part on land once owned by the Patricks.

Five

Close-by Neighbors

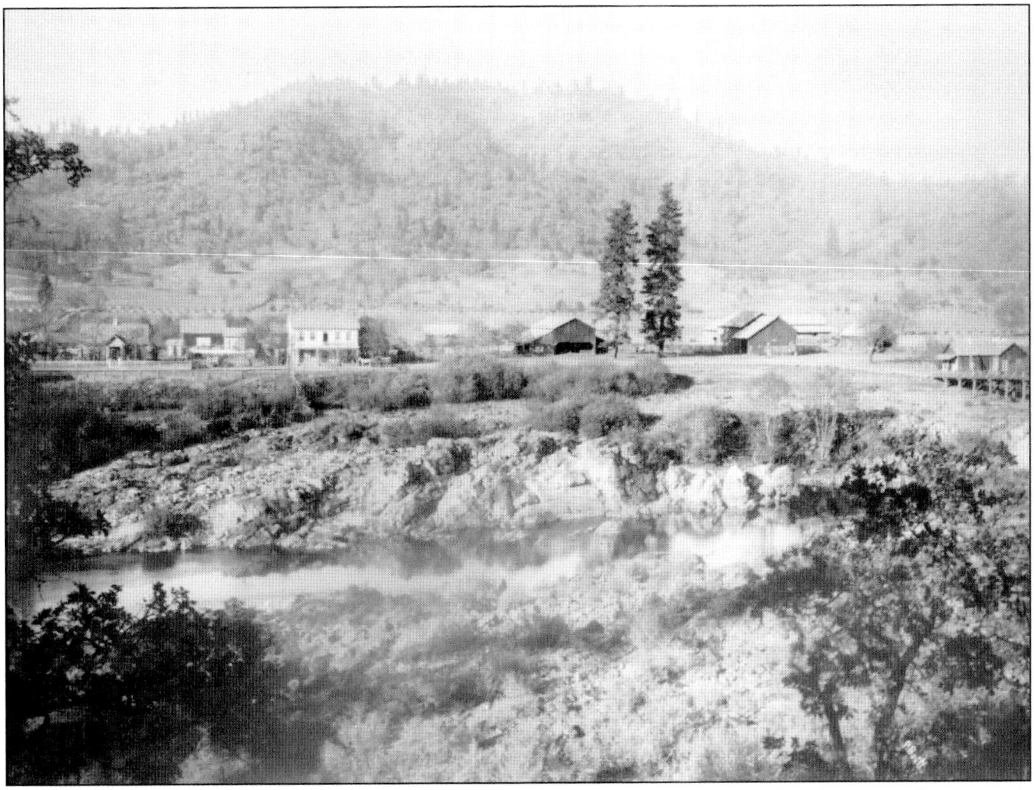

In 1852, John B. White established Rock Point, named for the large rocks there, on the Rogue's banks some 3 miles downstream from Gold Hill. L. J. White (not related) arrived and built a hotel at the point in 1865 with one of the area's first telegraph stations. In the early 1880s, the village of 200 had its own post office, general store, blacksmith shop, hotel, saloon, school, livery, and homes. (SOHS.)

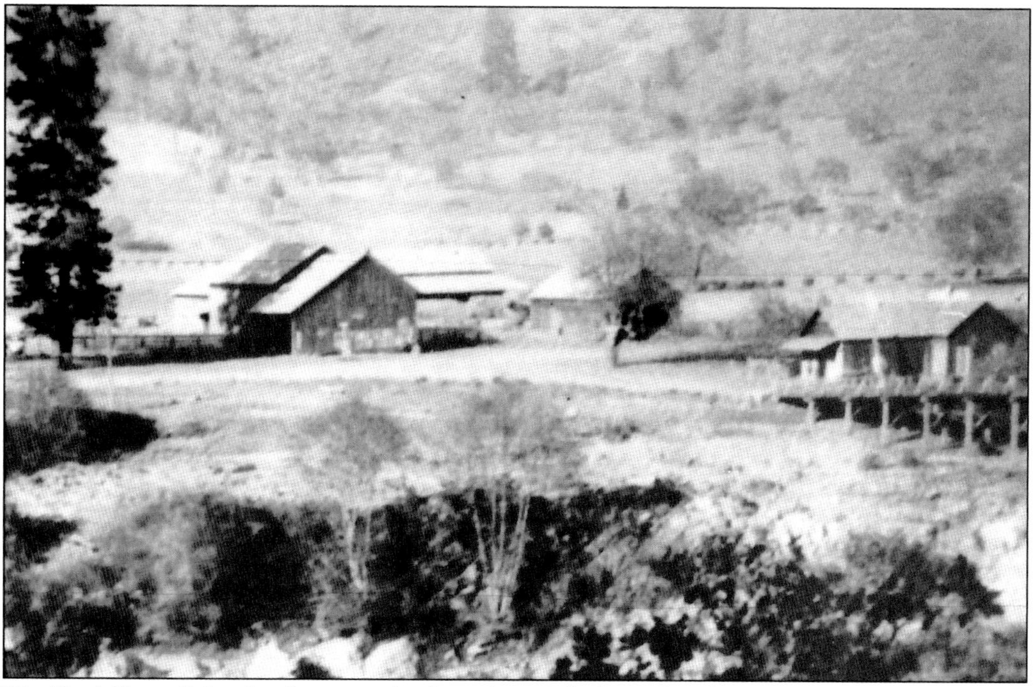

The Rock Point School is shown at the far right. With the railroad's bypassing of the settlement in favor of Gold Hill, the village slowly moved there over time. Only a house, an original barn, and the hotel remain today, and the former settlement is now the site of a fine vineyard and wine-tasting facility, Del Rio Vineyards.

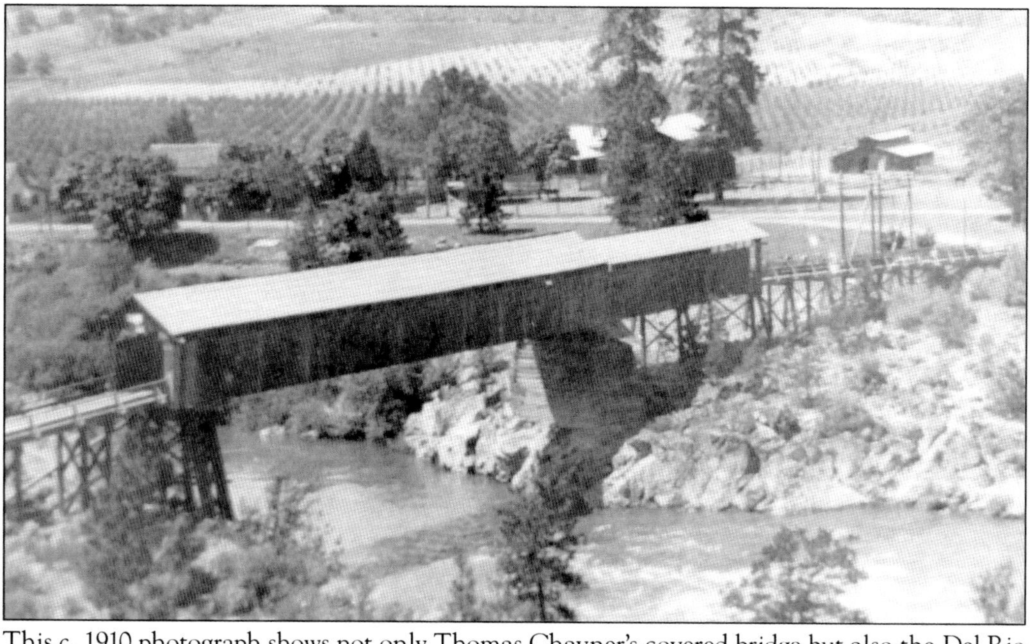

This c. 1910 photograph shows not only Thomas Chavner's covered bridge but also the Del Rio Orchards behind. Through booms and busts, hundreds of acres of pear, peach, and walnut trees produced into the late 20th century. An extensive winery and vineyards eventually replaced the orchards, and a concrete bridge replaced the covered one.

In 1874, John B. White and his wife donated 27 acres adjacent to Rock Point for a cemetery. The Rock Point Pioneer Cemetery is presently administered by two different trustees, including the IOOF. This area marks both White families, and the obelisk at the right marks L. J. White. Both pioneers and 21st-century residents are buried in this tranquil setting.

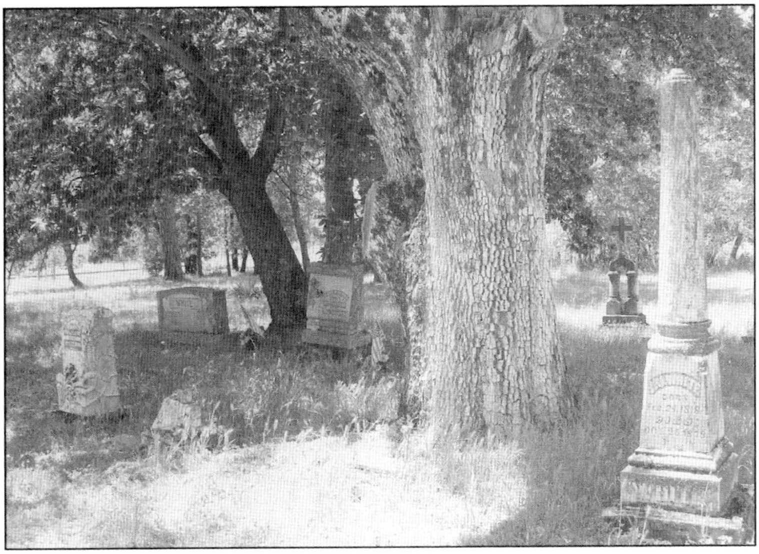

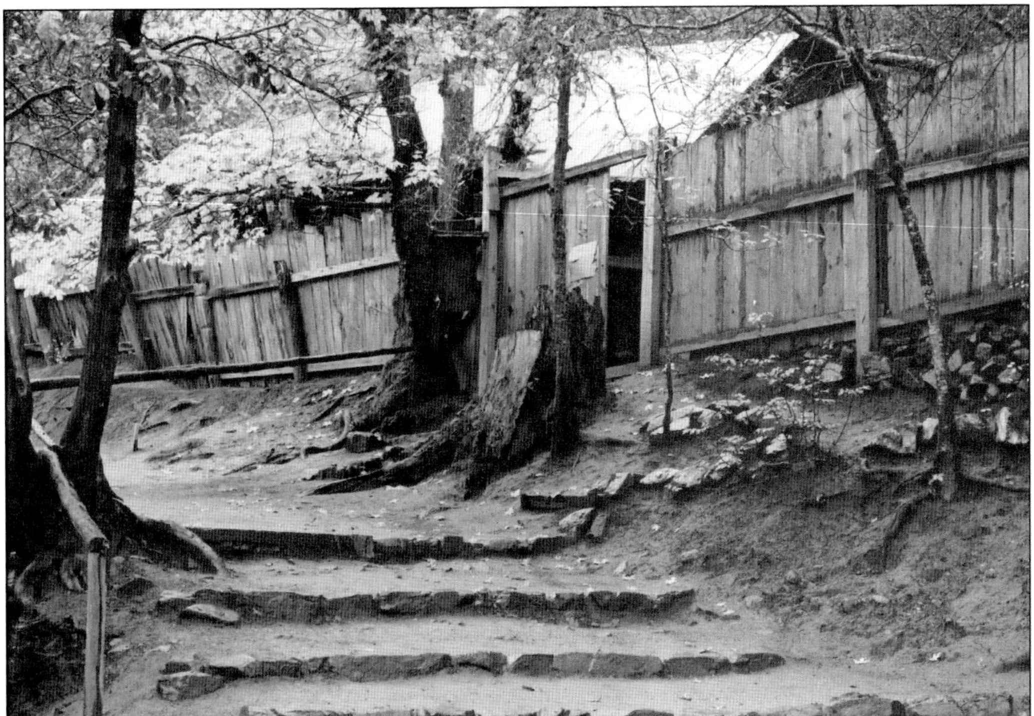

An unusual 22-acre lot lies 5 miles up Sardine Creek, with the Lucky Bart mine to the left and the Gray Eagle on the right fork. On one of these acreages lies the Oregon Vortex. As the result of an apparent confluence of magnetic fields, the laws of physics there seem to be temporarily suspended. Maria Cooper's family bought the property in 1960 from the wife of a local scientist and mining engineer, John Litster, who had conducted experiments on the vortex and died in 1959.

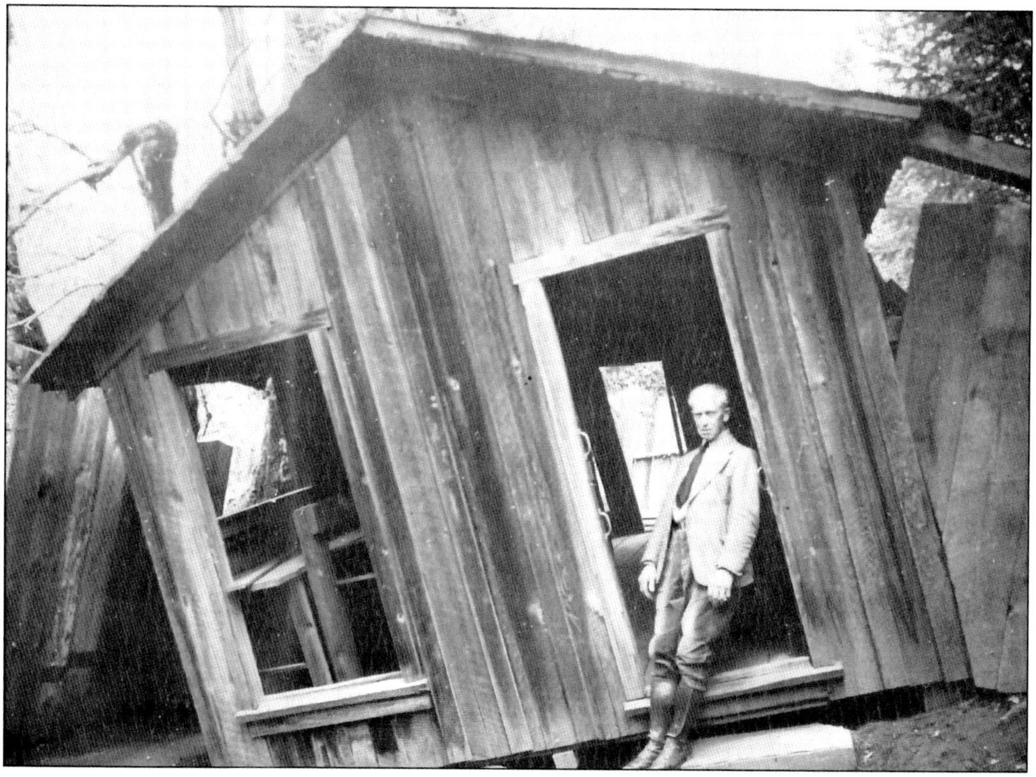

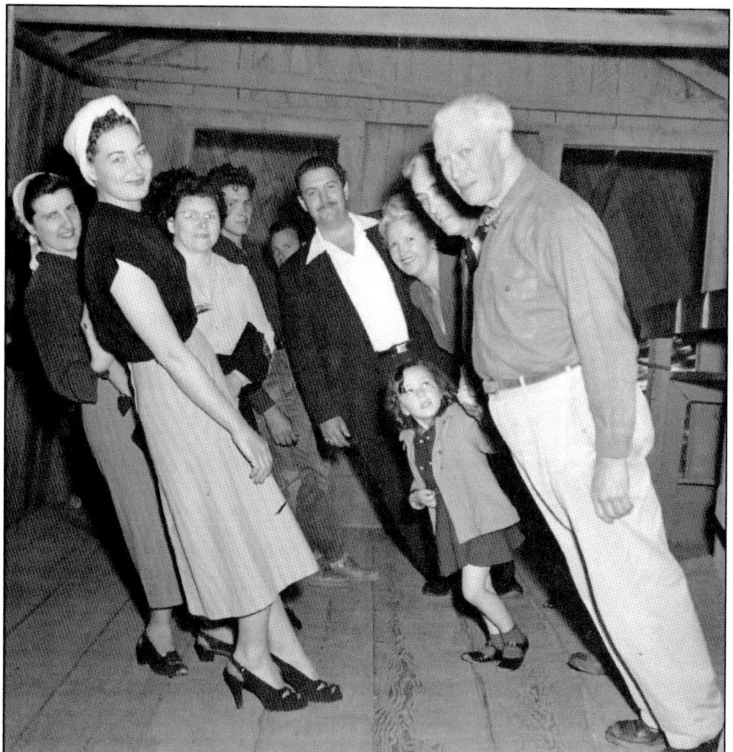

The grounds include the House of Mystery, a slanted, 1890 assay shack of the old Grey Eagle mine that slid off its foundation. Inside, balls roll uphill, while people stand at weird angles and brooms stand on end. Outside, people appear dramatically taller as they shift positions. John Litster is in front in both pictures. The other visitors at left in the background are unidentified.

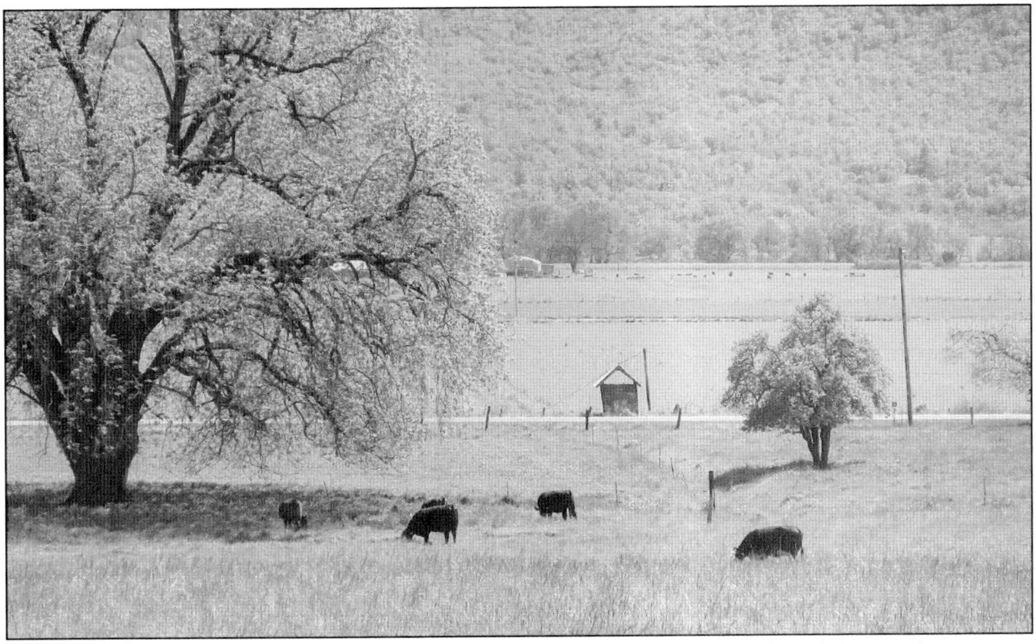

Sams Valley was named in honor of Chief Sam of the Rogue River tribe of Native Americans, who signed the peace treaty, was on the Table Rock reservation, and subsequently removed with the tribe in 1856 to southeastern Oregon. Located 5 miles from Gold Hill, the rich valley produced grains, livestock, dairy products, vegetables, and other produce. Although farmers grew what they needed, their excess production—especially corn, wheat, and barley—were wagoned to Gold Hill's depot for shipment. At Highway 234 and Ramsey Road is one of the earliest homes in Sams Valley. A noted horseman, marksman, and farmer, C. C. McClendon designed and built the farm house (below) in 1856. The outlying structures were added later, and the farm was a dairy, as well as growing hay and grains. The barns are shown above from a distance.

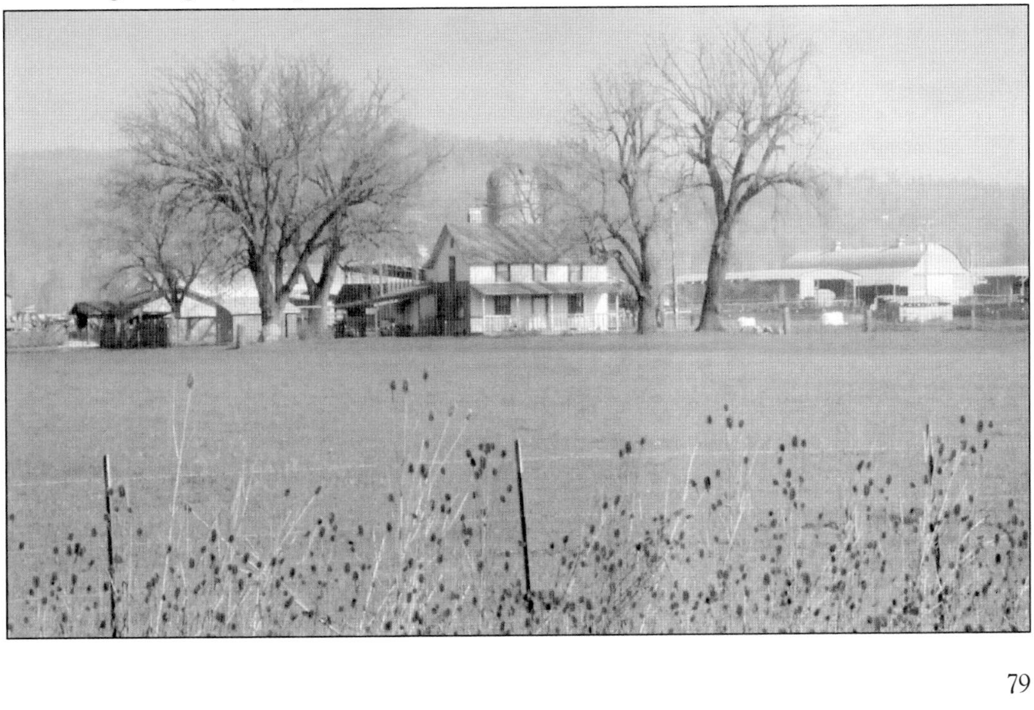

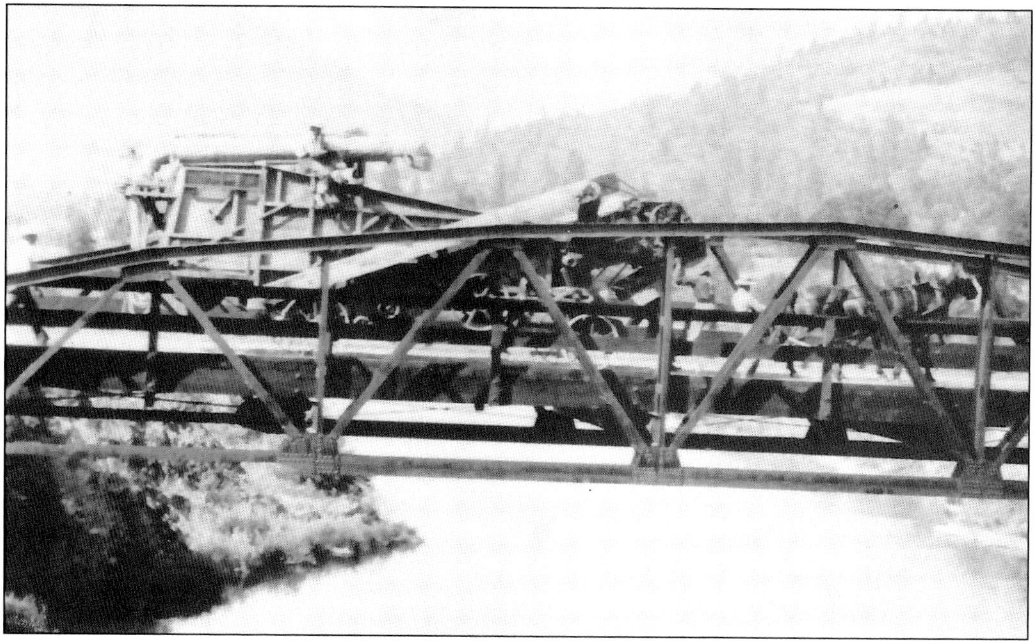

In 1918 Bill Tresham (above) is crossing the Gold Hill auto route over the Rogue River to Sams Valley while seated on his steam combine, pulled by a horse team. He and his three sons owned threshing equipment and traveled throughout the valley to work the farms during the season. Tresham owned a 160-acre ranch in Sams Valley, and Tresham Lane is named in his honor. Below, Bill's wife Lena and daughter-in-law Ella pose at the ranch in 1918.

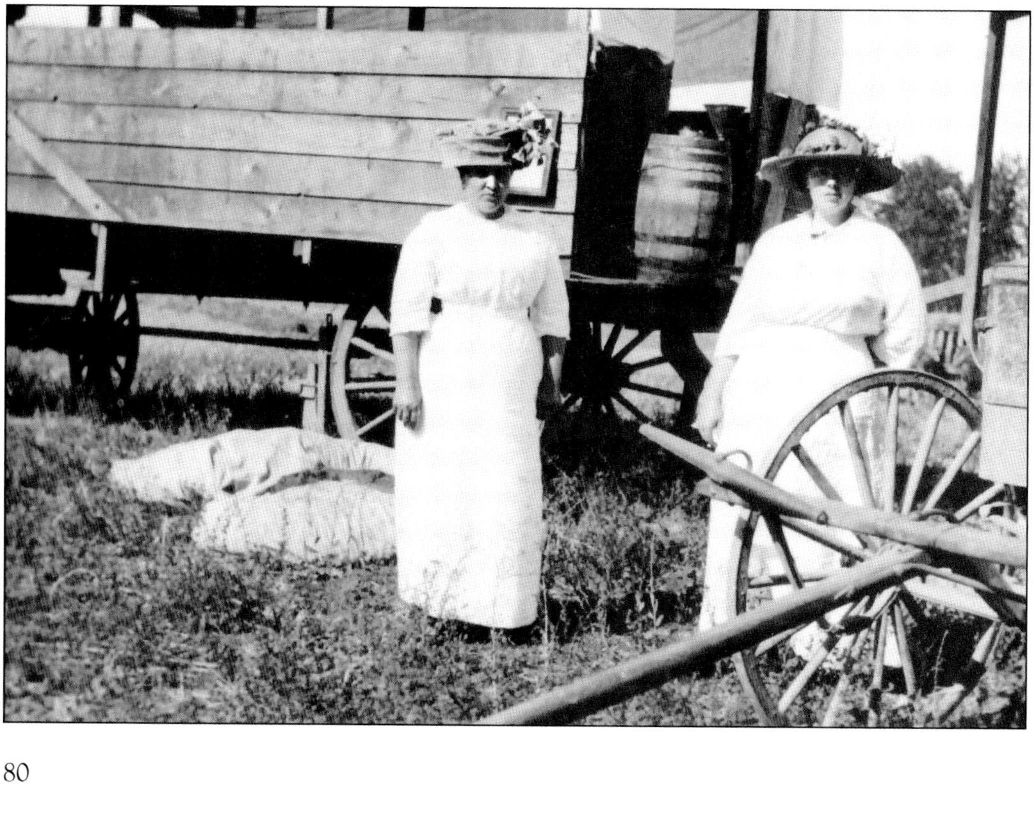

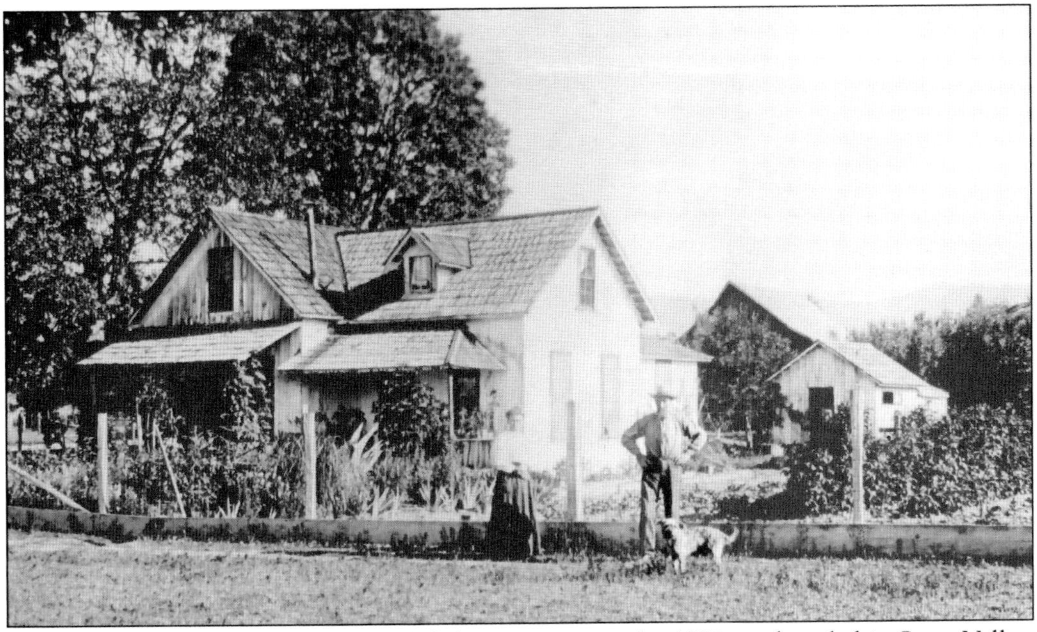

"Grandpa" Hinrich Holst and his wife left Minnesota in the 1890s and settled in Sams Valley. He was a farmer and the local banker; he loaned the money and—like Thomas Chavner—would foreclose when debts could not be repaid, although he would usually give a grace period or two. This is the Holst farmhouse in Sams Valley in 1911.

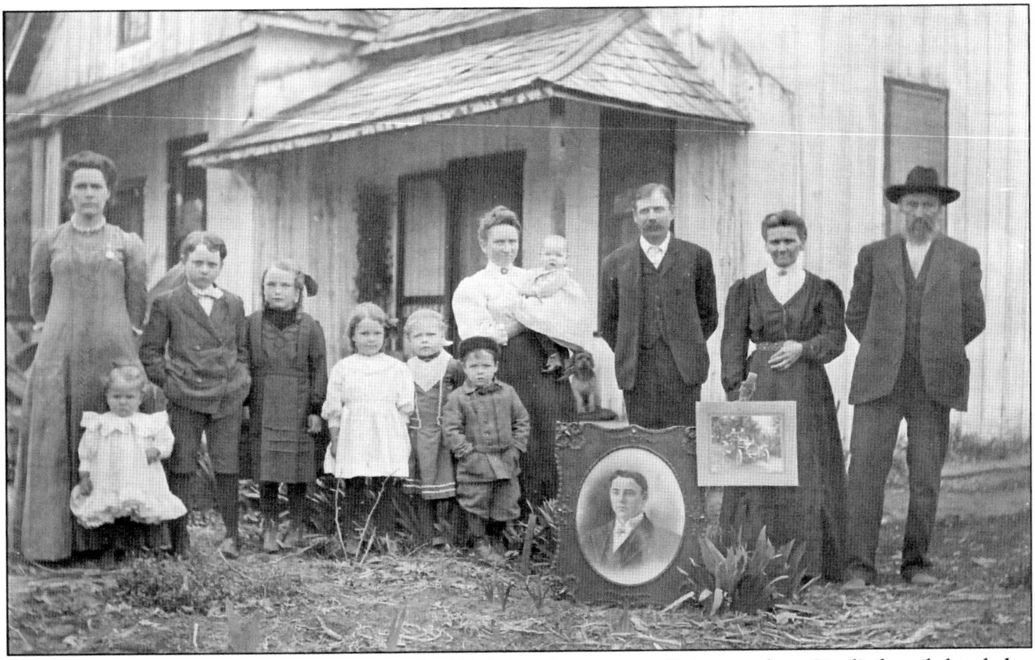

The occasion for this picture was Grandpa Holst's celebration of his grandson Paul's fourth birthday on March 31, 1912. Celebrants are, from left to right, Bertha Holst, Glen Holst (baby in front), Ray Holst, Juenesse Holst, Ivern Holst, Henrietta Schulz, Paul Schulz, Alina Holst Schulz, Gladys Schulz (baby being held), Max Schulz, Grandma Holst, and Grandpa Holst. The man in the portrait is John Holst; the other picture to the right shows Grandma Holst's parents, the Hoffmans.

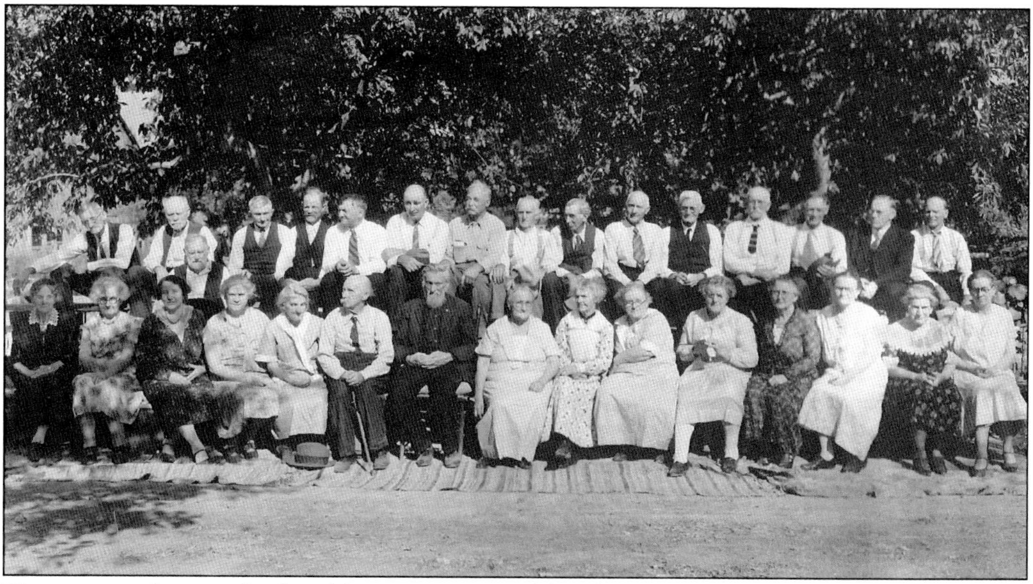

This picture shows only the older generations of family, relatives, and friends that celebrated Grandpa H. Holst's 80th birthday on August 30, 1932. Over 235 people attended. Each year, Holst had a birthday celebration and invited nearly everyone he knew. However, Grandpa was really celebrating his 79th birthday at this time, as he felt "When I was born, I already was a year old." So every year he celebrated one year early.

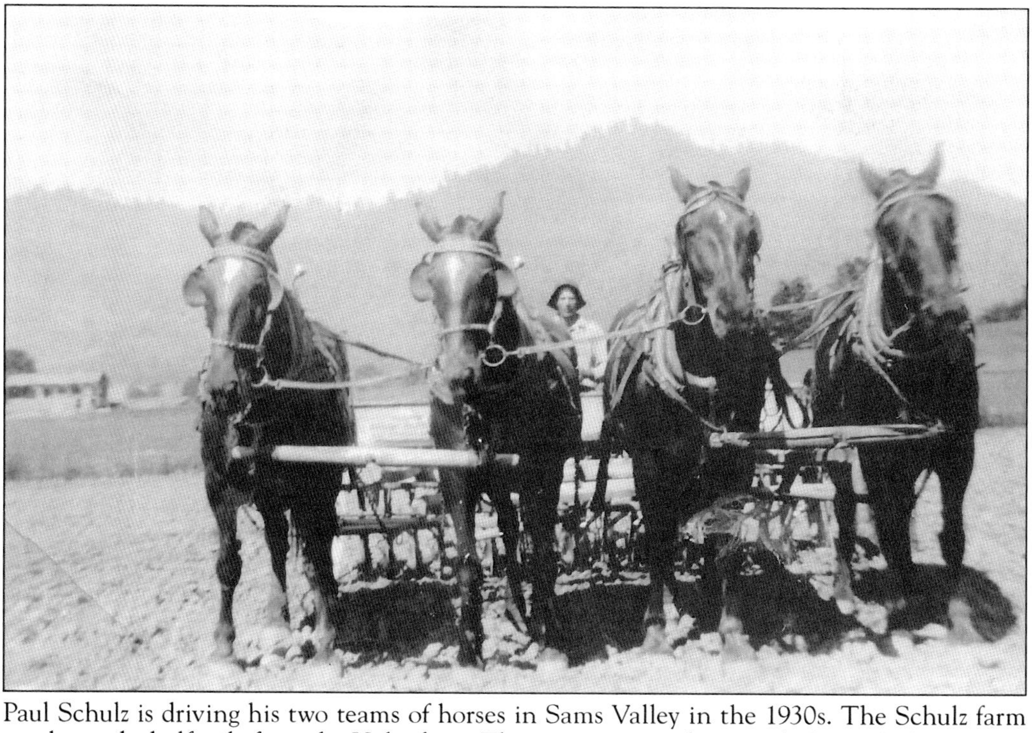

Paul Schulz is driving his two teams of horses in Sams Valley in the 1930s. The Schulz farm was located a half mile from the Holst farm. This picture was taken just before Schulz bought a tractor; even after that, he still used his horses for the easy jobs. The farms grew corn to feed the pigs and cows and hay for the livestock along with wheat, oats, and other crops.

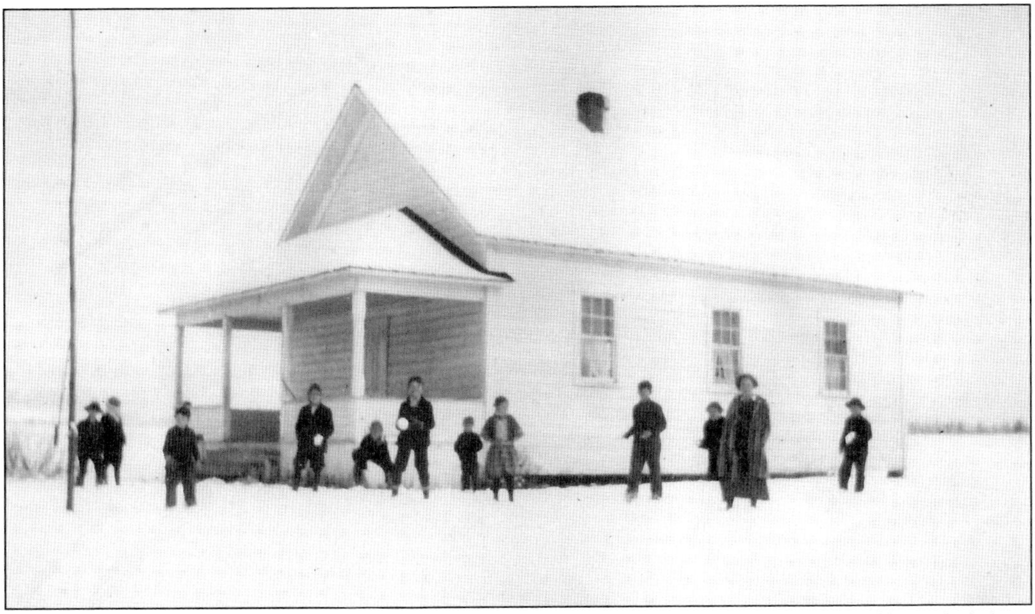

Although Sams Valley in the 1910s had only around 100 inhabitants, children still needed their own school due to the distances. This 1915 picture shows the all-grade school in winter. The Old Sams Valley School that opened in 1921 on Old Sams Valley Road replaced it.

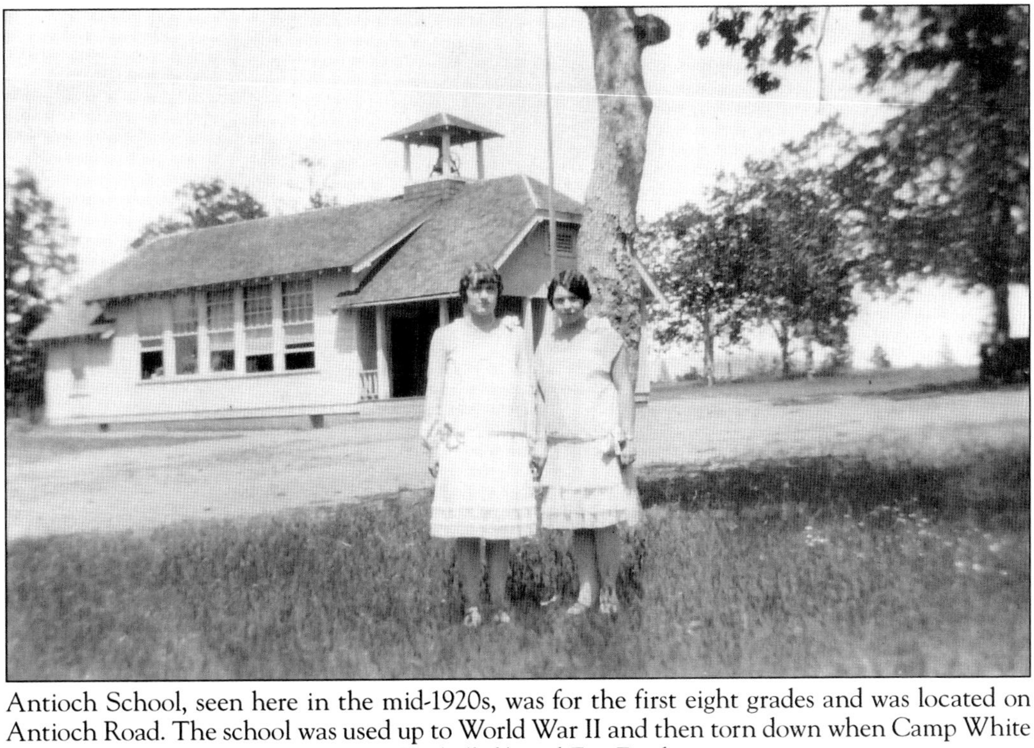

Antioch School, seen here in the mid-1920s, was for the first eight grades and was located on Antioch Road. The school was used up to World War II and then torn down when Camp White was constructed. Pictured are sisters Ruth (left) and Eva Frink.

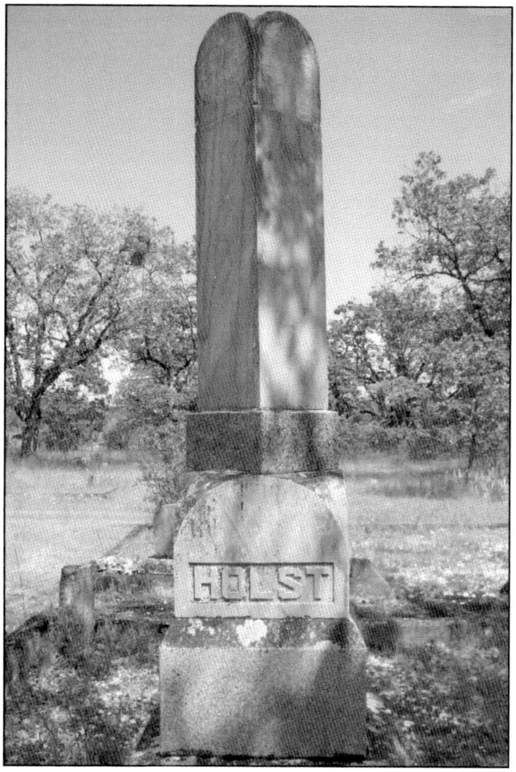

The H. Holst monument is located in the small Pankey Park Cemetery, which is on Ramsey Road in Sams Valley. Before his death, Grandpa Holst walked regularly in the 1930s to the cemetery from his home and made a plot plan of all of the graves. The Pankeys were another early pioneer family in Sams Valley and donated land for the cemetery, which dates back to 1863.

The original owners of the land surrounding this house were Joab and Marzee Rowe in 1864. After Joab died one year later, Marzee remarried in 1870 to G. W. Cooksey. Constructed in the 1920s, this home is typical of the farm residences of the time in Sams Valley. Paul and Ruth Schulz purchased it in the mid-1930s from a bank foreclosure.

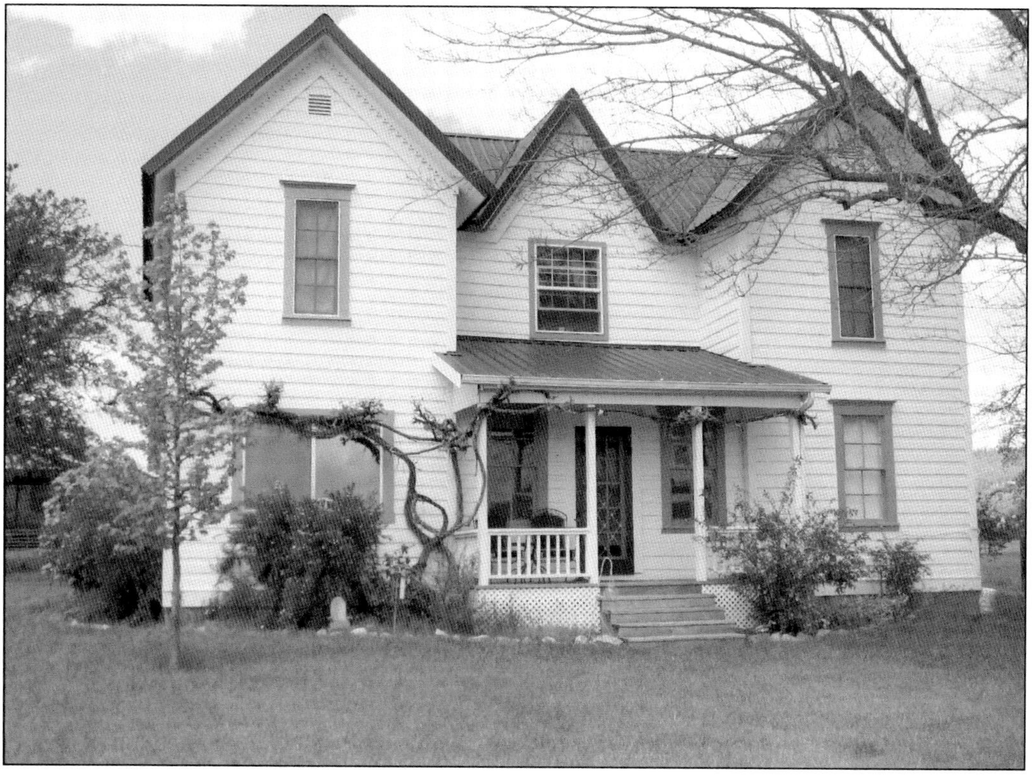

Six

The Mighty Rogue and Its Crossings

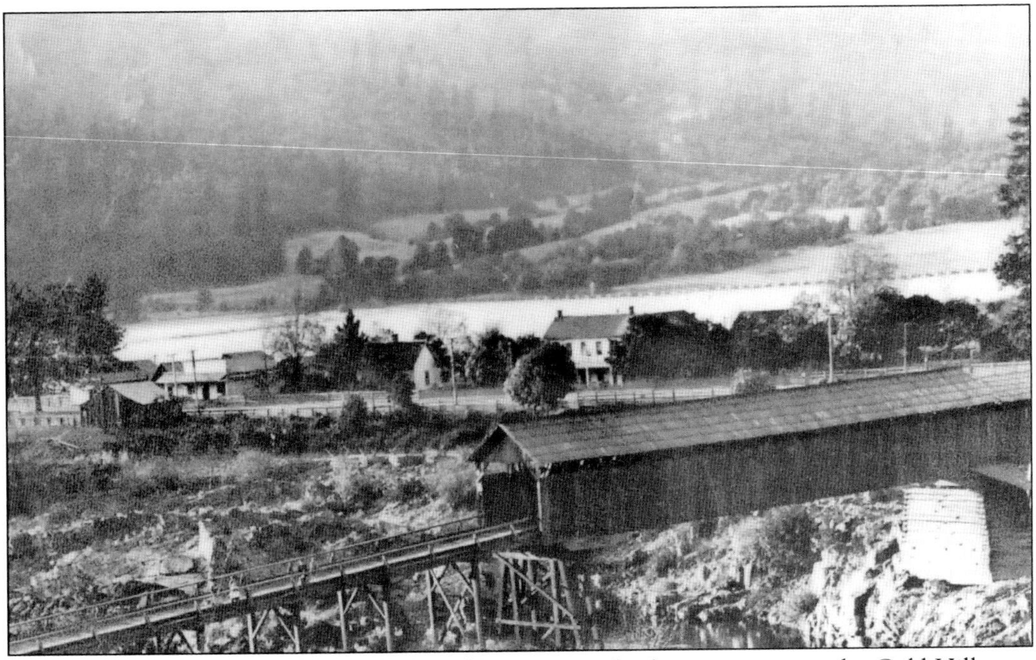

No city in Oregon south of Portland can claim as many bridges over time as the Gold Hill area. Sixteen were built to cross the Rogue and its wide tributary creeks, in addition to Gold Ray Dam. In 1858, J. B. White and Davis Evans built the first bridge by Rock Point that crossed this river between the Table Rocks and distant Pacific Ocean. Four years later, Thomas Chavner built the pictured toll bridge after floods wiped out the first one in 1861. Chavner's bridge lasted another ten years before being replaced. This 1910 image shows the tiny Rock Point settlement in the background.

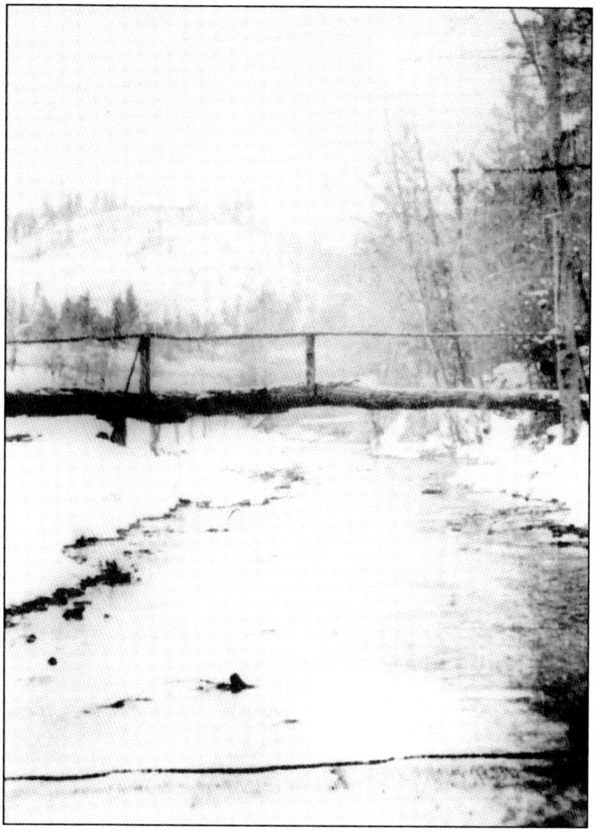

This footbridge crossed Sardine Creek in the late 1800s, near where the creek forked and Alderbrook School was built. Constructed from felled trees, this crossing was undoubtedly slippery when wet and risky when torrential floods roared down the creek to the Rogue River.

The Rogue River has rapids and rough water along with its lazy passages during the summer. From fishing to rafting and swimming, people have enjoyed the river since first settling here, but they always need to be careful. This is Douden Falls just above Gold Hill on Highway 234 to Sams Valley.

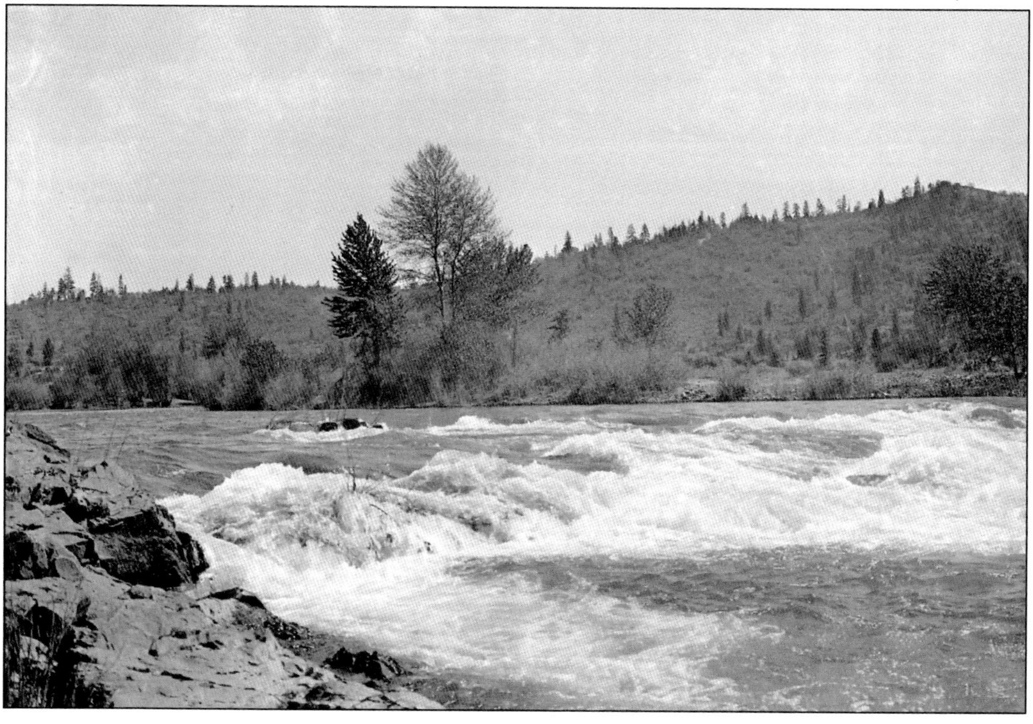

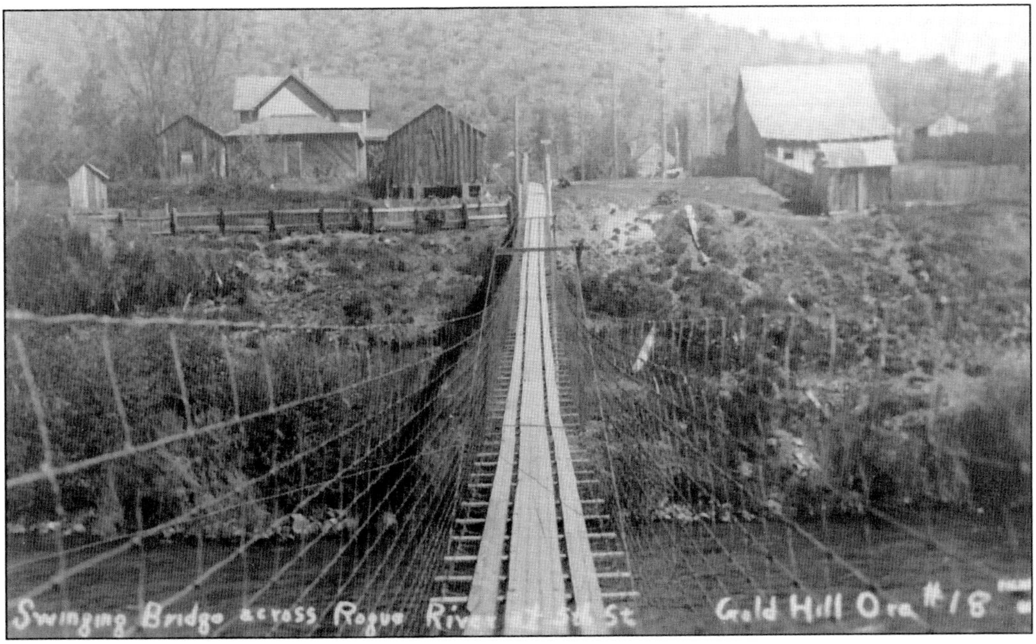

Built in the 1880s, this suspension footbridge (above) crossed the Rogue River from Sixth Street. It was held in place by cables attached to the Hay home and bedrock on the Gold Hill side, then to a tree and the Fleming home on the Echo Mountain side (the Dardanelles side). If walking over this trembling walkway was not bad enough, the town's boys waited until an unsuspecting traveler was midway and then jumped on the ends to make it sway violently. A flood in 1927 swept this crossing away, and it was not replaced. The image below is the view from the center of the footbridge, looking to the northwest.

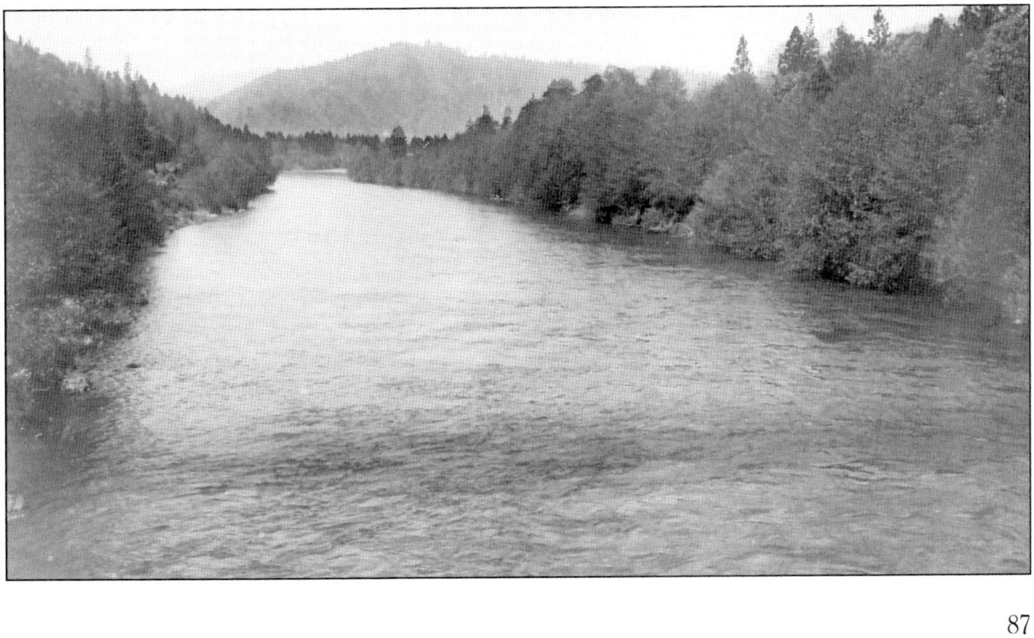

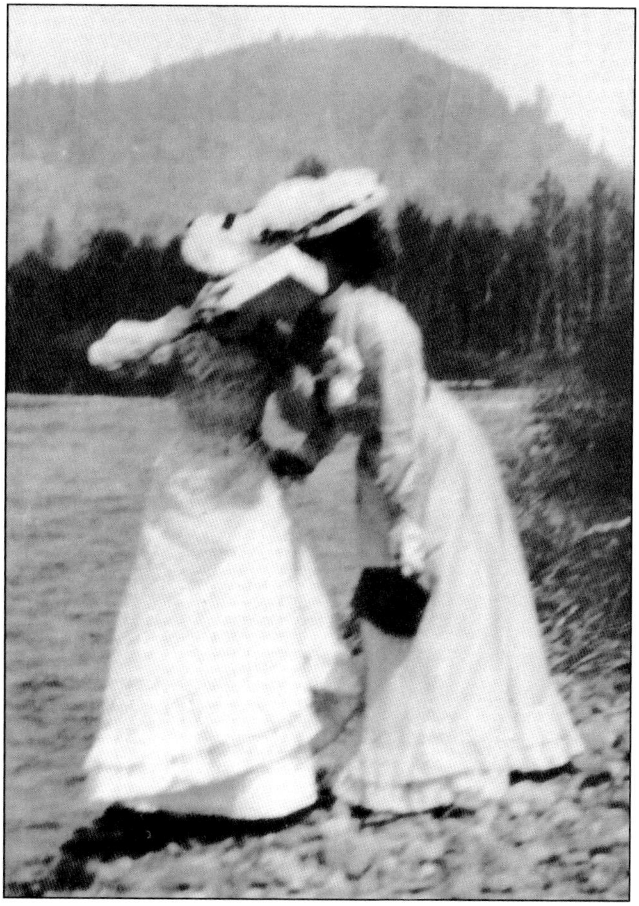

Hull and Becket Pickwick pose for this 1900s picture by the river, as they playfully use a cardboard picnic box to hide from the photographer's camera. The location appears to be north of the city and toward the hills where the Gold Hill Pocket was.

An unidentified lady is fishing below the first railroad bridge, built in 1883. The roof and sides were added in 1890. This photograph was taken about 1900, and the bridge was replaced in 1905. Looking upstream on the southeast side of the Rogue, Gold Hill is to the left. While women were avid fishermen, they dressed differently than this. This picture—as beautiful as it is—is more than likely posed.

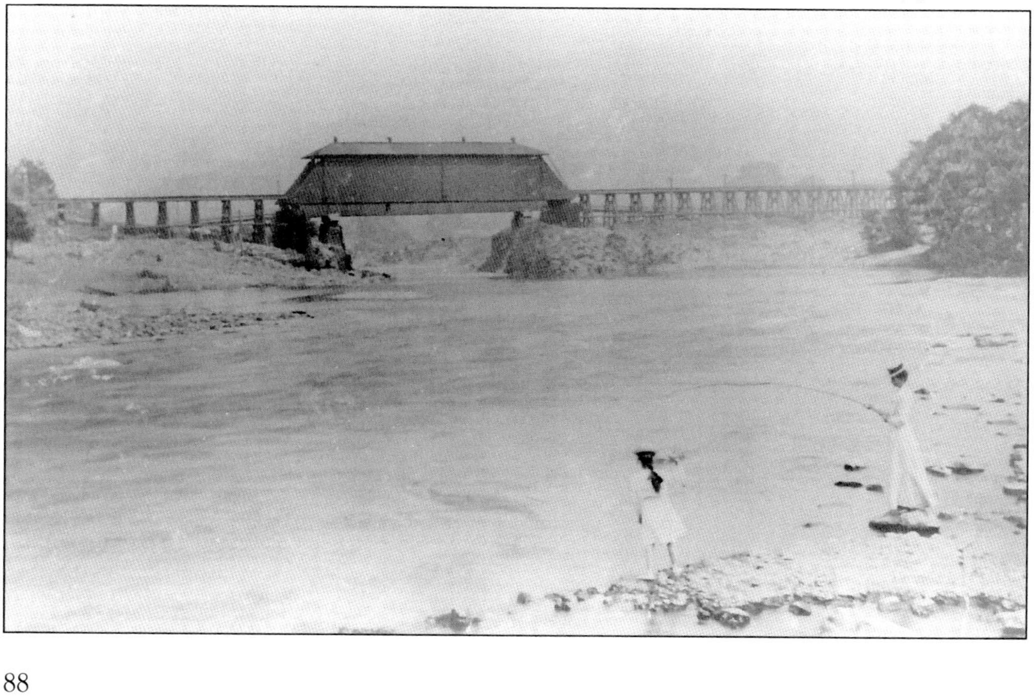

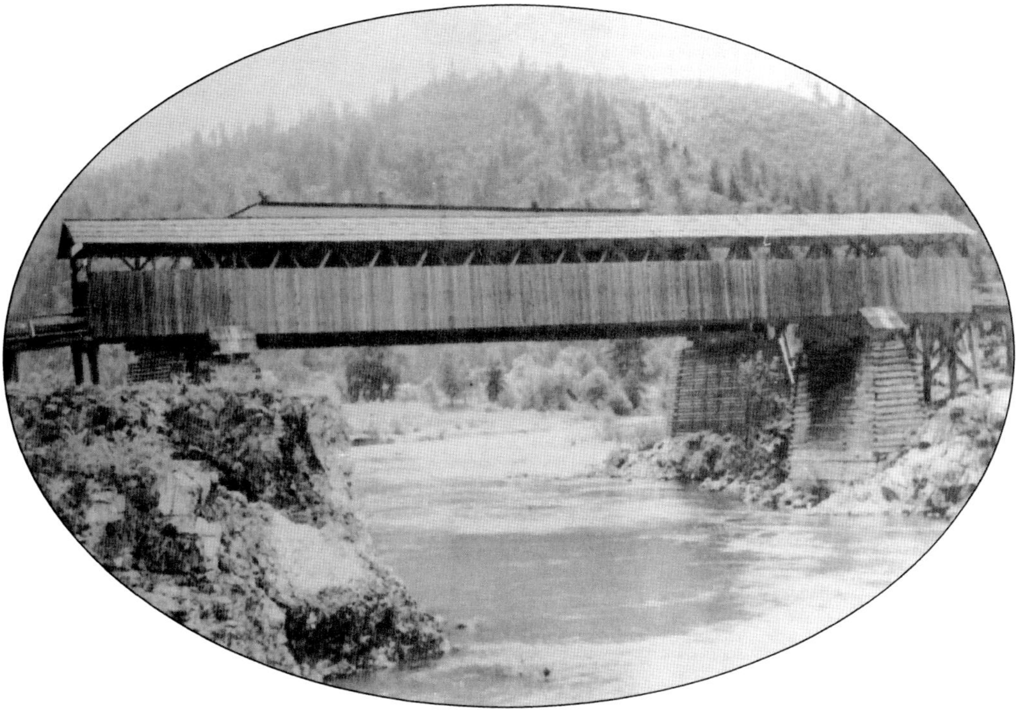

These two images show the wooden Centennial Wagon Bridge that Thomas Chavner built in 1876. It operated as a toll bridge until Chavner sold it to the county 12 years later. The first railroad bridge is behind the toll bridge in the picture above, and to the right in the image below. Pete Amse lived in the tollhouse on the Gold Hill side, and the gate to the bridge is seen in the lower left. The photograph below was taken about 1900 after Chavner's death. The wooden supports under the bridges would not be able to withstand the savage floods that came later.

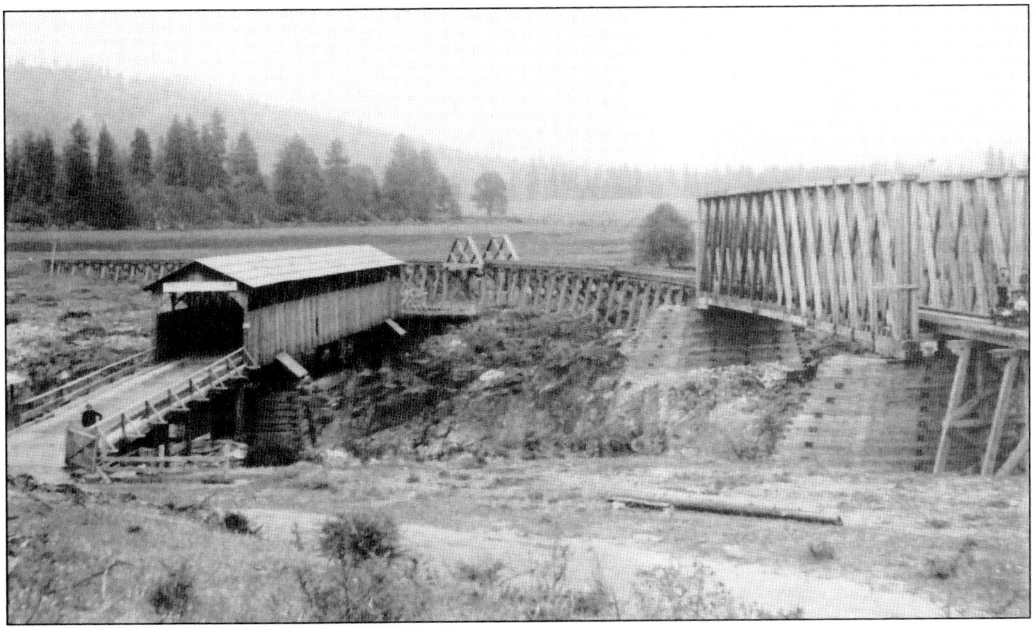

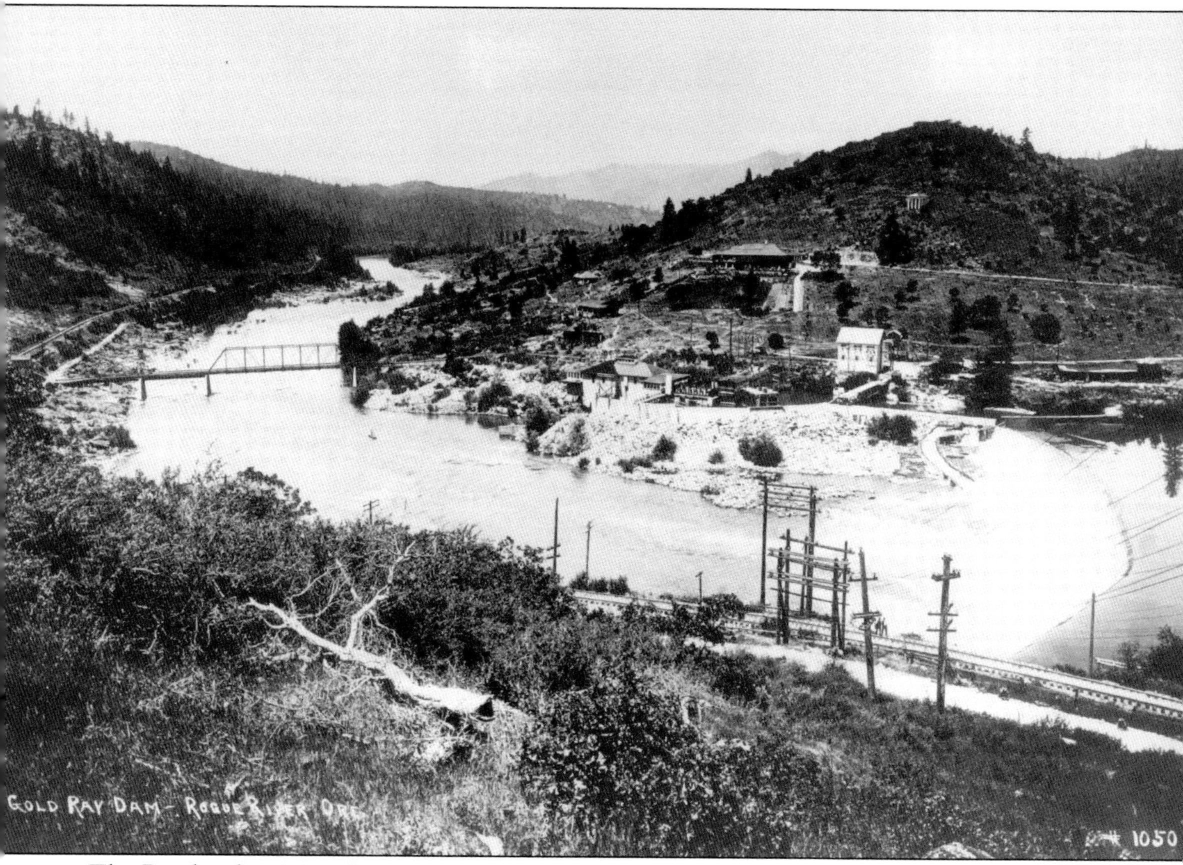

The Ray brothers' Condor Water and Power Company made the largest single investment in Southern Oregon at the time in building the large dam at Tolo, 4 miles above Gold Hill where the Rogue leaves its valley basin. When the log-and-concrete horseshoe dam was completed in 1904, it was 17 feet tall and 350 feet long. The impounded river was diverted through a powerhouse, whose unique rope-driven turbines created the first hydroelectric power in Southern Oregon. This 1918 image shows the complex. The large building in the center is the Ray brothers' hunting lodge. On December 7, 1904, electric bulbs burned in Medford and the surrounding areas with a new energy that took the place of coal-powered generators, both for mining and residential uses. In 1941, a concrete overflow dam was built in its place, which diverted water through a new powerhouse. Pacific Power and Light Company shut down the plant in 1971 and donated the facilities to Jackson County. In 2010 the dam was demolished, and the Rogue River again flows without any interference to the Pacific Ocean. (SOHS.)

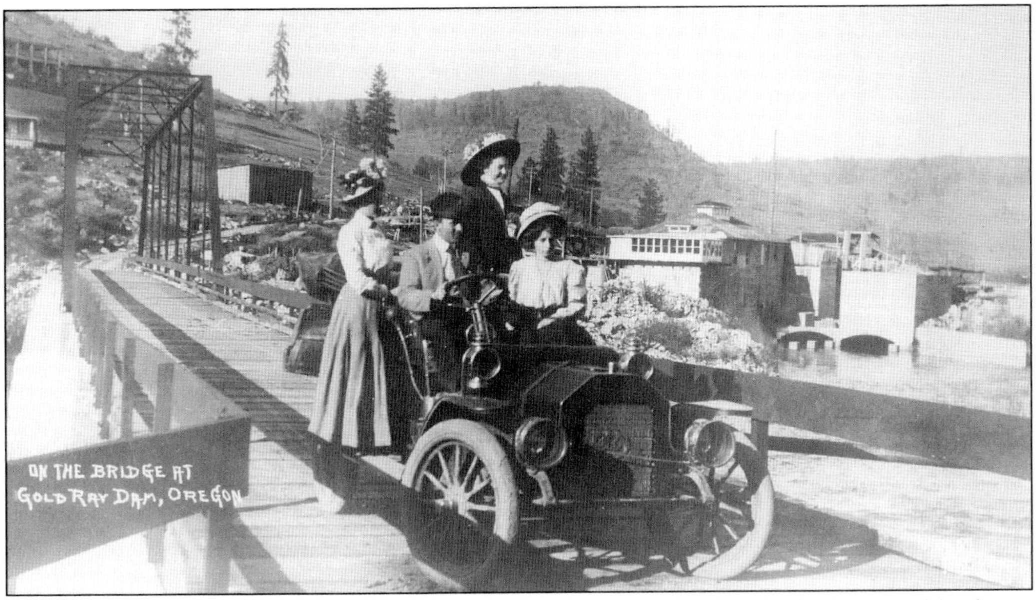

Photographer Frank Hull is shown with his wife in a Reo car crossing the new steel bridge at Gold Ray that connected Sams Valley with Tolo and Central Point. The ladies standing in the back seat are unidentified. Behind the bridge and car is the powerplant, with its two 750 kilowatt-generating units and rope-driven, submerged turbines. Power was supplied throughout the county, from Grants Pass to Ashland. (SOHS.)

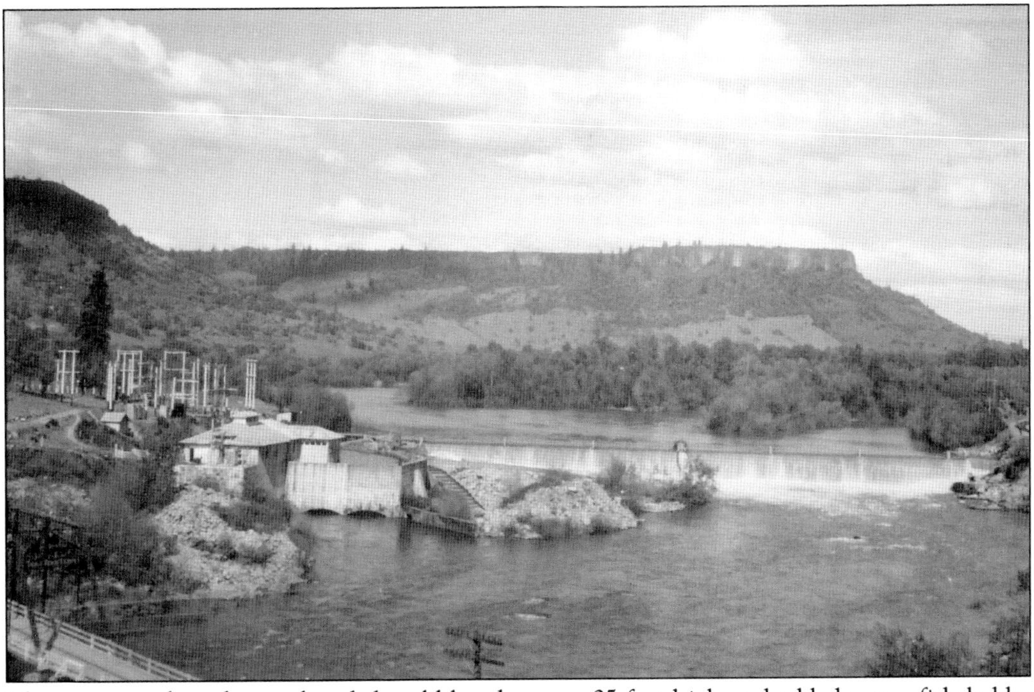

The concrete dam that replaced the old log dam was 35 feet high and added a new fish ladder and fish-counting station. The larger powerplant with the transmission lines to the left was constructed during World War II to bring more hydroelectric power to Gold Hill's cement plant and neighboring towns.

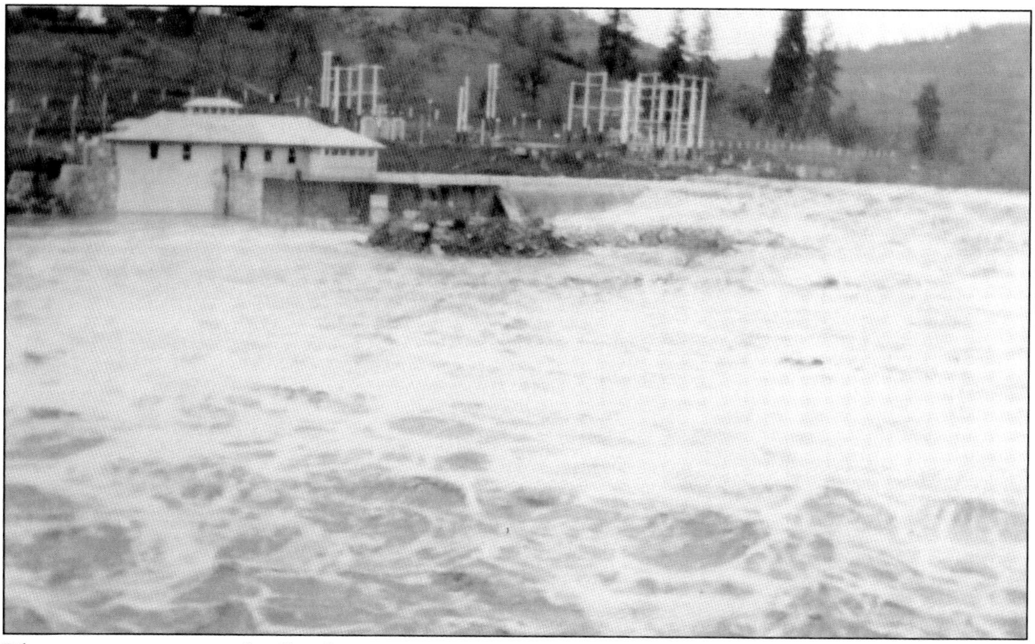

The awesome power of a flooding, rampaging Rogue River even affects Gold Ray Dam and its powerhouse. This flood during January 1947 did not do great damage, but a later one in 1964 washed away the steel bridge downstream from it. Although threatening the powerhouse itself, this great flood did not cause a need for significant repairs.

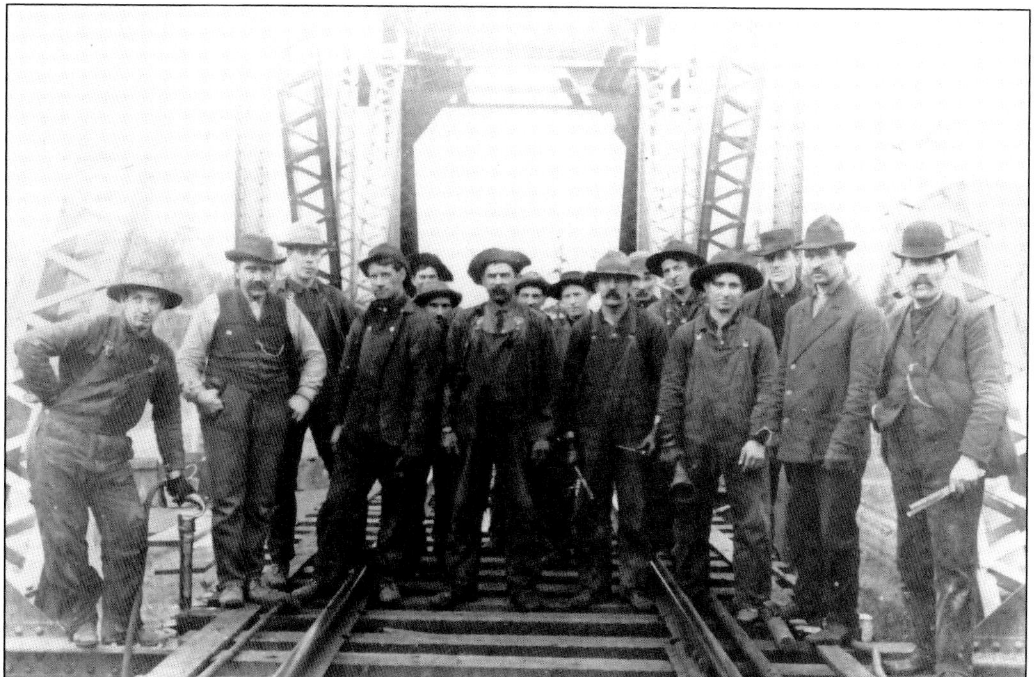

Whether due to floods, overloading, or age, bridges needed to be constantly inspected and repaired. This 1906 image shows a typical crew after the new railroad bridge was built. The two superintendents, or managers, stand out by reason of their vests, watch chains, and hats.

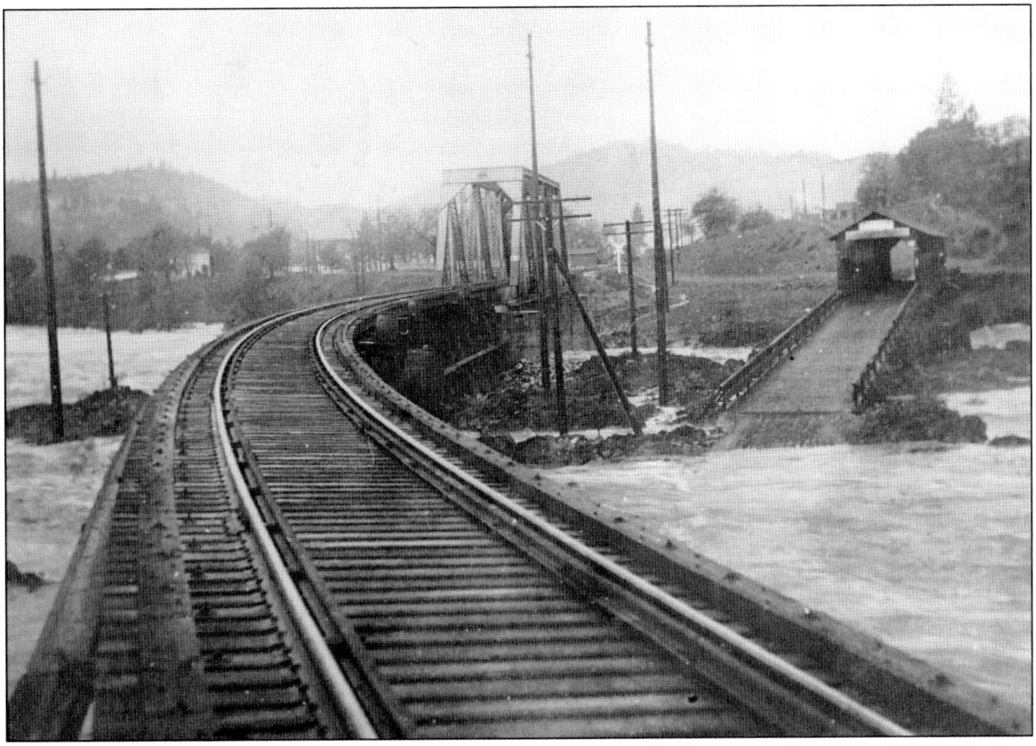

A savage 1911 flood threatened both the railroad bridge and Chavner's Centennial Toll Bridge. Although Chavner's structure lasted through high waters for 35 years, this flood washed away the roofed thoroughfare used by both horses and cars. The bridge was replaced. This view is looking west toward the city. Built sturdily with a steel frame and huge wood stanchions bolted to concrete blocks, the six-year-old railroad bridge survived.

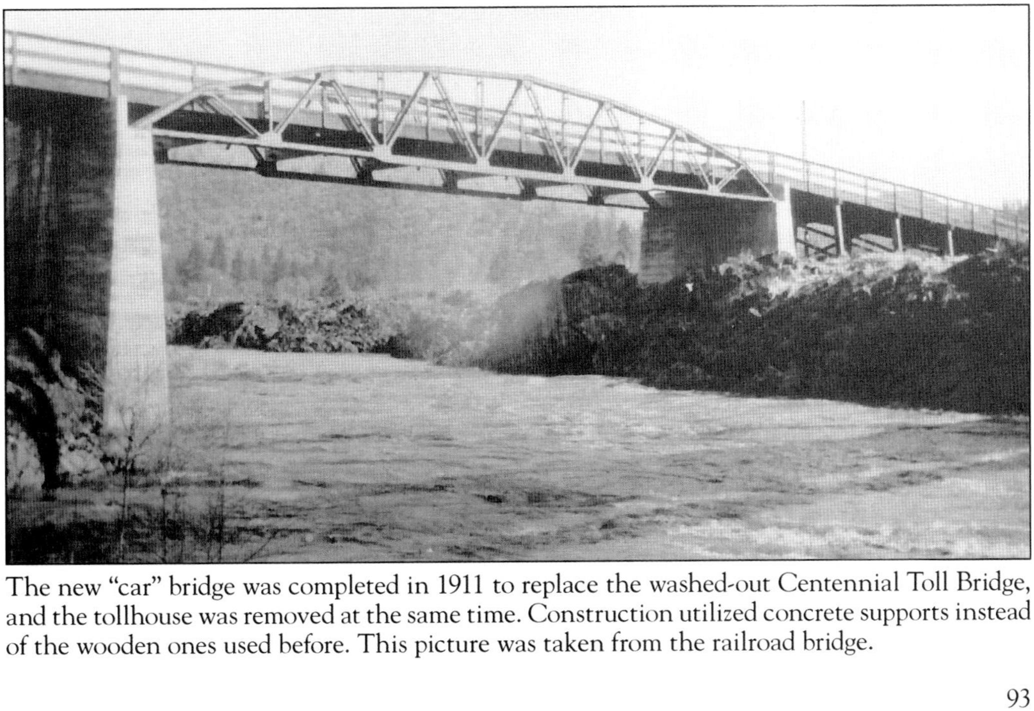

The new "car" bridge was completed in 1911 to replace the washed-out Centennial Toll Bridge, and the tollhouse was removed at the same time. Construction utilized concrete supports instead of the wooden ones used before. This picture was taken from the railroad bridge.

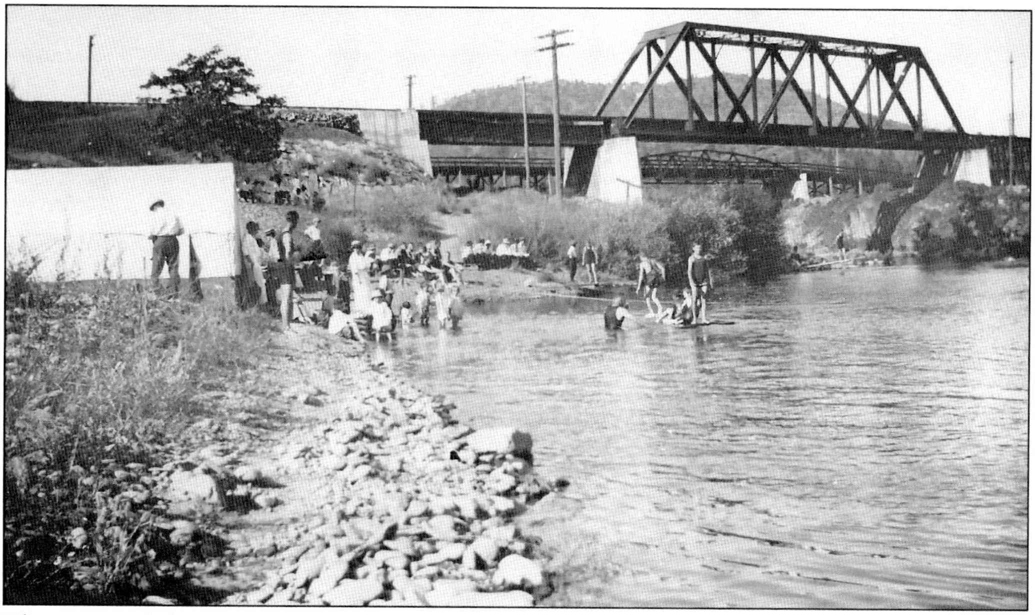

This postcard shows swimmers, a dressing tent, and a crowd by the Southern Pacific Railroad Bridge. The back of the postcard reads, "Self with straw hat near tent. July 1915." To the far right and under the bridge, a boy is standing on a diving board.

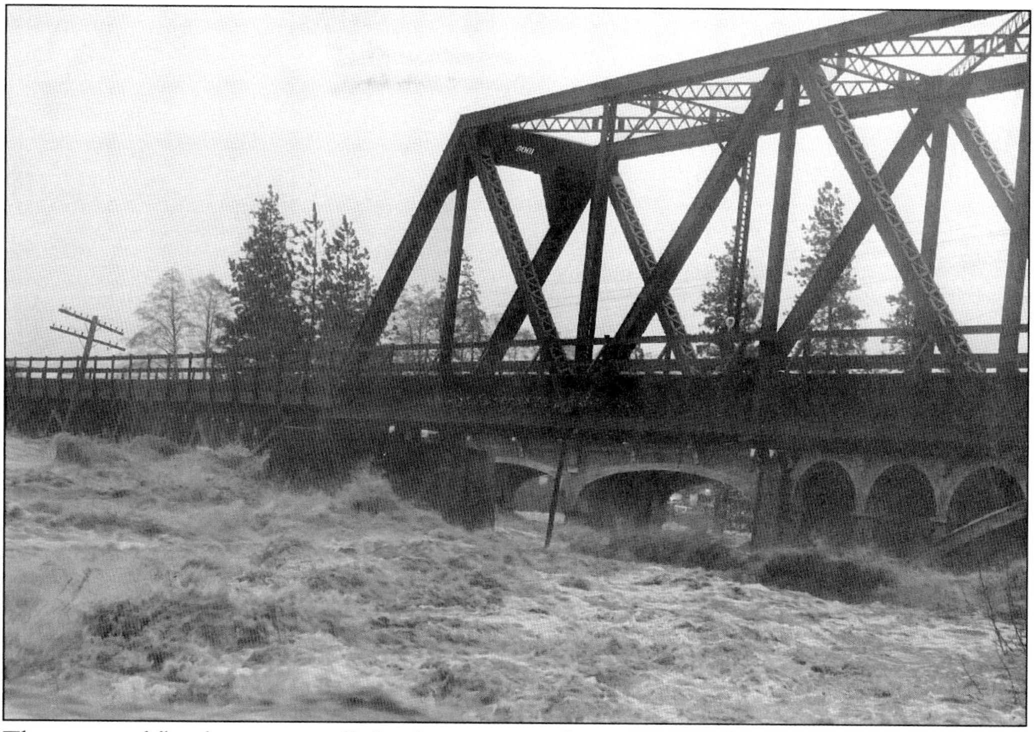

The power of floods cannot really be shown except by witnessing the event, but these pictures come close. Among the many Rogue River floods that surged over banks and destroyed bridges and houses, the 1964 flood, pictured here, was a notable one. The Gold Hill and Rock Point bridges survived. (RG.)

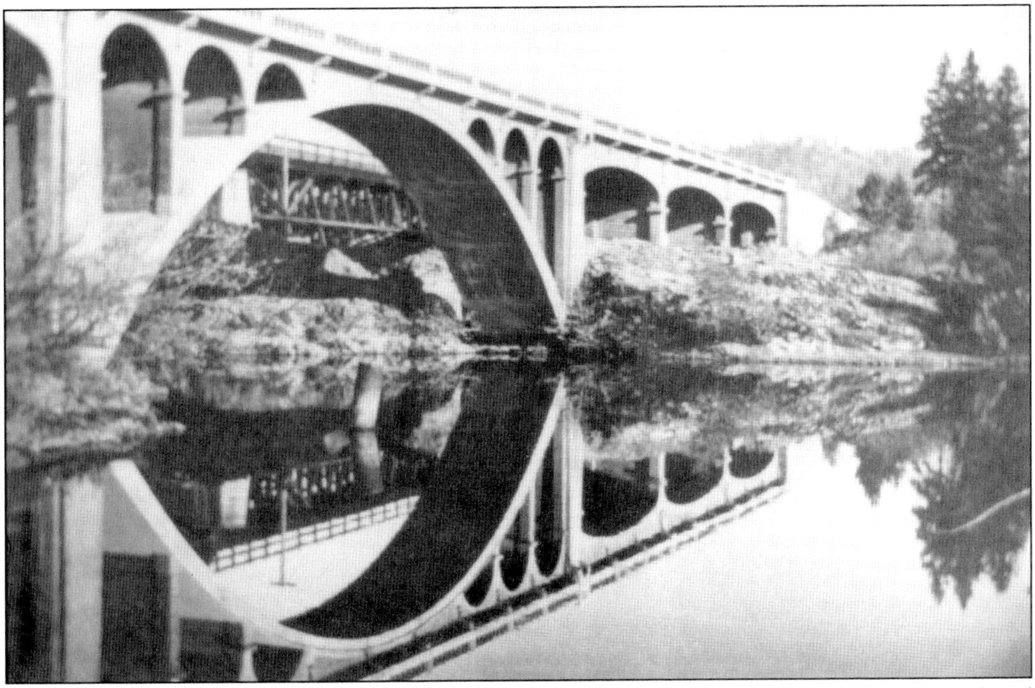

With the beauty of the present Gold Hill (or Pacific Highway) Bridge reflecting back, the railroad bridge's support ties are visible behind. This view is from the Gold Hill side, with its enjoyable park and beach.

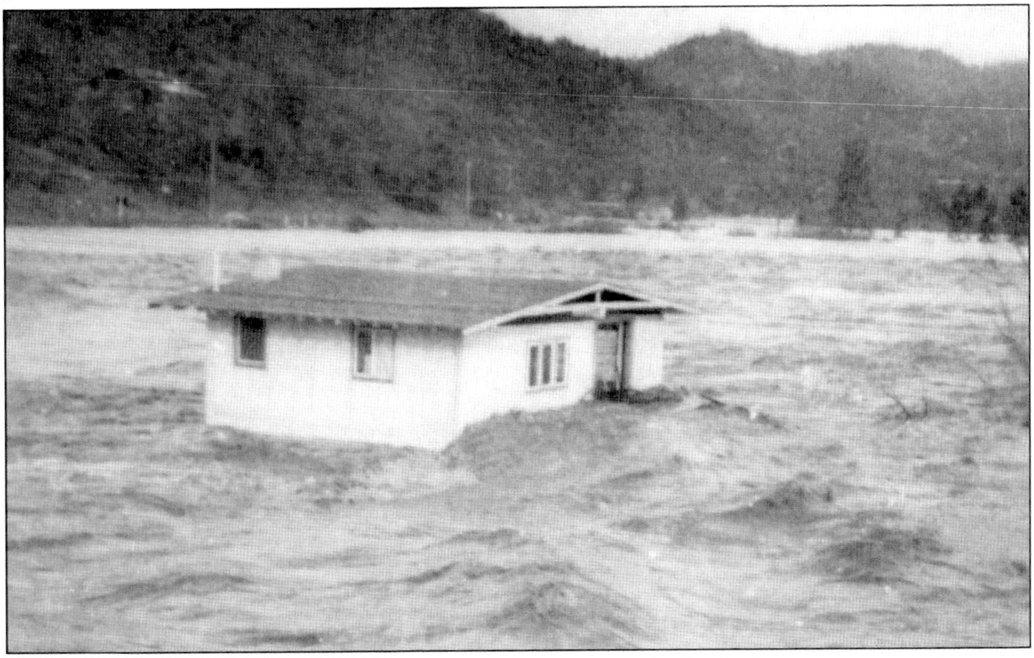

A 1955 flood trapped a man inside the house in this picture who had refused to evacuate. Rescuers took a cable from one side of the river, raced over the railroad tracks to the other side, and then winched the cable up. When the house finally slammed against a ridge to a swirling stop, they were able to rescue the man by the cable.

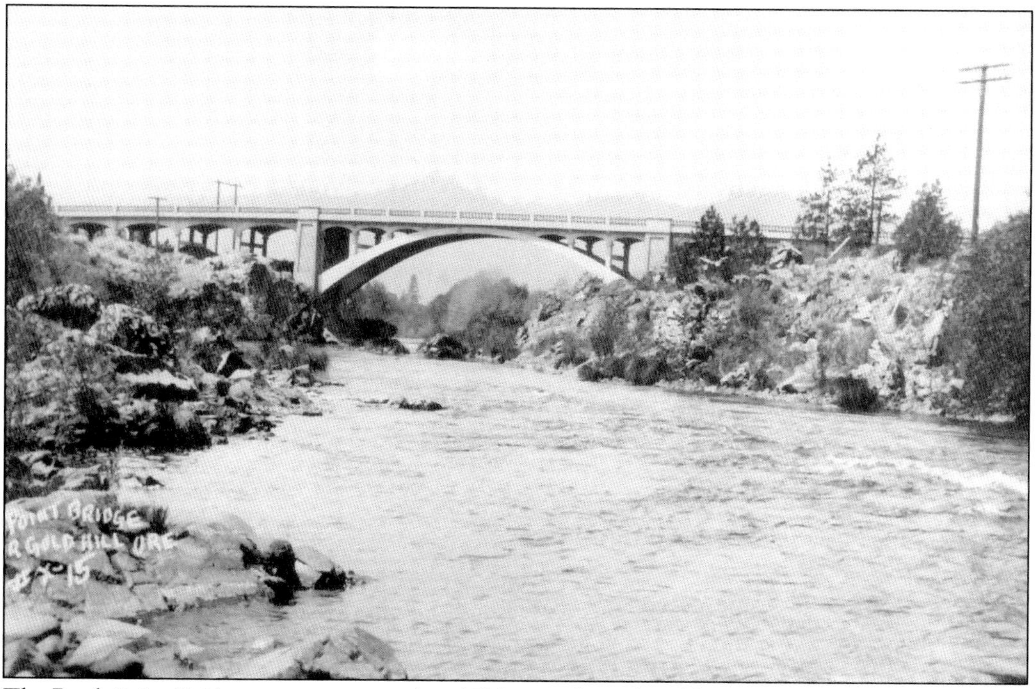

The Rock Point Bridge was constructed in 1920 to replace the old one. As with all aging bridges, different repair work has been made to this two-lane crossing, including in 1953 and 2000. It was extensively rebuilt from 2009 to late 2010 with structural modifications. The closing of this bridge for repairs caused residents to drive miles out of their way to get to town.

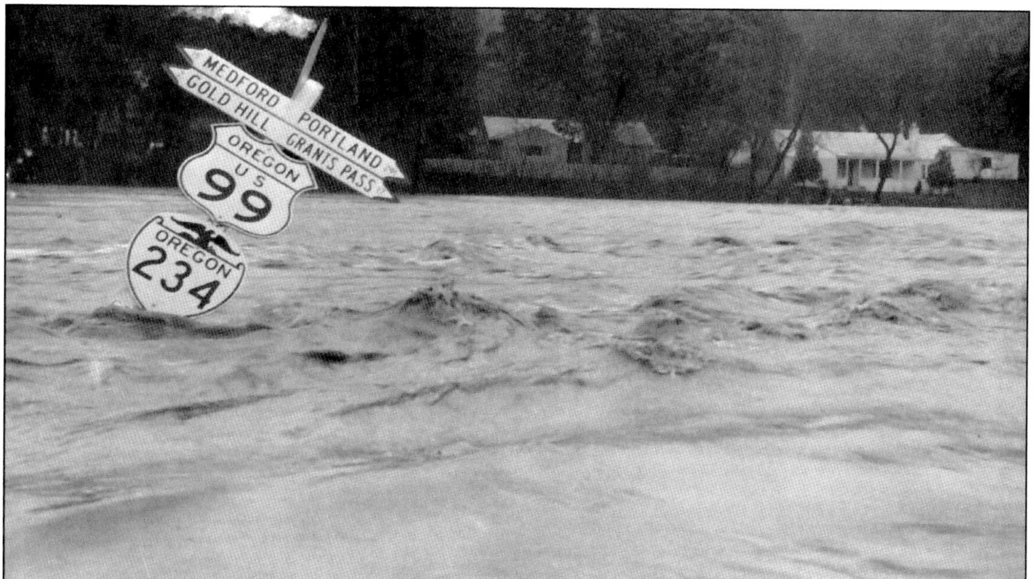

Floods were bad in 1955, 1964, and 1997, to name a few, and more problems arose apart from the imminent risks of destruction, death, and isolation. Taking baths, washing clothes, and finding potable water were real problems due to muddy water. Shown during the 1964 flood, this spot is where Sardine Creek empties into the Rogue River close to Rock Point. The Rock Point Bridge survived. (RG.)

Seven

Earning a Living

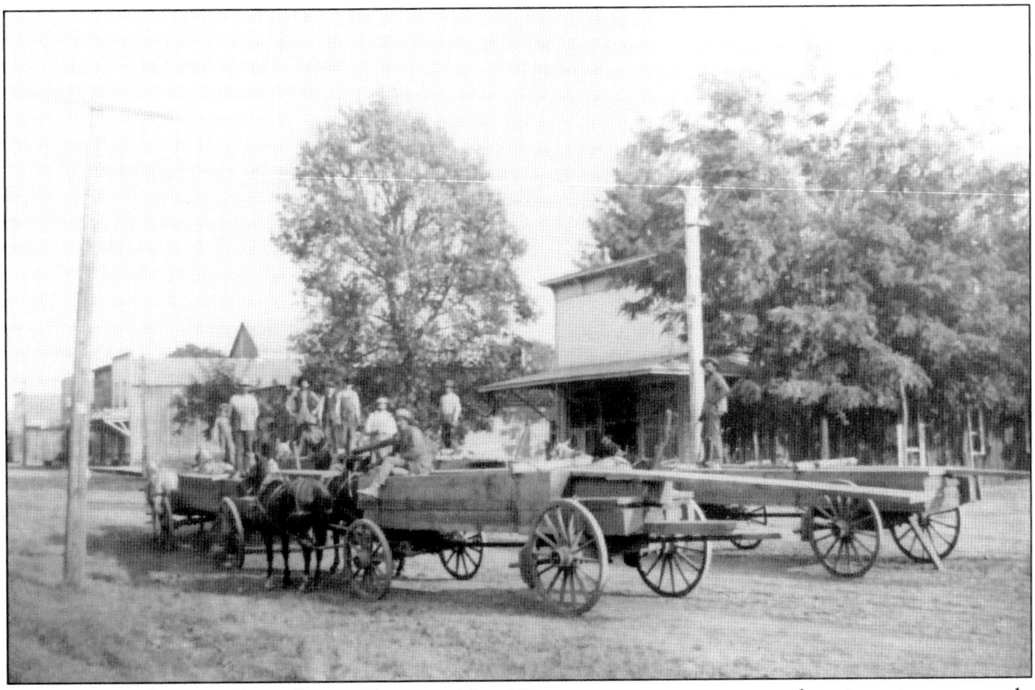

Since unemployment benefits, welfare, and healthcare programs were not then in existence, early Americans had to work to live. Whether laboring at farming, fishing, lumbering, gold mining, or in a cement plant, Gold Hill folks were no different than anyone else. Lumbering was a big business until the late 20th century, when environmental restrictions and economic developments curtailed it. These lumber wagons on Second Avenue were used to haul lumber from the Dusenberry Mill on Sardine Creek in the late 1890s.

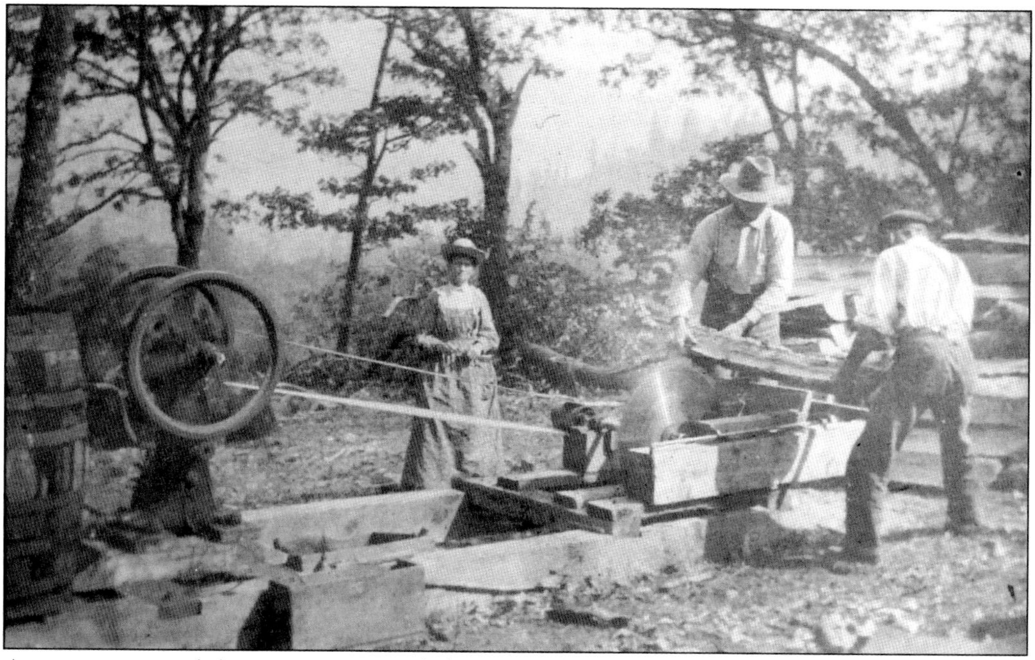

As a woman stands by, two men run a belt-operated saw at Rock Point in the late 1800s. Large mills were already running, but these smaller operators could earn a living as well as meet their own needs. Once they sawed the logs into planks and lumber, the next step was to transport the wood to market. (SOHS.)

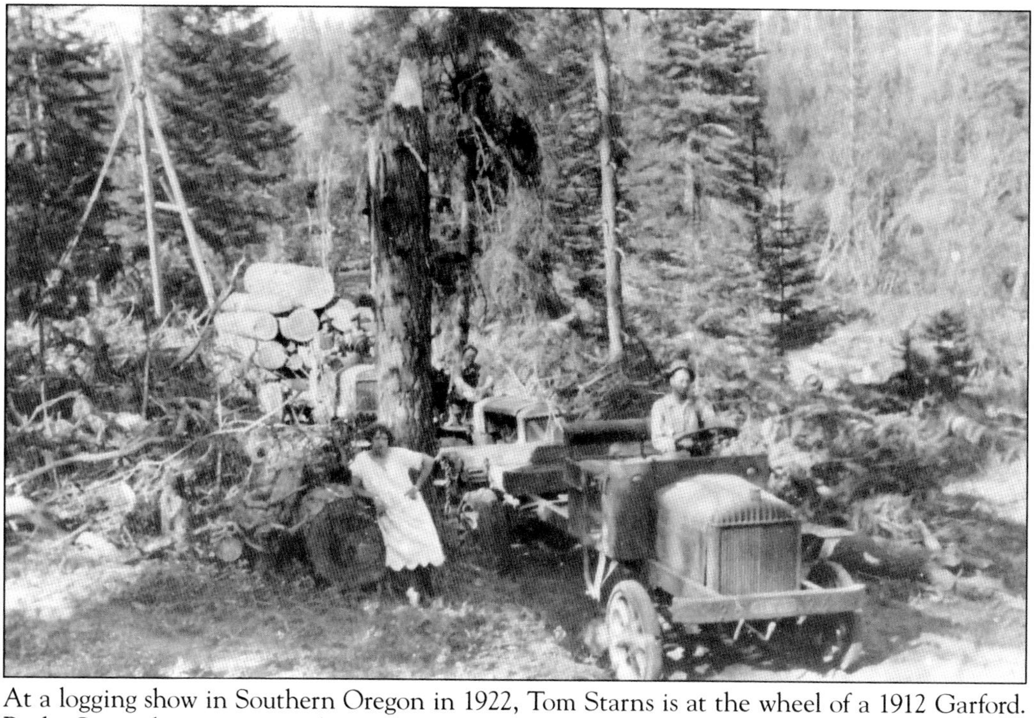

At a logging show in Southern Oregon in 1922, Tom Starns is at the wheel of a 1912 Garford. Birdie Starns leans against a large cut stump, while the crews behind them are driving a 1908 crawler tractor; a 1909 Garford follows with a high stack of large logs.

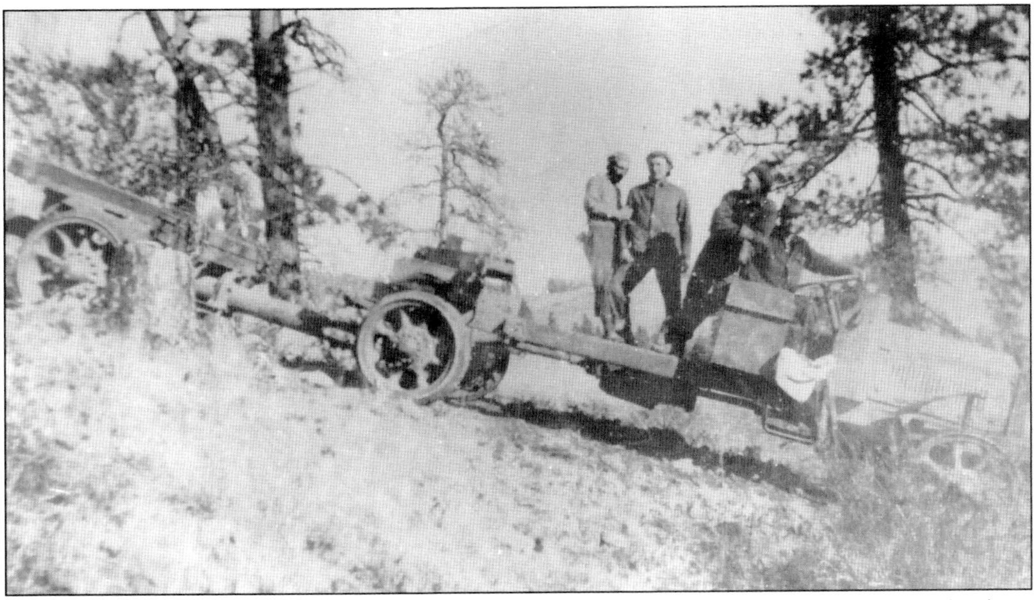

Tom Starns is at the wheel of an old Sterling log truck. Once a large log was ready for loading, horses dragged it up a ramp to the truck. Powerful winches could then be used. The dangerous work continued as the truck was driven over tough terrain to the closest sawmill. Working and driving on an incline like this required considerable experience, to say the least.

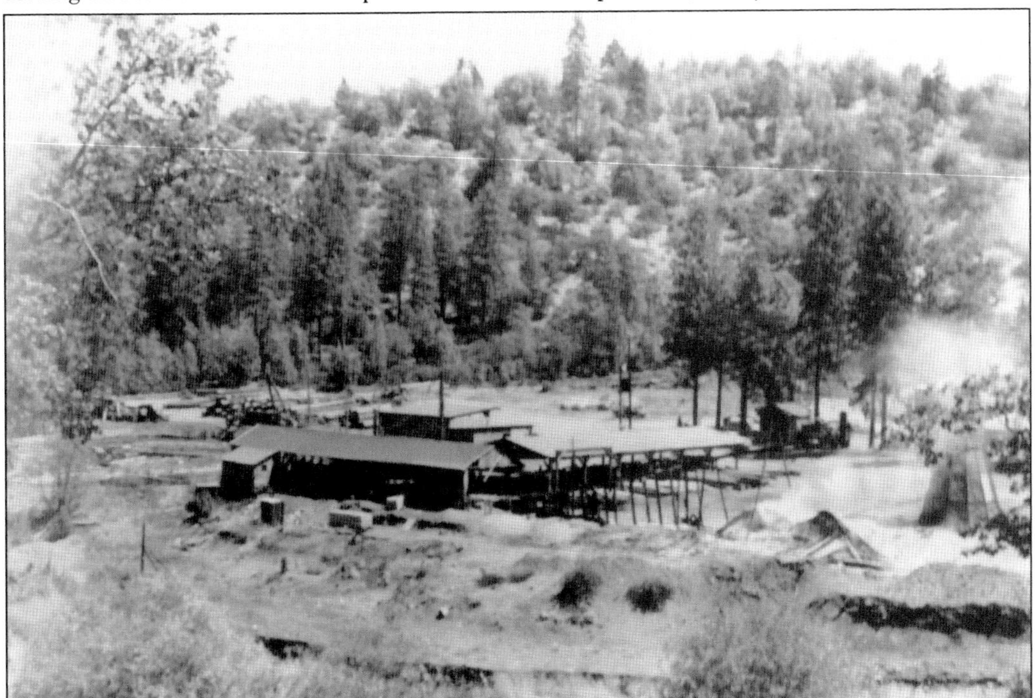

The Jeddeloh Brothers owned and ran this extensive 1930s sawmill on Galls Creek. Similar operations took place for years on Sardine Creek and other tributaries. These enterprises employed local men and were good employers, but when the economic cycle brought downturns, the mills had to lay off men.

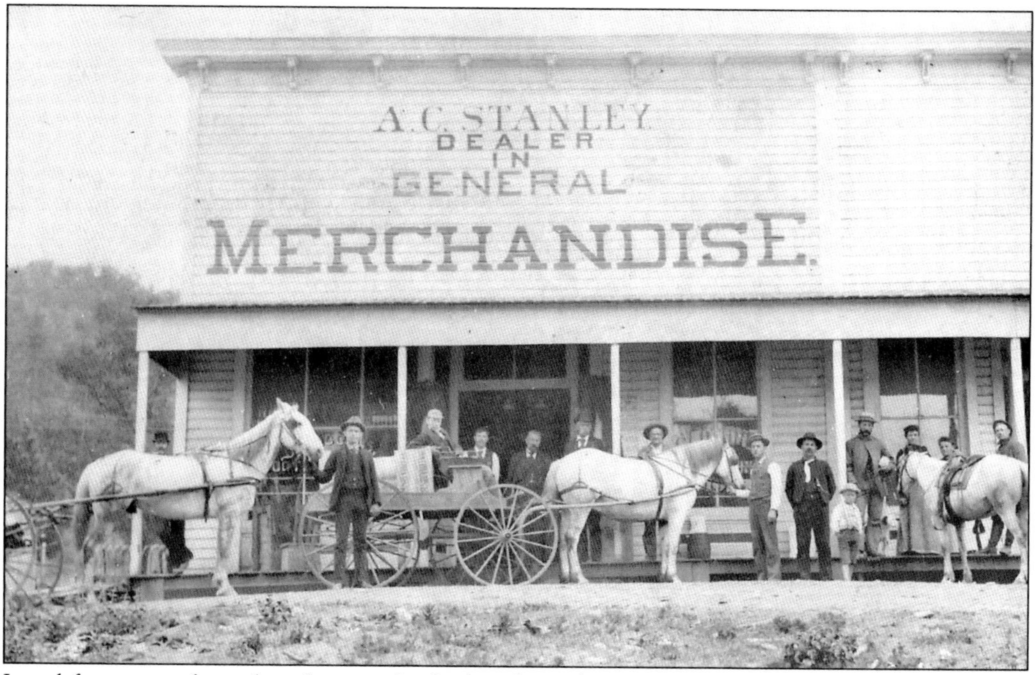

Local farmers and ranchers line up for feed and supplies in front of the A. C. Stanley general merchandise store in the 1890s. Dressed in suits and ties, the owners stand by the front door. These businesses tried to carry whatever would sell. This store was another early Gold Hill Fourth Avenue operation above the railroad tracks.

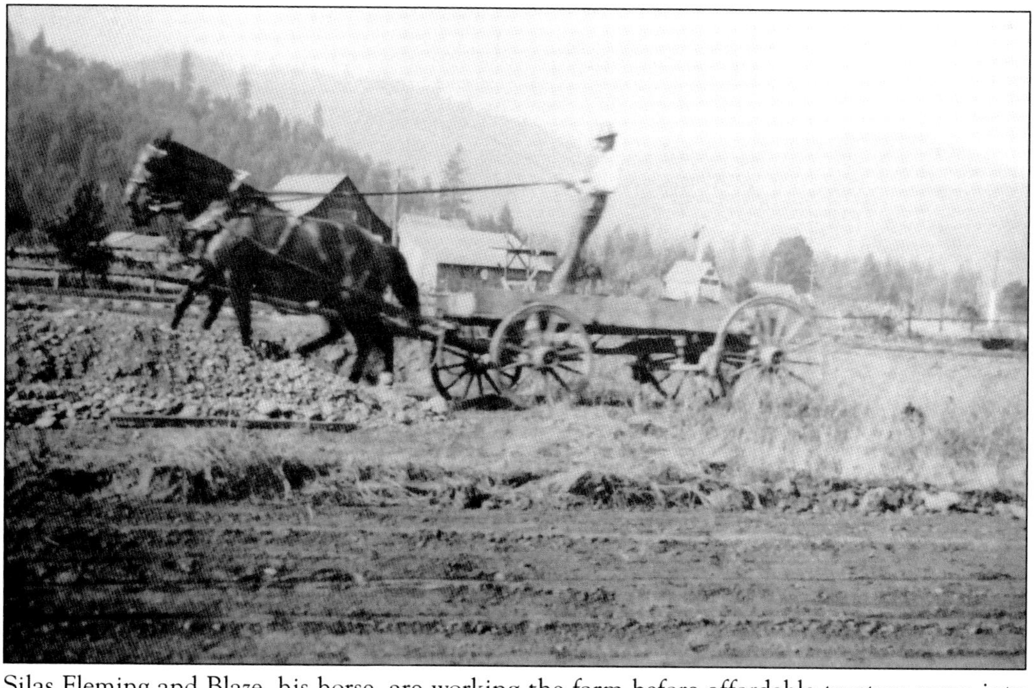

Silas Fleming and Blaze, his horse, are working the farm before affordable tractors came into existence. A resident of Gold Hill, Silas also worked in excavating the right-of-way for the railroads, along with plowing and working his own land.

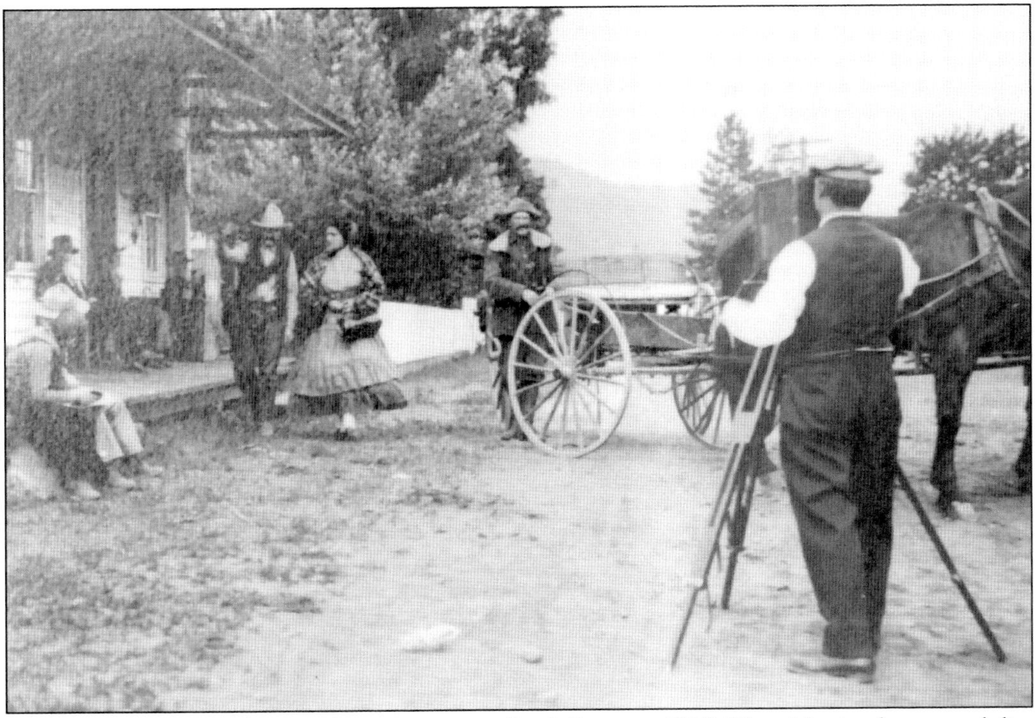

A traveling photographer is taking pictures at Rock Point in 1915. The old tripod, unpaved dirt street, clothes, and horse-pulled cart testify to the times. The photographer's apparatus would now be an expensive ticket on *Antiques Roadshow*.

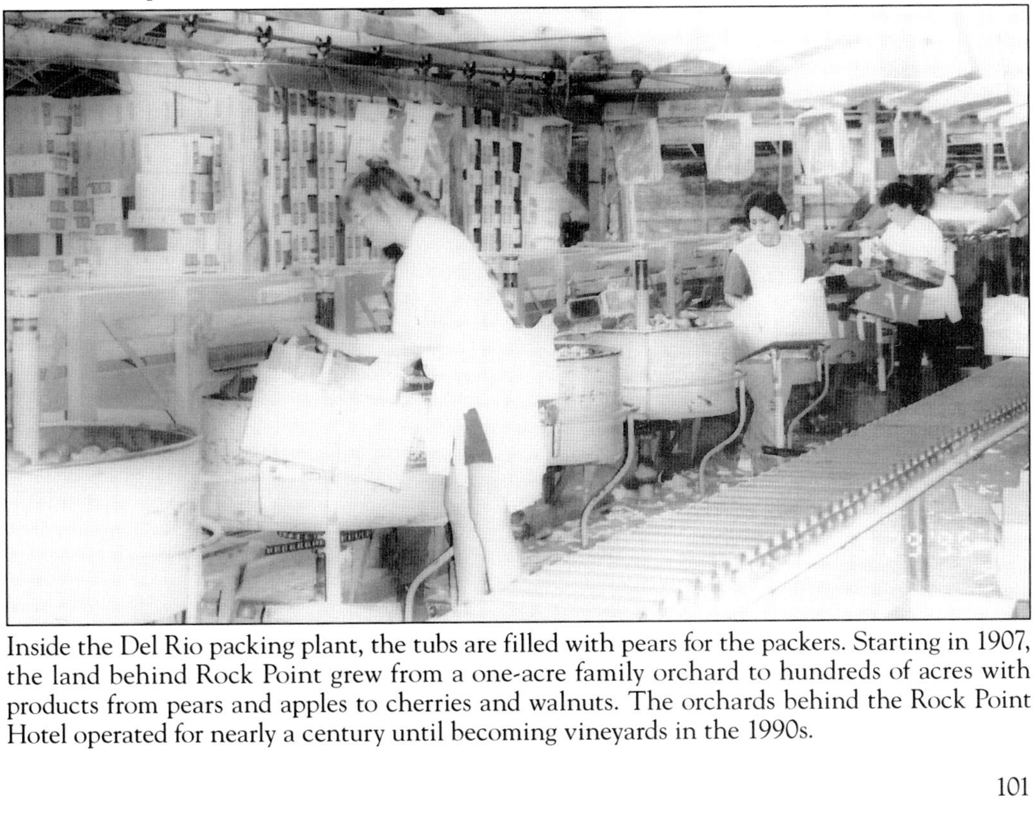

Inside the Del Rio packing plant, the tubs are filled with pears for the packers. Starting in 1907, the land behind Rock Point grew from a one-acre family orchard to hundreds of acres with products from pears and apples to cherries and walnuts. The orchards behind the Rock Point Hotel operated for nearly a century until becoming vineyards in the 1990s.

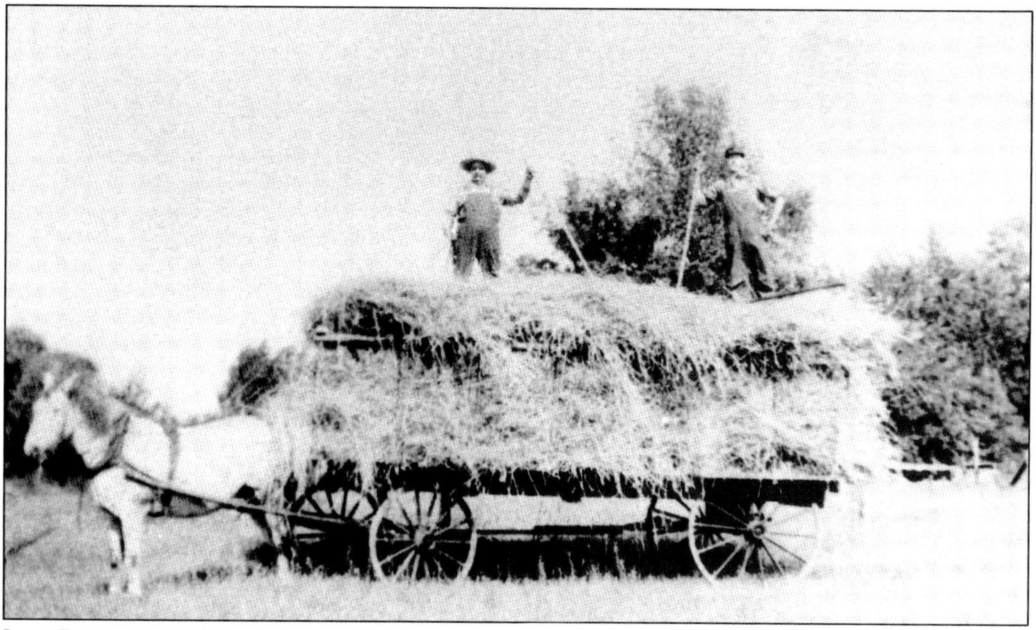

Jesse D. Starns and his son Robert are bringing in the hay in June 1938. The old horse is named Prince, and the amount of hay that was stuffed on the wagon took ingenuity. Farming and ranching continues in the area today, especially in Sams Valley.

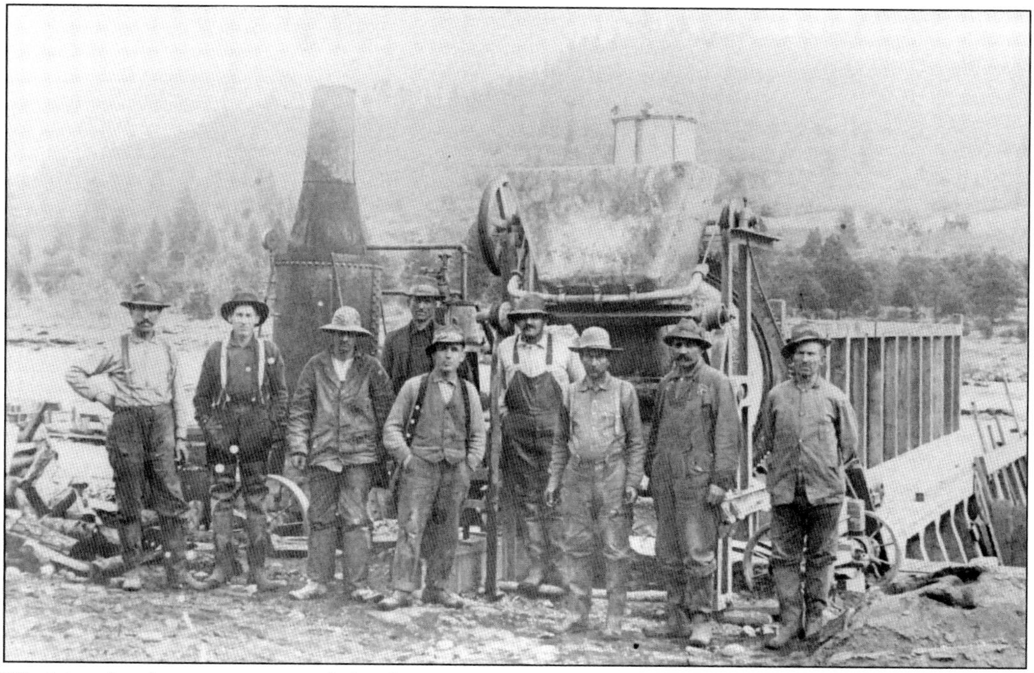

Working for the city, state, or federal governments was always an option, especially when times were bad. This picture is of the workers at the Gold Hill Water Works with its filtration system to provide potable water for drinking, washing, and other needs. The Rogue River is in the background, and one wonders what high water would have done.

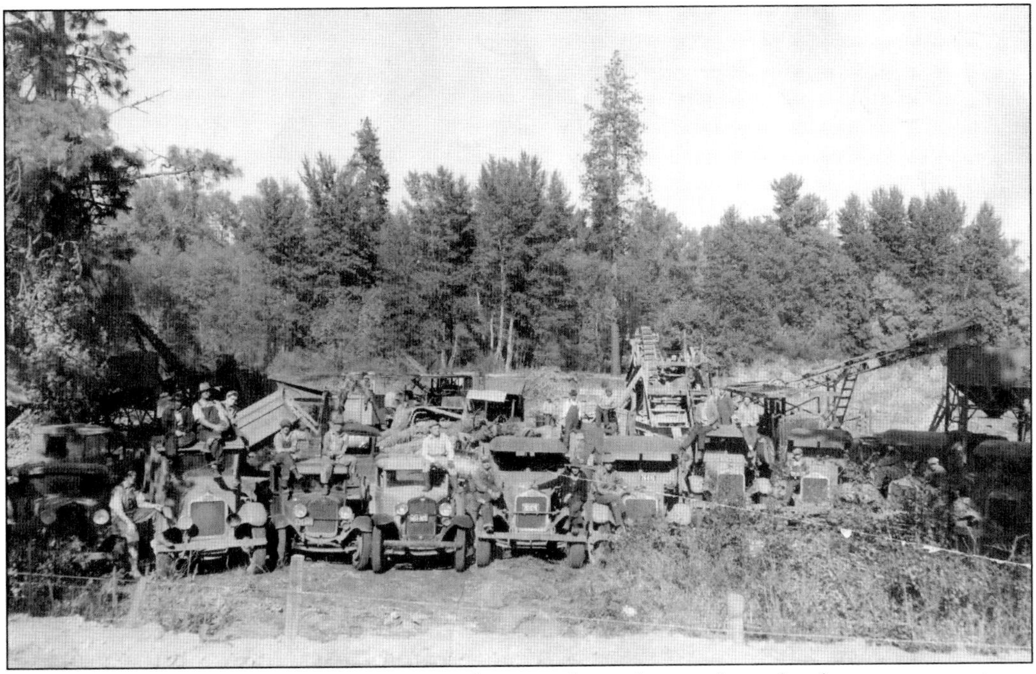

This classic picture shows a 1930s crew with its trucks, either working for the state or a private contractor. The excavation and conveyor equipment indicates that the operation was a gravel or rock pit, and the trucks were used to transport the rock to construction or road sites.

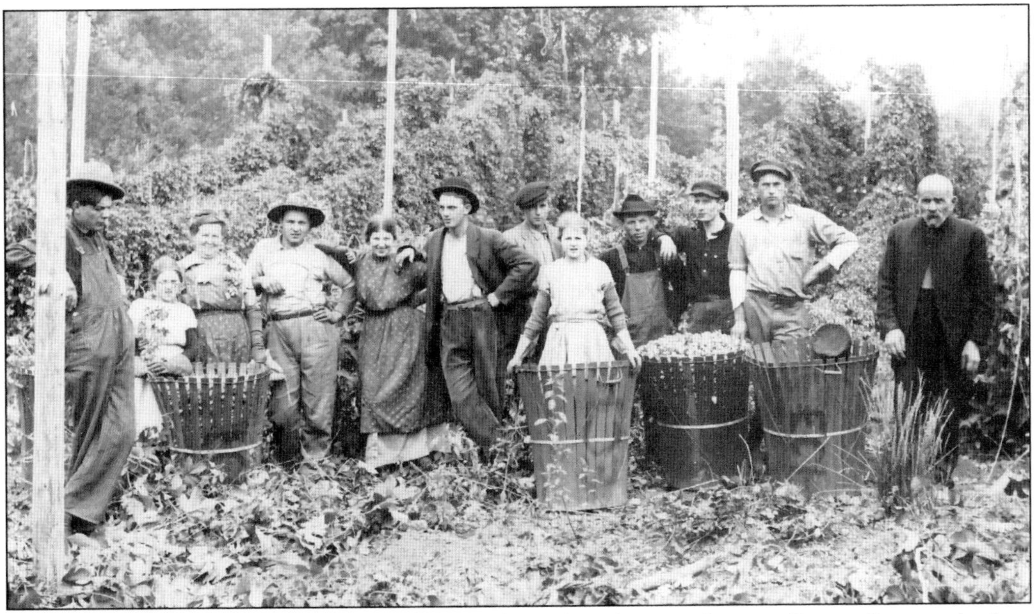

From the 1920s on, residents camped out at the Hilton hop yards near Grants Pass in the late summer to earn money picking hops, used in making beer. Workers strapped a large basket onto their backs and then tossed the hops into it over their shoulders. These were emptied into a large, truck-pulled hopper; before trucks, horses were used. The tall poles were used to hold the hops, which were green, squishy, and looked like pine cones.

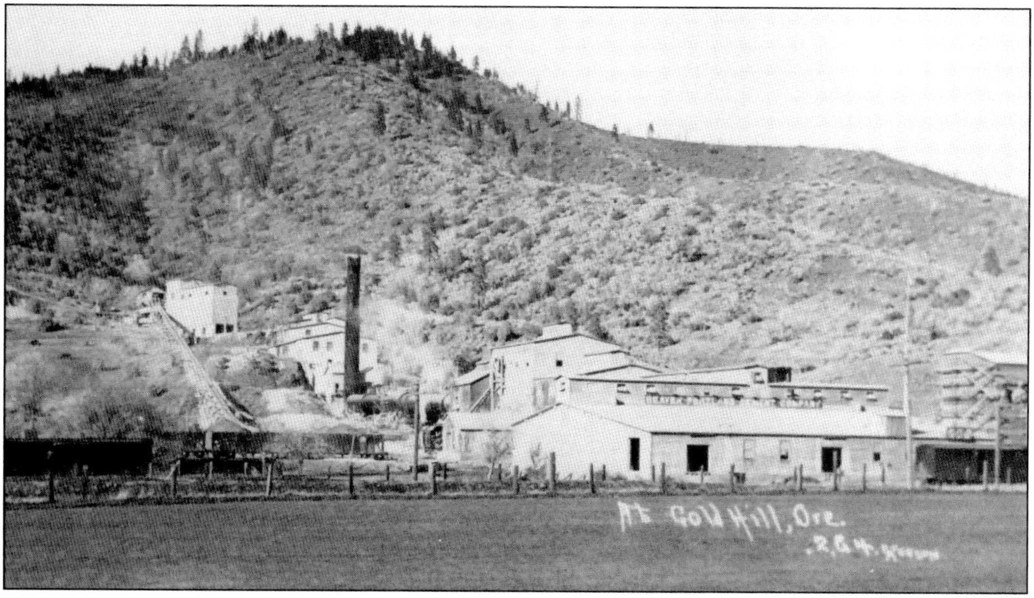

Given the nearby high-quality limestone deposits, railroad depot, and central location, Gold Hill became the site for a large cement plant in 1913 on 18 adjacent city acres by the Beaver Portland Cement Company. Making cement basically requires mixing crushed limestone with shale, adding water to form a slurry, and then firing the mixture in a huge kiln. After cooling, gypsum is mixed, and this is then ground into a fine powder. Much of the required lime rock was first quarried at Zacher Crossing, where the Bristol Silica Plant is now located, and loaded onto railroad cars for shipment 1 mile east to the plant; later, the limestone came from Marble Mountain to the north and was transported again by rail. The picture below is from the early 1900s. The old cement mixer has drum wheels; the train depot and Gold Hill Hotel are in the background.

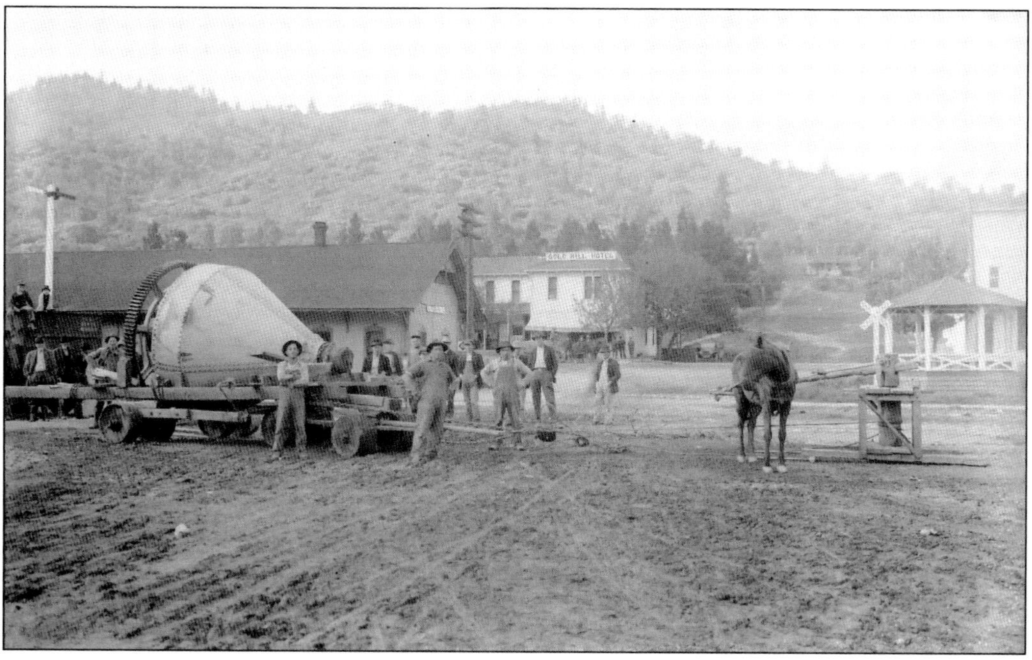

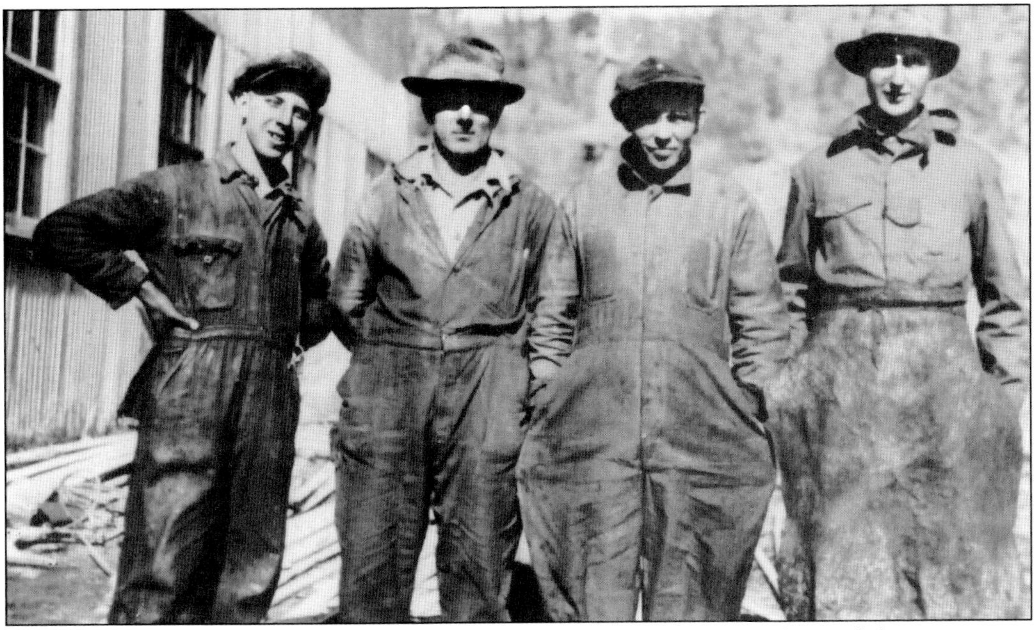

Once completed in 1915, the cement plant was the largest in Oregon and served the community for 60 years, employing between 100 and 150 people. This continued after Pacific Portland merged in 1952 with Ideal Cement. The workers are, from left to right, Frenchy Meunier, Earl Adams, Joe Blair, and Frank Carter. The plant closed in 1967, and the economic shock to the community took time to work out.

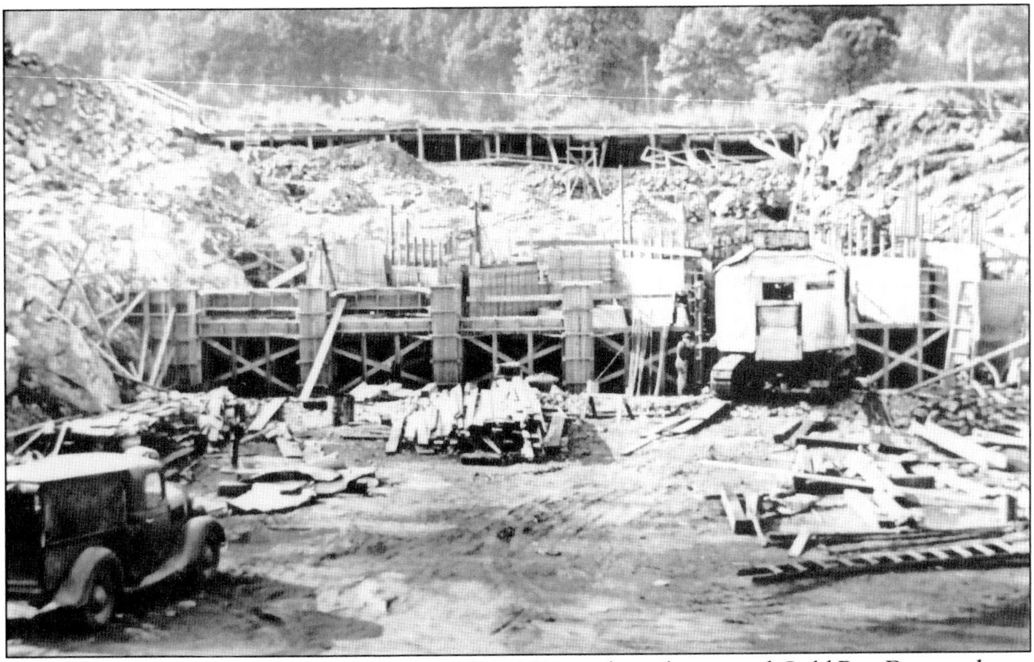

Construction was also a big employer into the 1950s, such as the second Gold Ray Dam and new power plant projects. Portland Cement started construction of a new power plant in 1944, close to Gold Hill where the city's sports park is now on Highway 234. This was a large undertaking and employed numbers of workers. The power plant was abandoned when the cement plant closed.

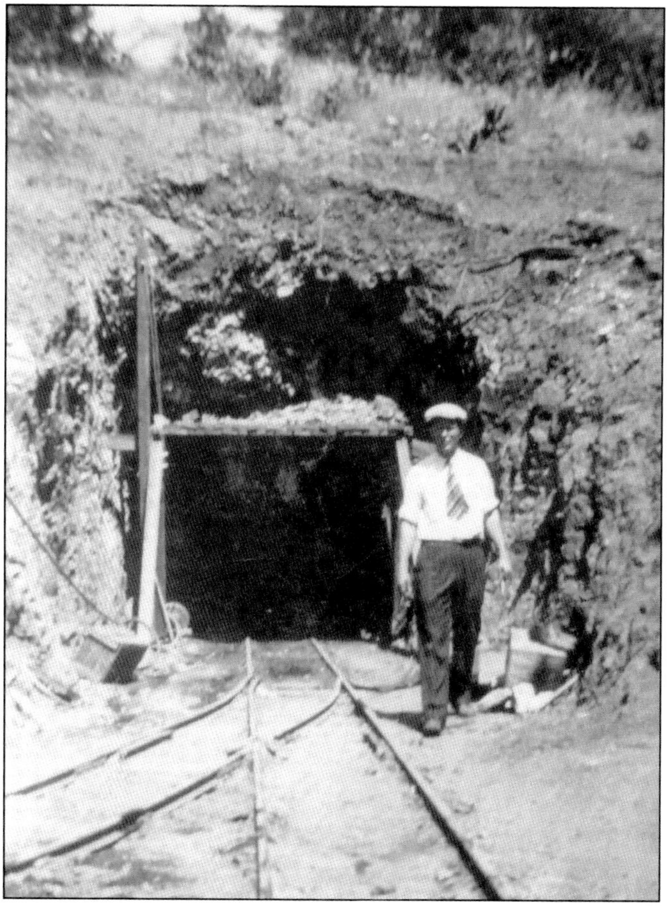

Jim Lively is shown at left in the 1930s at his Lively Lime mine and quarry on Kane Creek, which was a large industry in Gold Hill for many years and was close to town. The limestone or "paper rock" was trucked over Blackwell Road to the train depot, loaded onto cars, and shipped out to make paper. (Paper rock is still used today.) In the picture below, a steam engine drove the tram and hoist that carried the cart on rails. Wooden blocks on the friction bands were used as a brake and clutch. The limestone chunks were sizeable.

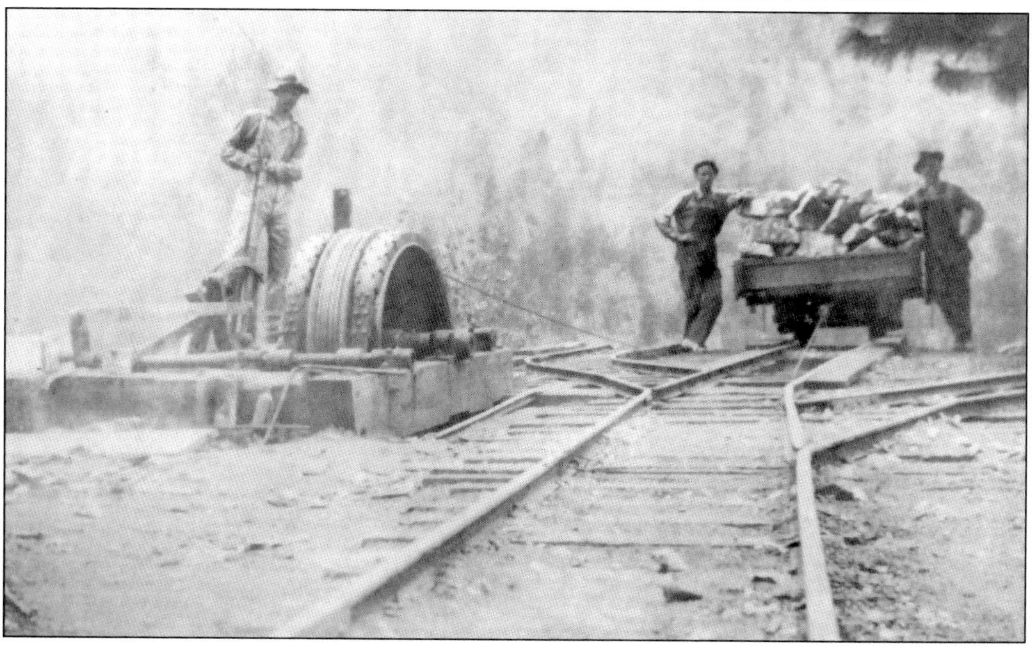

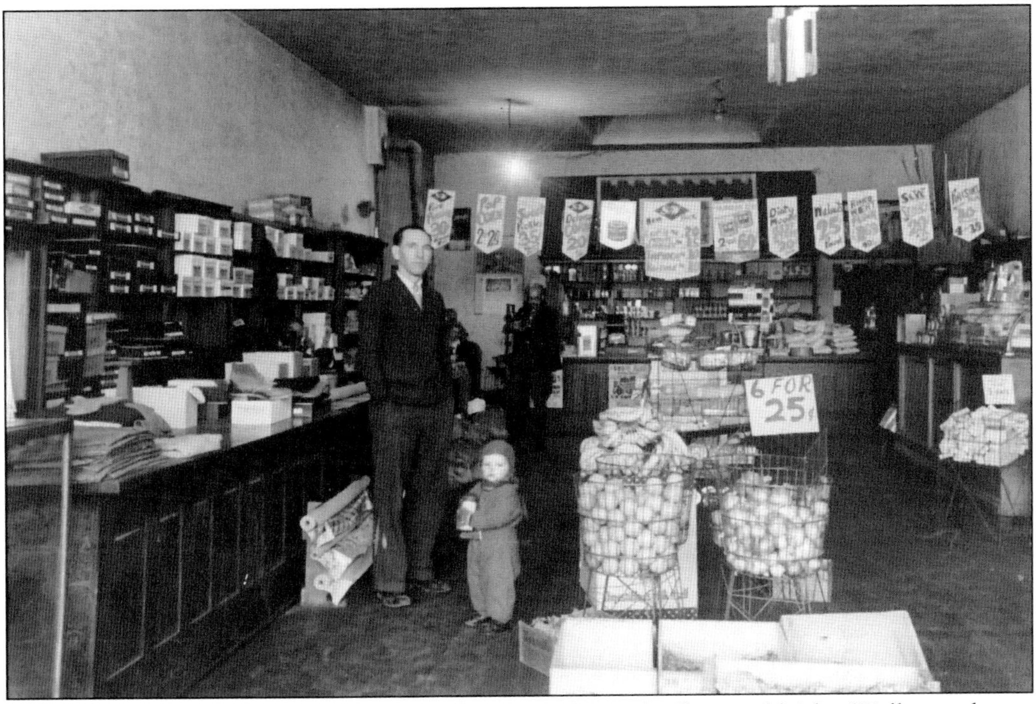

Walker's Gold Hill Grocery Store is seen here in 1938, with 45-year-old Alva Walker and two-year-old Dick Walker. The open fruit and vegetable cases with hand-printed signs attest to the operations then. As more people worked for outside employers, they simply bought what they needed to eat from stores like this.

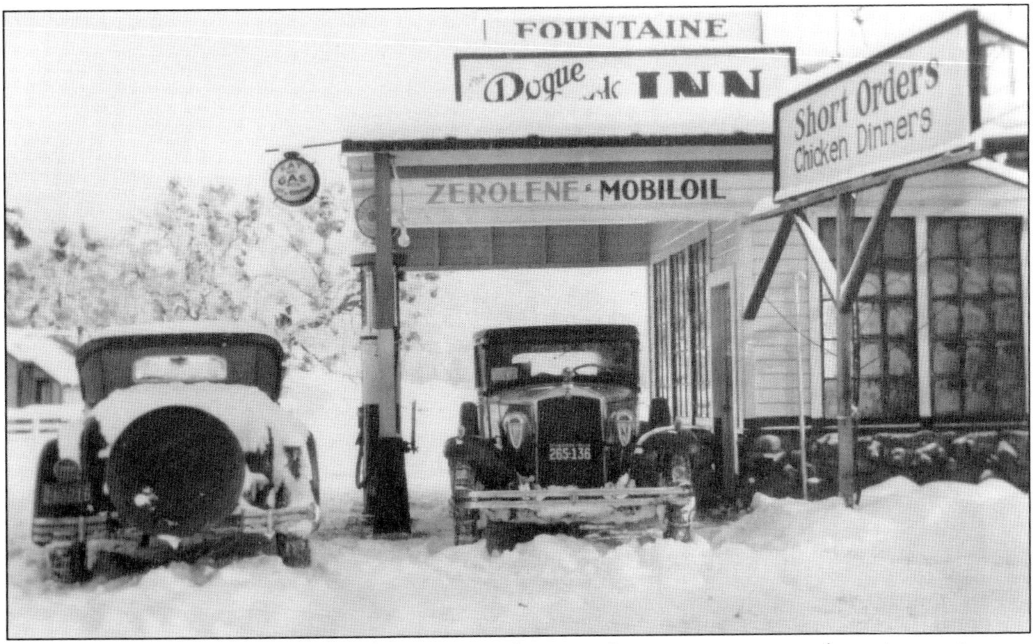

People in the area ran their own businesses, of course, from restaurants and service stations to fishing tackle shops and drugstores. This 1937 picture shows Seth Coy's service station on Second Avenue. A 1928 Durant is in the bay. This was the year of a rare, large snow.

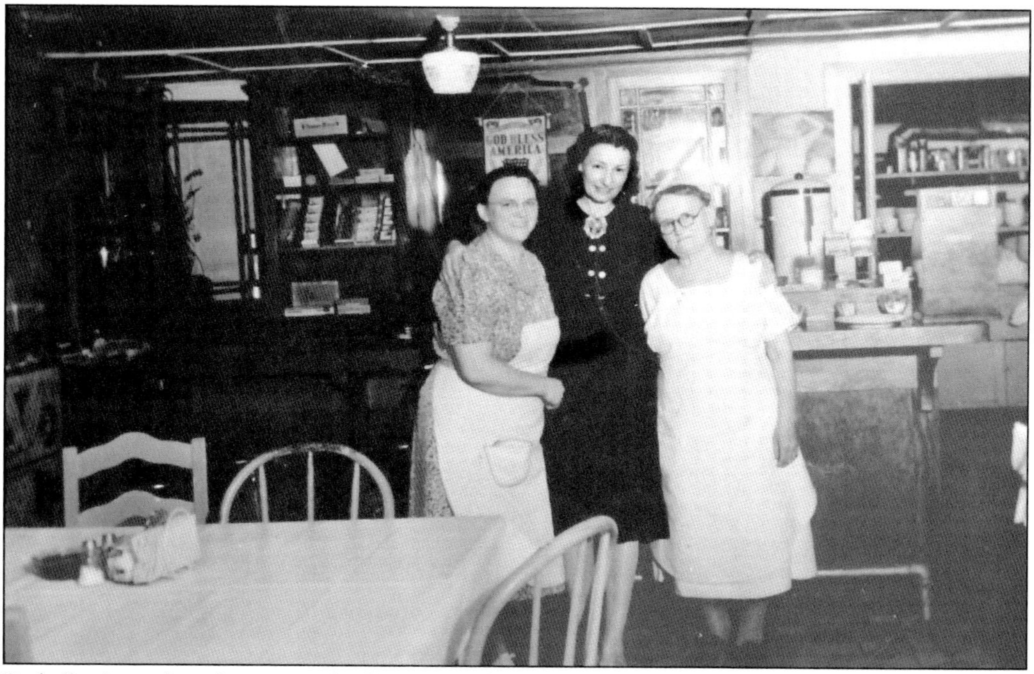

Seth Coy's mother, Susie, ran the Rogue Nook Inn adjacent to the service station. In this 1950s picture, from left to right, are teacher Maude Coy Robinson (helping out during a summer break), Bertha Coy, and their mother, Susie.

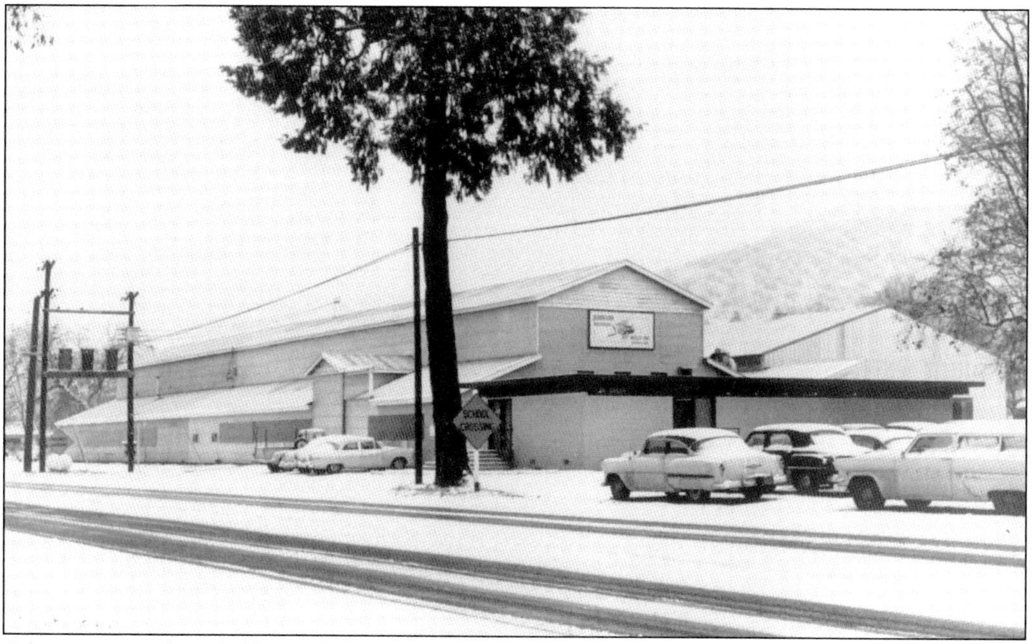

After running their Galls Creek sawmill for years, the three Jeddeloh brothers began building saws for other mills in 1955 as Jeddeloh Brothers Sweed Mill. They later branched out to manufacturing a variety of recycling equipment with custom engineering and systems manufacturing. Cascade Wood Products bought the company in 1986. Now called Sweed Machinery, Inc., the largest business in Gold Hill, it is still located on Second Avenue.

Eight

When Work Is Done

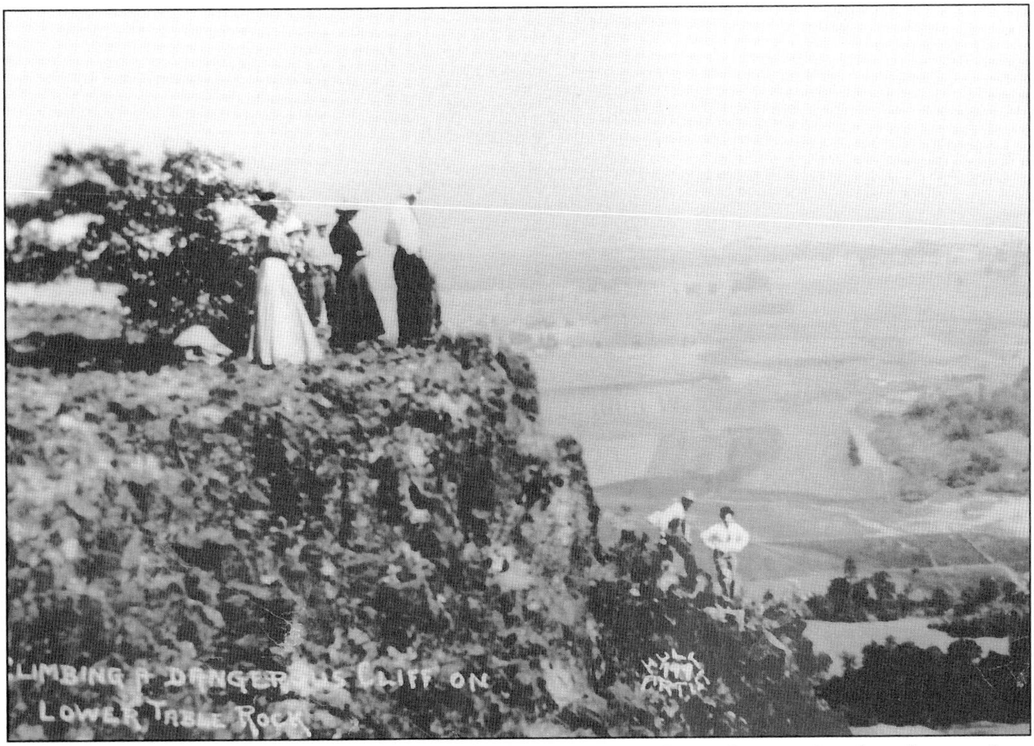

The Table Rocks in Sams Valley near Medford are a Southern Oregon landmark, standing high above the Rogue River valley. A gathering place for settlers, the flat, high plateau stands approximately 750 feet above the valley floor with 200-foot drop-offs from the cliffs. The area has two sections—Lower and Upper Table Rocks—and the Nature Conservancy dedicated Lower Table Rock as a preserve.

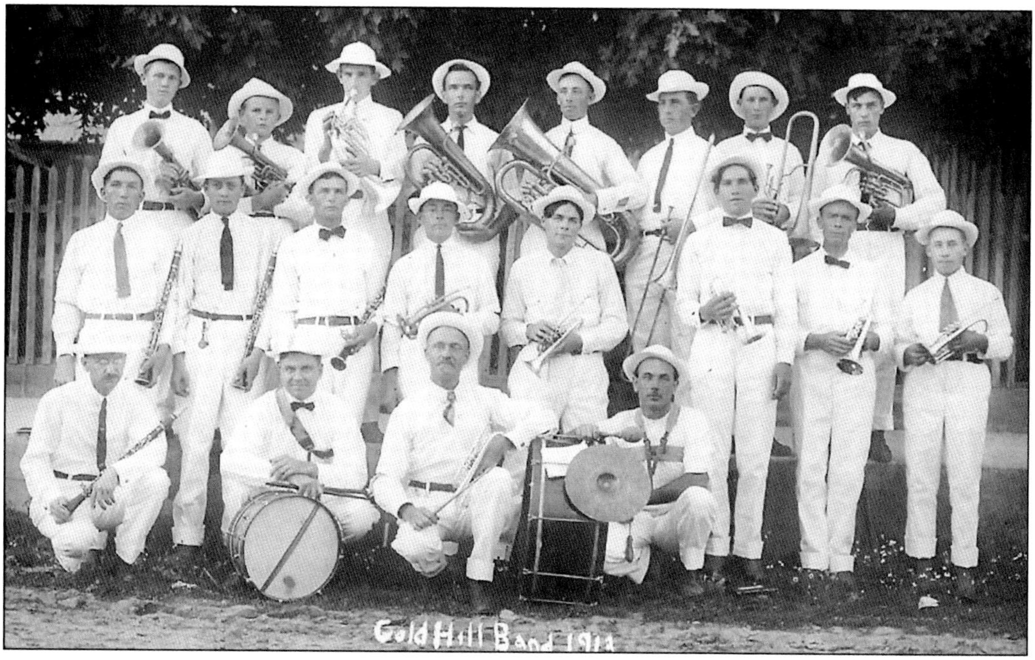

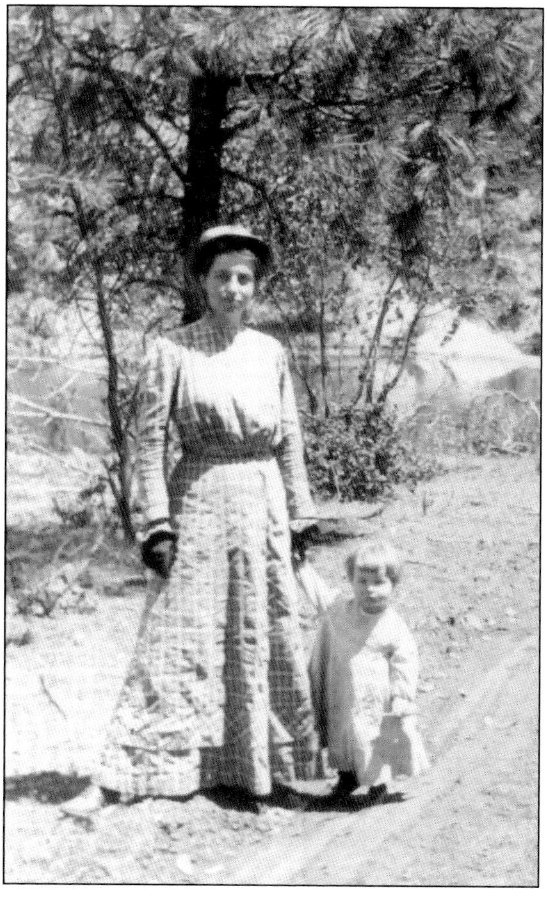

Long before television, video games, and texting began monopolizing people's free time, band music and its enjoyment was a way of life. Community bands practiced and played in town after work, sometimes while being pulled through city streets on a horse and wagon. The 1913 Gold Hill Band (above) has a striking modern look compared to previous groups.

This early 1900s picture shows Fanny Sims and her son Oscar enjoying a walk in a picturesque natural setting.

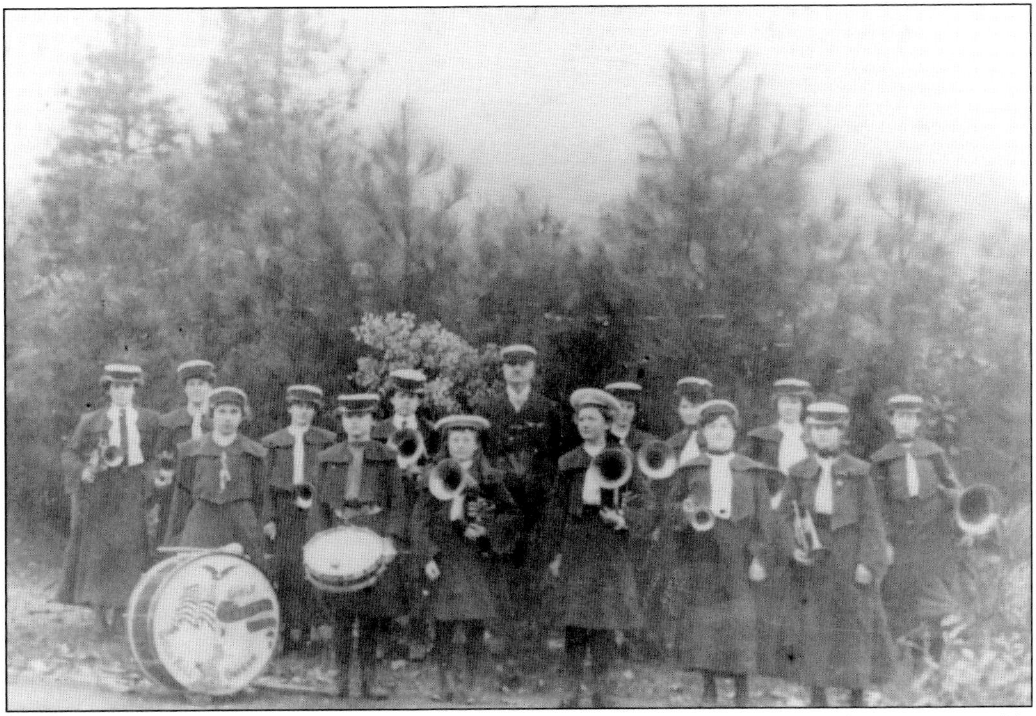

This 1915 image shows the girls' Gold Hill Band. Owing to the young-looking faces, it is possible that this band was made up primarily of high school students. The conductor is standing in the center; brass instruments predominate, and this group would look smart in their uniforms when marching down Fourth Avenue.

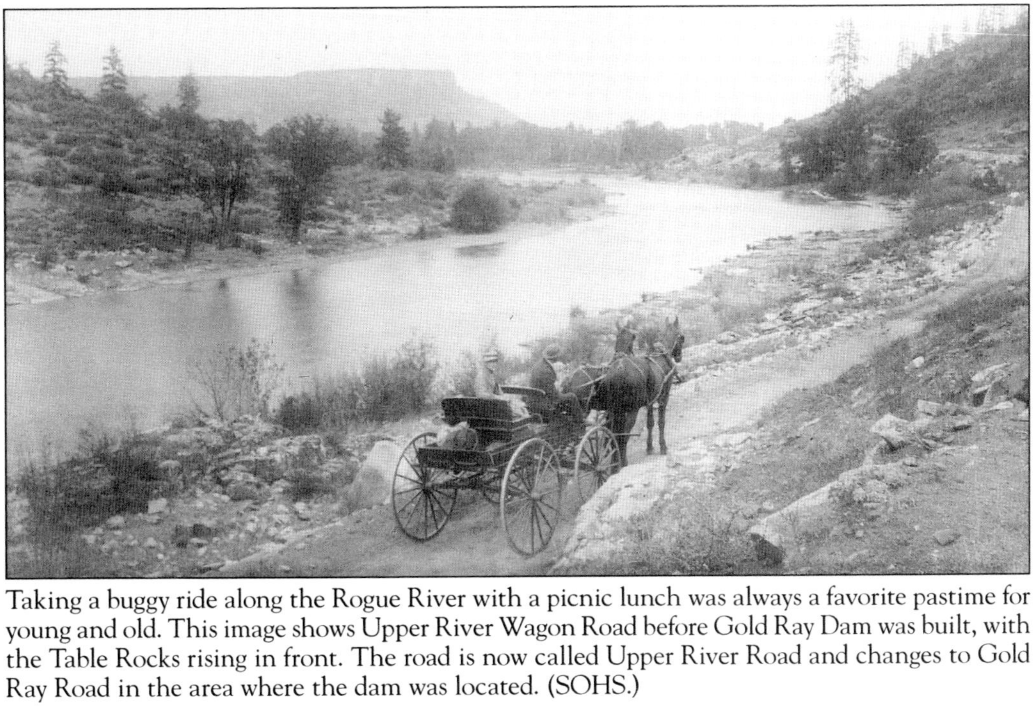

Taking a buggy ride along the Rogue River with a picnic lunch was always a favorite pastime for young and old. This image shows Upper River Wagon Road before Gold Ray Dam was built, with the Table Rocks rising in front. The road is now called Upper River Road and changes to Gold Ray Road in the area where the dam was located. (SOHS.)

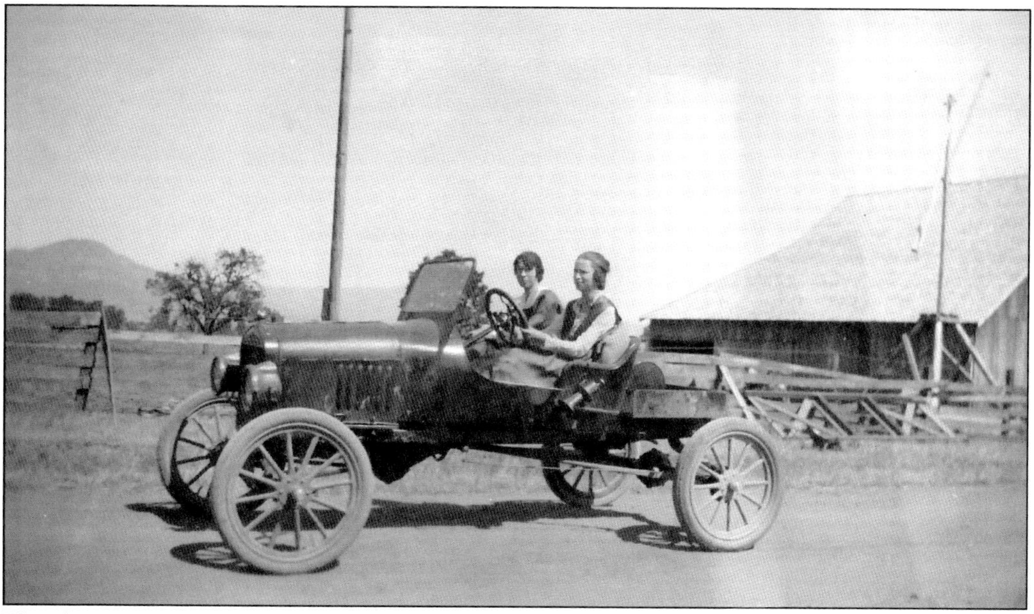

Blanche Merriman is driving her stripped-down Model T Ford pickup with her sister Edith Martin in 1919. The picture was taken at the Merriman Ranch on Highway 99 between Central Point and Medford, close to Sams Valley, with the plains and hills evident in the background.

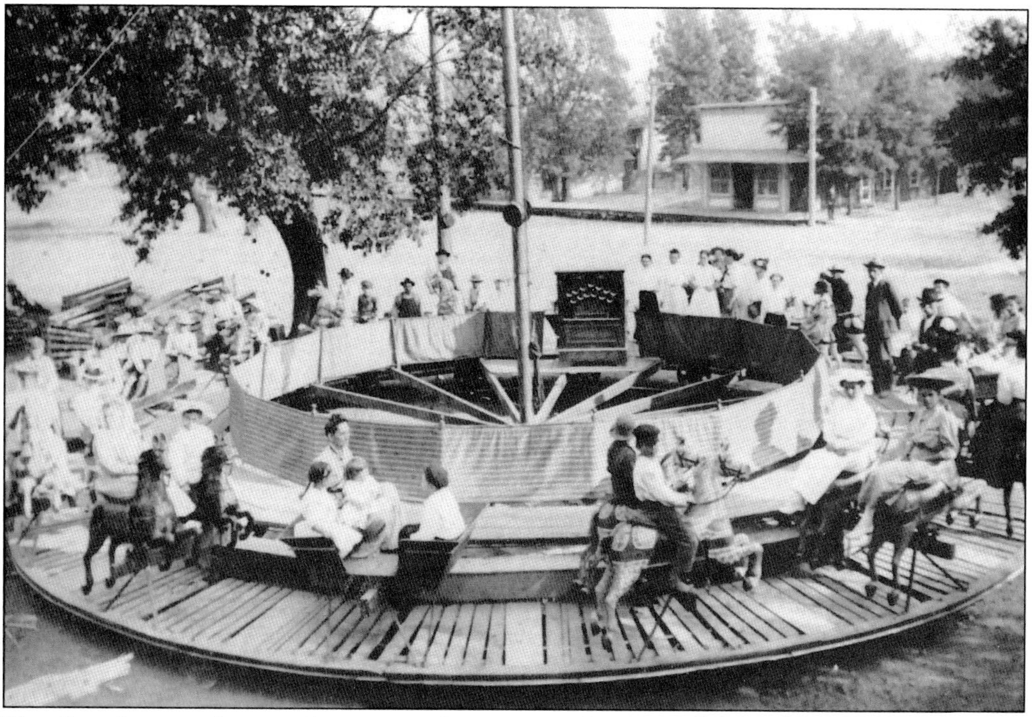

Traveling shows and carousels came on the trains as they passed through Gold Hill and other towns. This particular carousel in the early 1900s made more than one trip, and both parents and their children enjoyed the rides. The building in the background was on the corner of Fifth Street and Second Avenue.

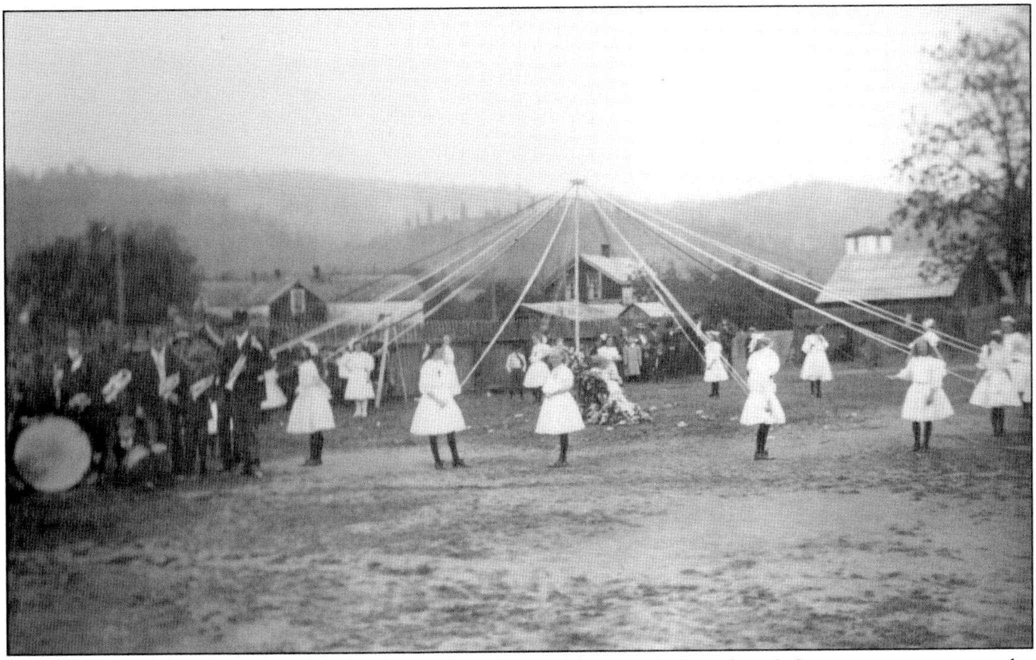

This May Day celebration at Dardanelles in the 1890s featured a band and the customary maypole. Marking the traditional end of winter on May 1, girls dressed in white danced around the maypole while holding the ends of long, colorful streamers. (SOHS.)

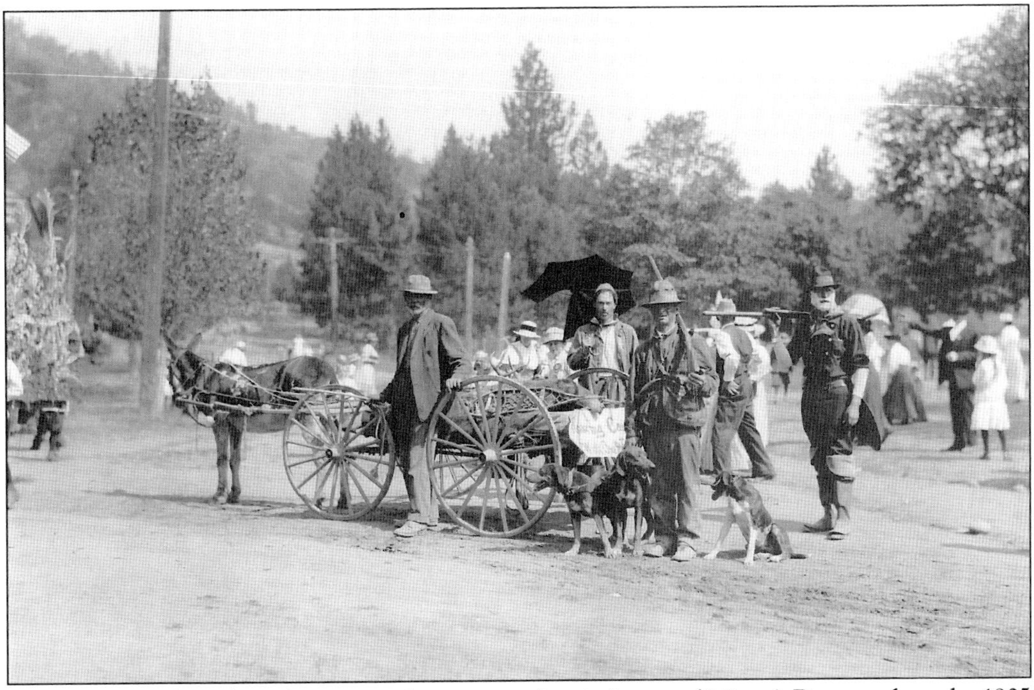

These costumed residents have just taken part in the city's annual Miner's Day parade at the 1905 Industrial Fair, a gala festival with a free salmon feed, bands, dancing, and game booths. In 1972, the annual June event was renamed Gold Dust Days, which continues today.

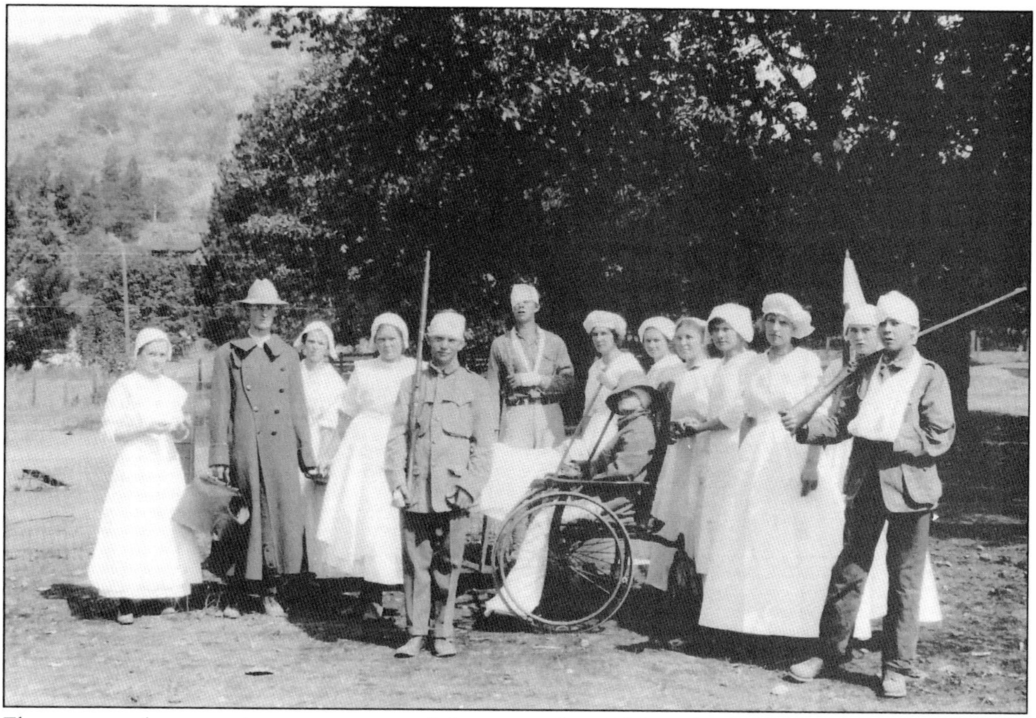

Floats were always an important part of these parades. Although reminding modern observers of World War I, this Red Cross float for the 1900 Gold Hill Industrial Fair was more likely in remembrance of the 1898 Spanish-American War.

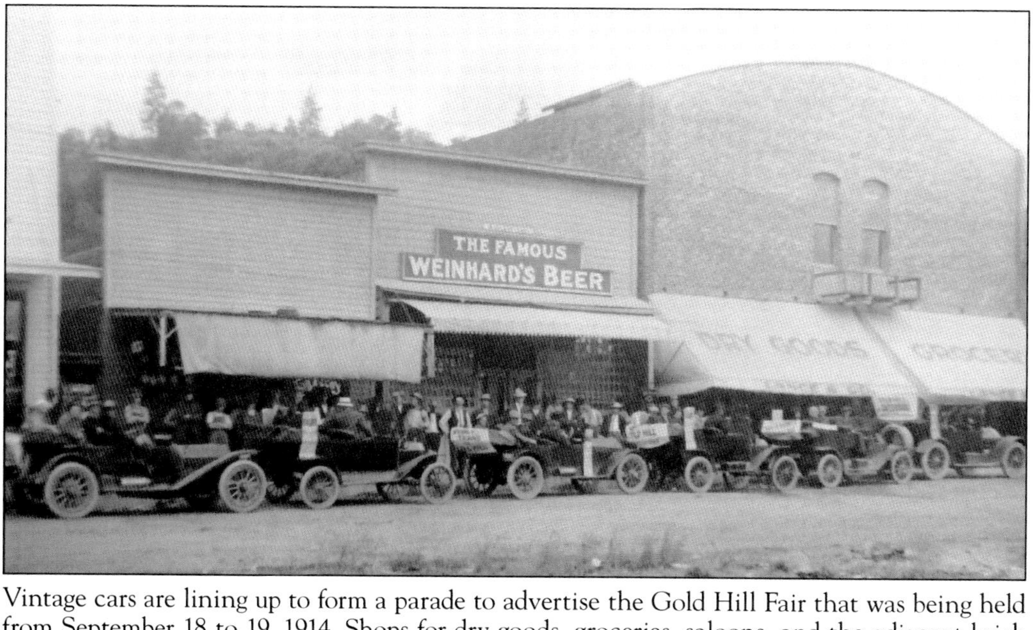

Vintage cars are lining up to form a parade to advertise the Gold Hill Fair that was being held from September 18 to 19, 1914. Shops for dry goods, groceries, saloons, and the adjacent brick opera house over Lance and Company's Dry Goods front the street.

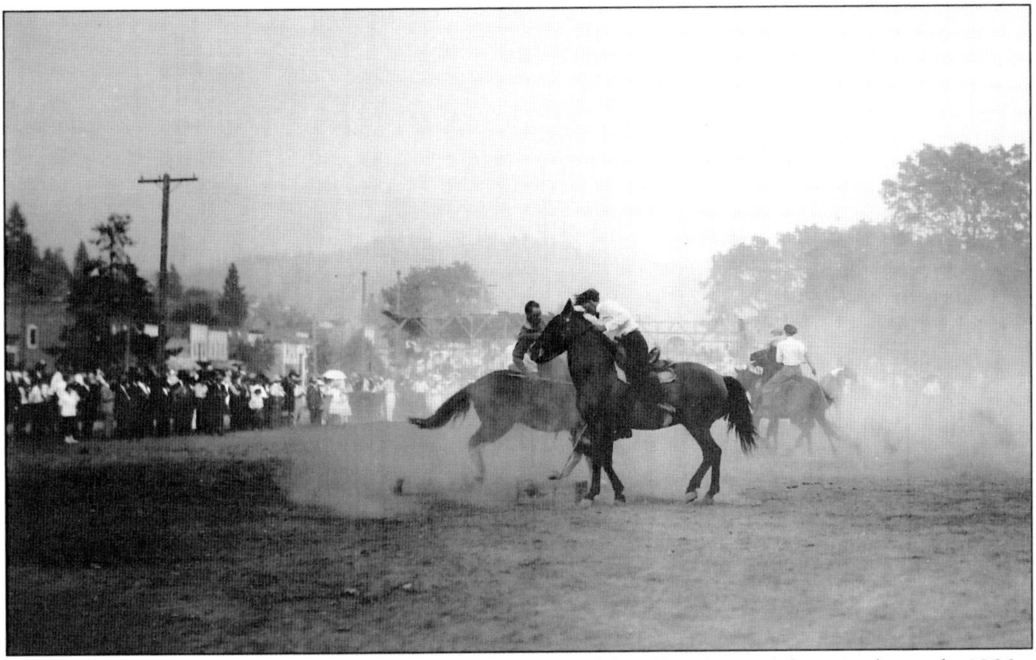

A different approach to polo was introduced at the Gold Hill industrial fairs in the early 1900s. The usual objective in polo is to score goals against the opposing team by hitting a small wooden ball with long-handled mallets while on horseback. Although the rules were basically the same, the Gold Hill version was a bit rougher and used a potato instead of a wooden ball. The polo field was where Sweed Machinery is now located. The image below is of the 1915 polo players and was taken across from the park.

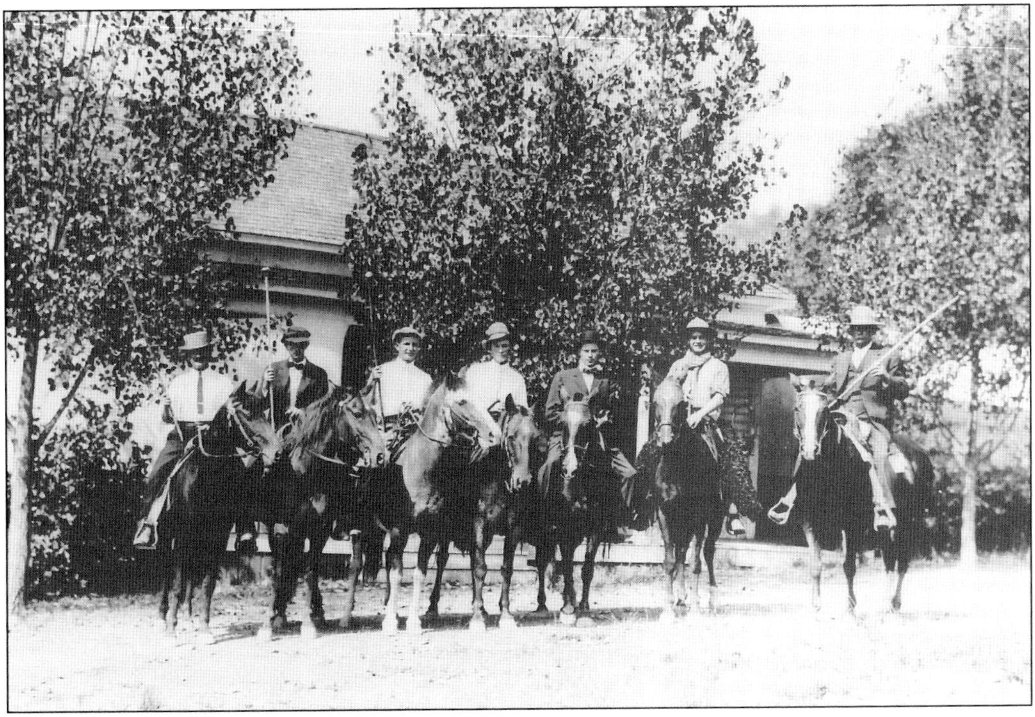

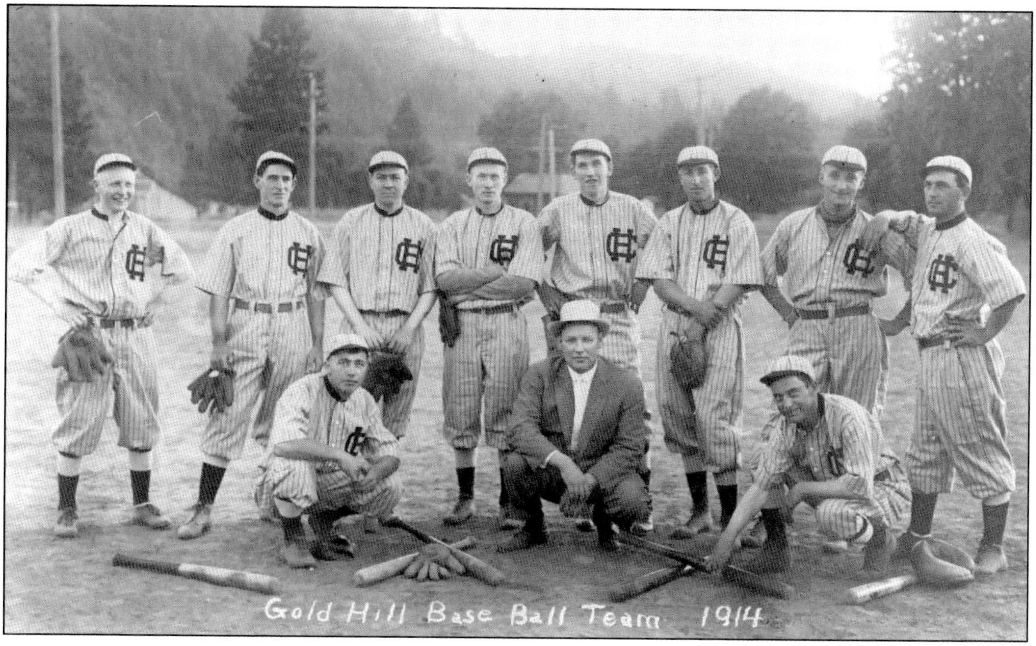

The local towns had their own baseball teams and league. From coastal Crescent City to Gold Hill and Ashland, the teams traveled back and forth to play in intense rivalries, with their fans following. The brawls that often followed a game's end were at times as entertaining as the actual play. Gold Hill's baseball field was also where the polo matches were played, between Second Avenue and the railroad tracks. The 1914 Gold Hill team (above) included, from left to right, (first row) Mr. Blackington, coach John Cameron, and unidentified; (second row) Charlie Reed, Harry Porter, two unidentified, Alvie Walker, Bill Kelsey, and Doc Eddings. In the 1930s image below, the crowd stands along the third base line watching a home player at bat.

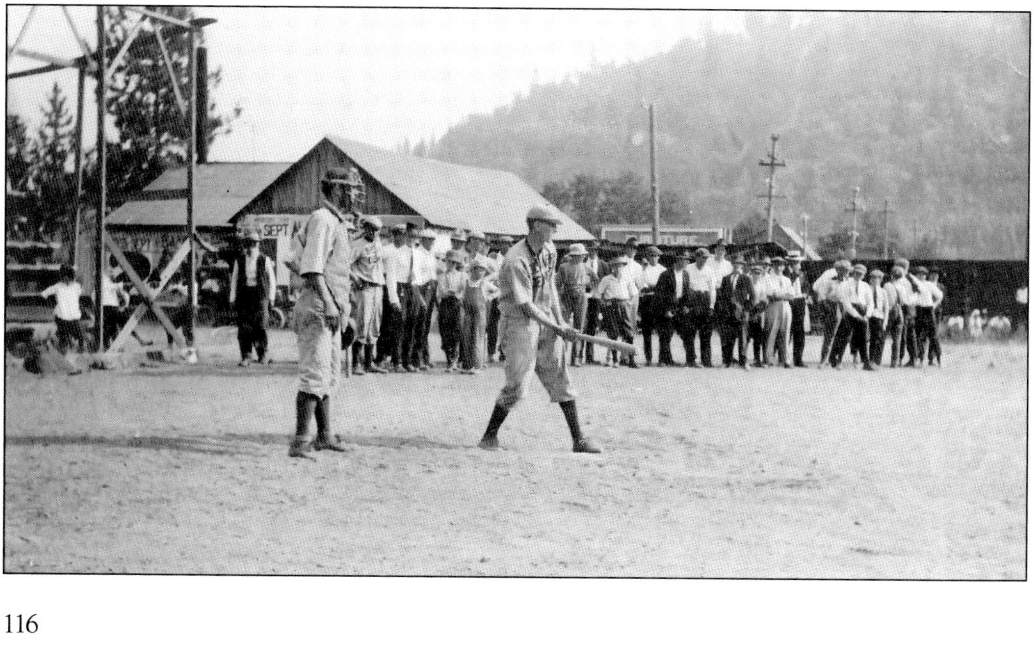

These two young girls with their clown makeup are believed to be members of the Coy family posing after a late 1930s parade. The picture was taken by the railroad tracks near the bridge, given that the water tower can be seen in the background.

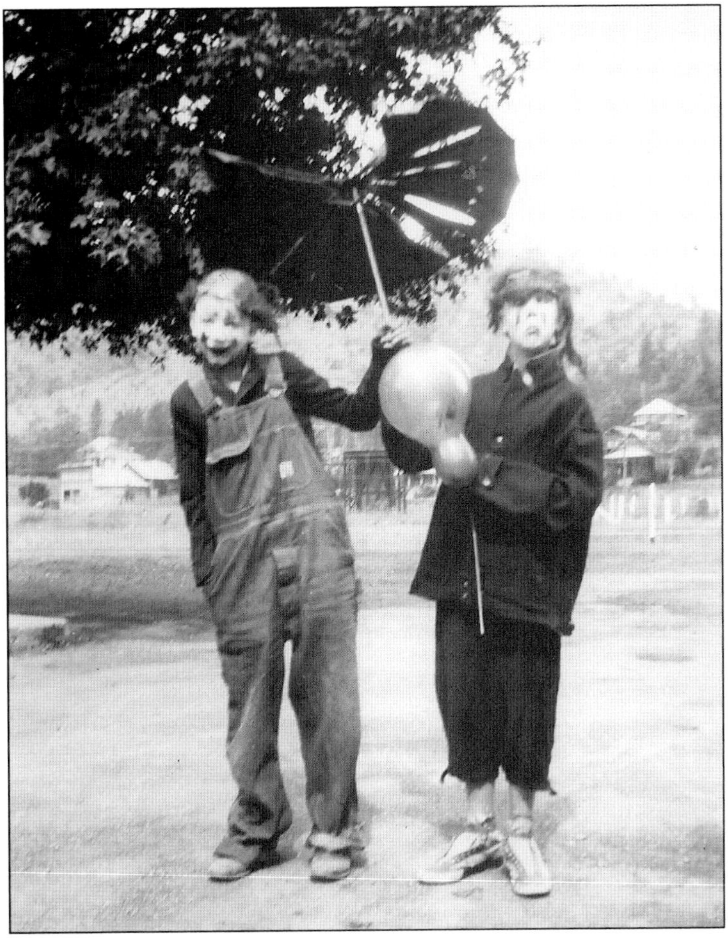

Well-dressed passengers in four cars posed in front of the Gold Hill Hotel after participating in a 1930s Gold Hill parade. American flags decorate the electric pole, and the white coats and hats stand out.

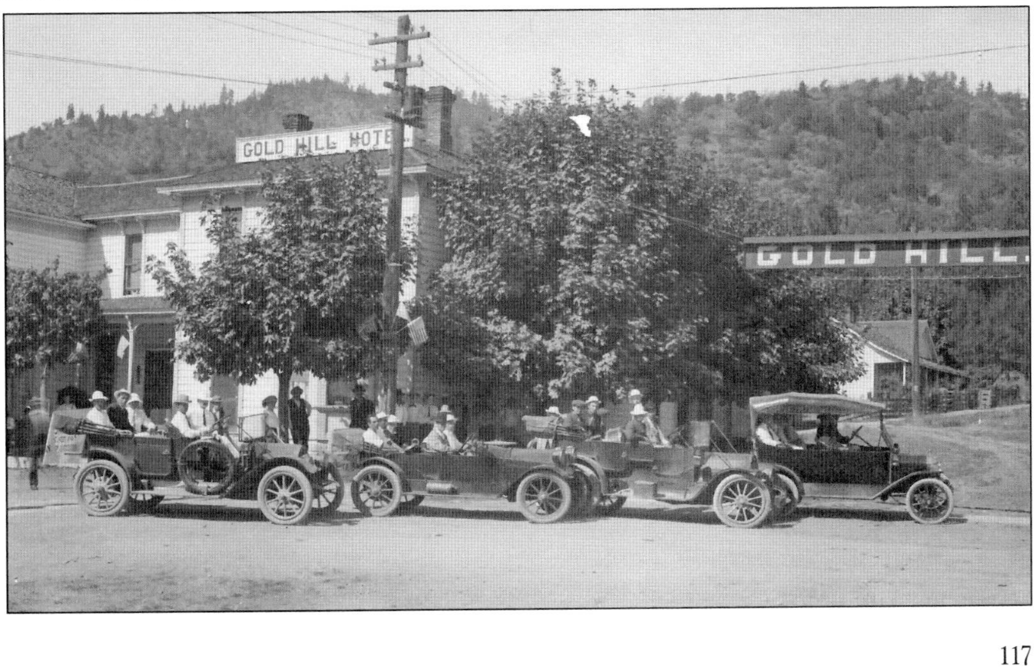

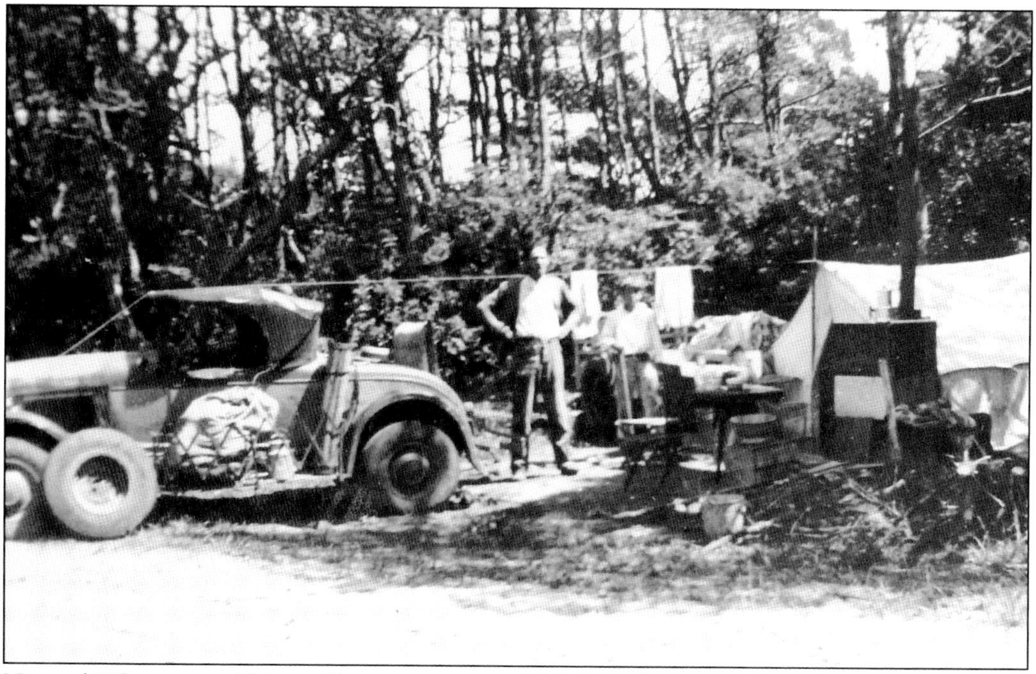

Howard Wharton and his son Ben camp out in 1938 with their 1925 Roadster. The tent is held up by a rope that stretches taut to the car. Judging from the elaborate setup, this was likely their hunting camp.

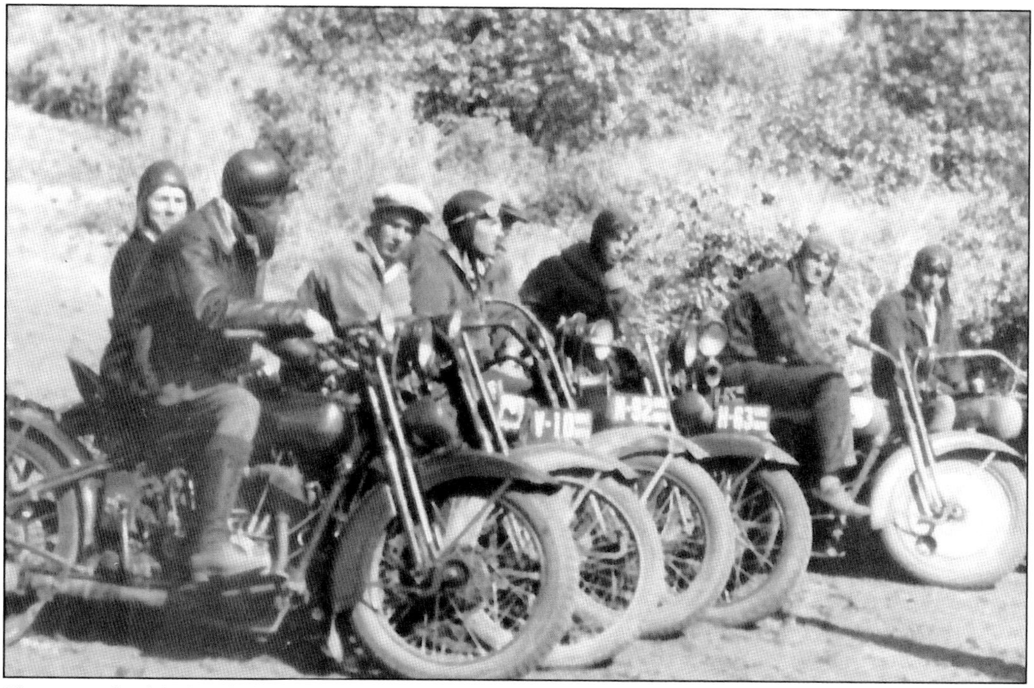

Photographed behind the school in Gold Hill near the bottom of Hill Climb Trail, these 1928 riders were the forerunners of modern motorcycle and motorcross clubs. Their leather helmets were not much protection, and it was probably a hot and noisy ride, although thrilling.

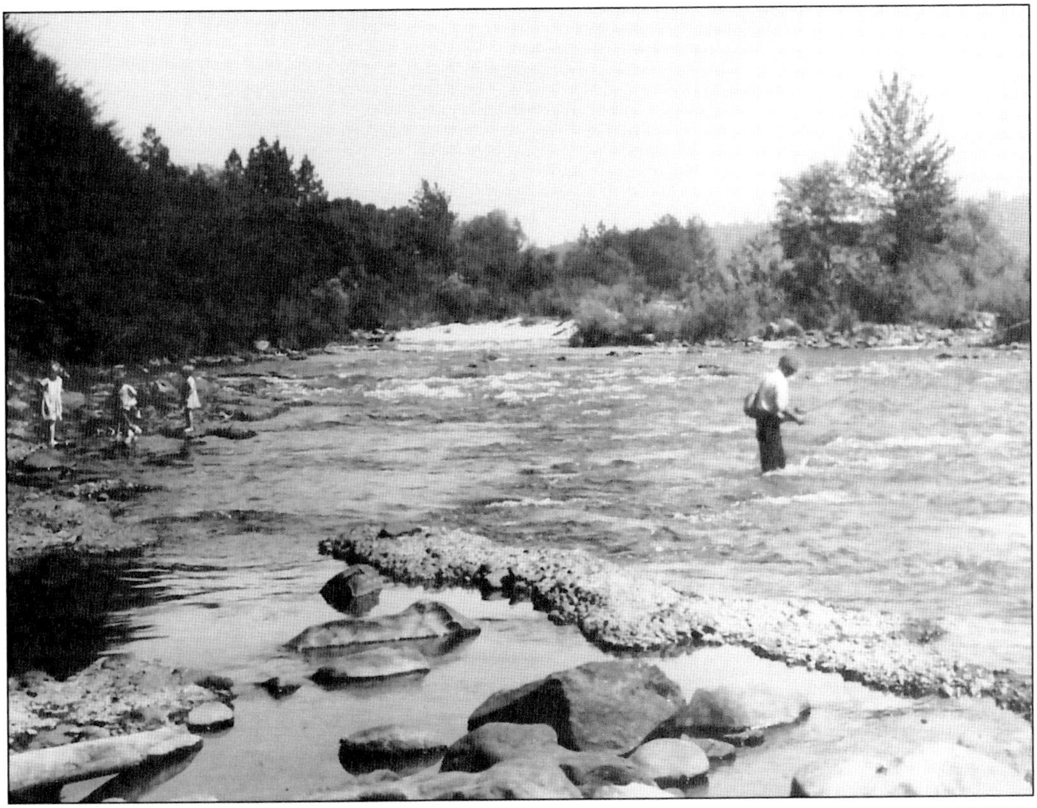

There is nothing grander than fishing on the renowned Rogue River for salmon or steelhead—and catching one! Three children (above) are playing on the riverbank at the left, while a lone fisherman, presumably their father, is in the river intently staring ahead. The 1930s picture at right shows five Chinook salmon by an old car, which is a 1929 Dodge or Studebaker. The fishing was certainly good then.

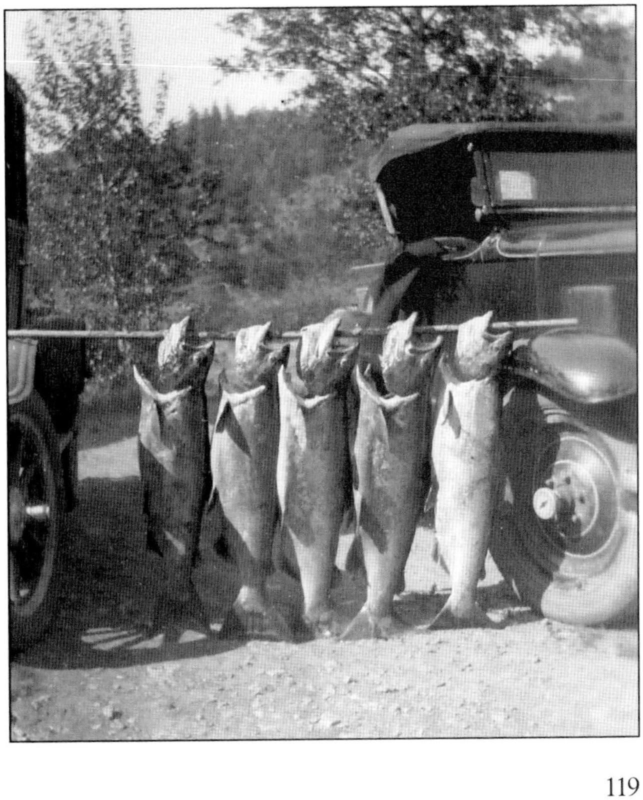

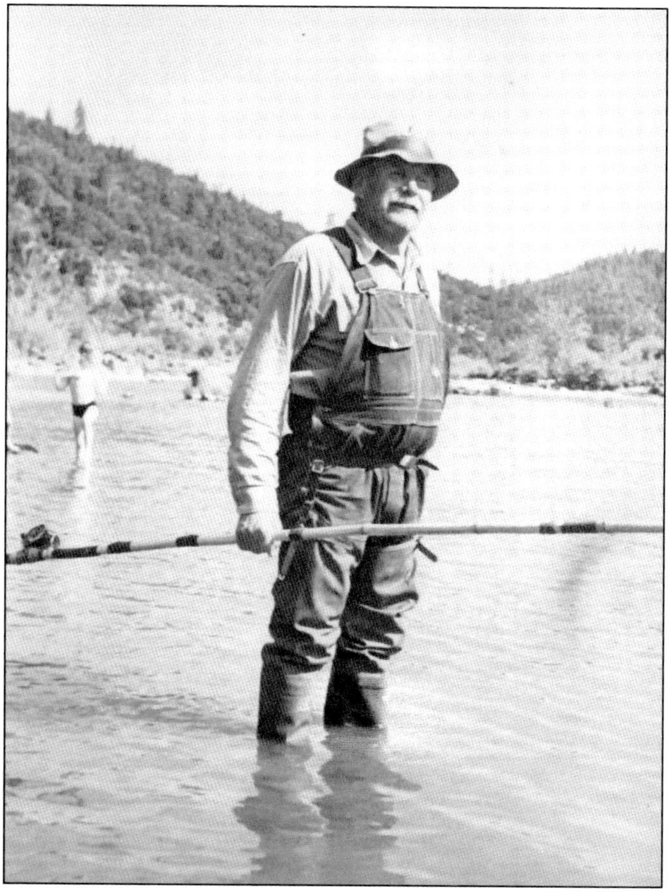

Max Schulz, a son-in-law of Hinrich Holst, is pictured on the Rogue River near Ernie Lyman's house. This was the swimming hole for Sams Valley and was known as the Biederman. Schulz was fishing for salmon with grasshoppers or worms, as many of the fishermen did at that time.

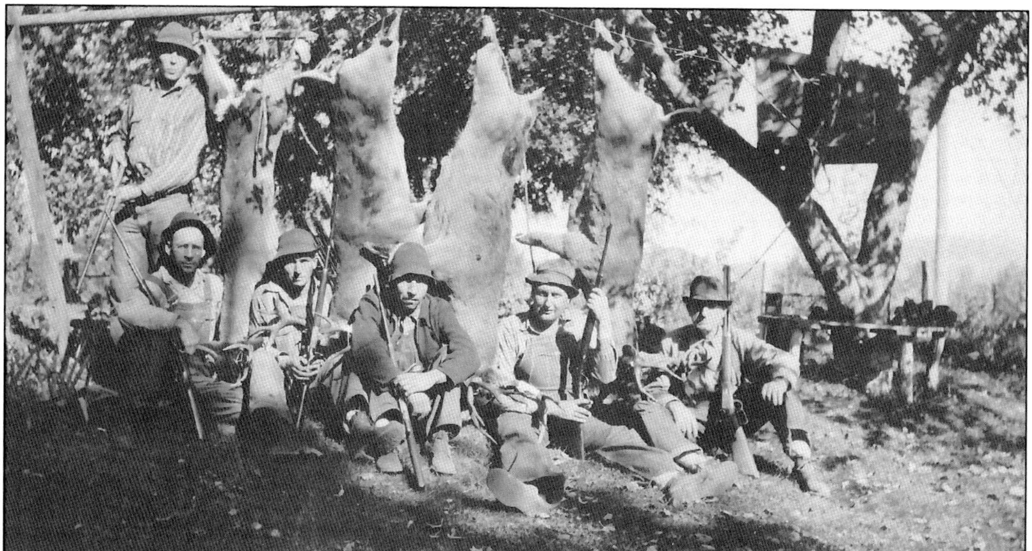

In the late 1930s, these Sams Valley and Gold Hill area friends had a fine hunt—with venison to be served later. The hunters include, from left to right, Leroy Carter, great-grandson of H. Holst; Paul Schulz, H. Holst's grandson; Lesley Walker, Clyde Walker, Frank Carter, and Charley Carter.

Ben Hur Lampman was raised in North Dakota and moved to Gold Hill to become the publisher of the weekly *Gold Hill News* from 1912 to 1916, when *The Oregonian* lured him away. A passionate fisherman, Lampman returned often to fish on the Rogue. A renowned editor, essayist, short story writer, and poet, he was named poet laureate of Oregon in 1951. Famous for his flowing Windsor ties, he won an O. Henry Award, authored six books, and had poems and stories printed in the *New York Times*, *Atlantic Monthly*, and *Saturday Evening Post*, among others. In recognition of this famous native son, the town held Ben Hur Lampman Day in his honor on June 21, 1947. People came from across the county. Clark Gable, Tyrone Power, and David Niven were fishing on the Rogue and showed up, as did invited governors, celebrities, and authors. The festivities included a baseball game, horseback stunts, horse race, salmon feast, and a parade. An estimated 2,500 people attended.

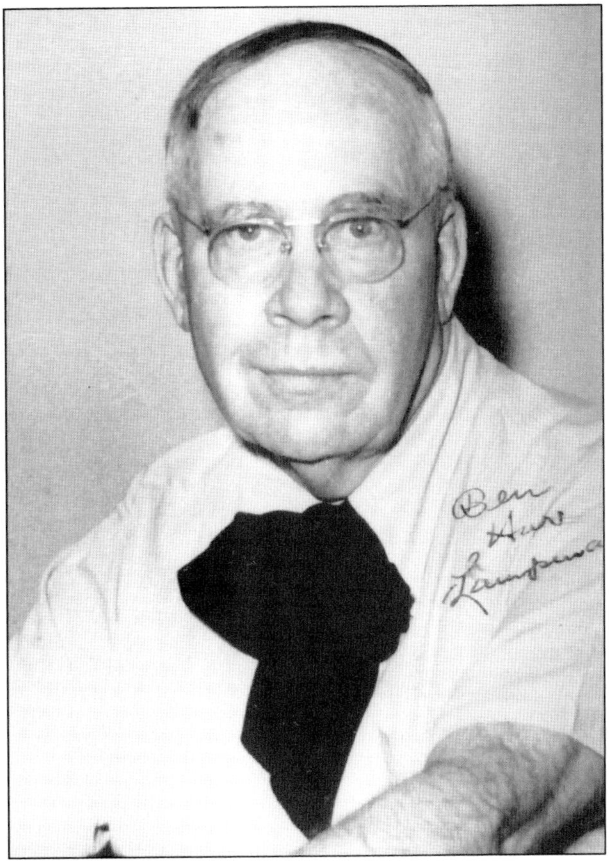

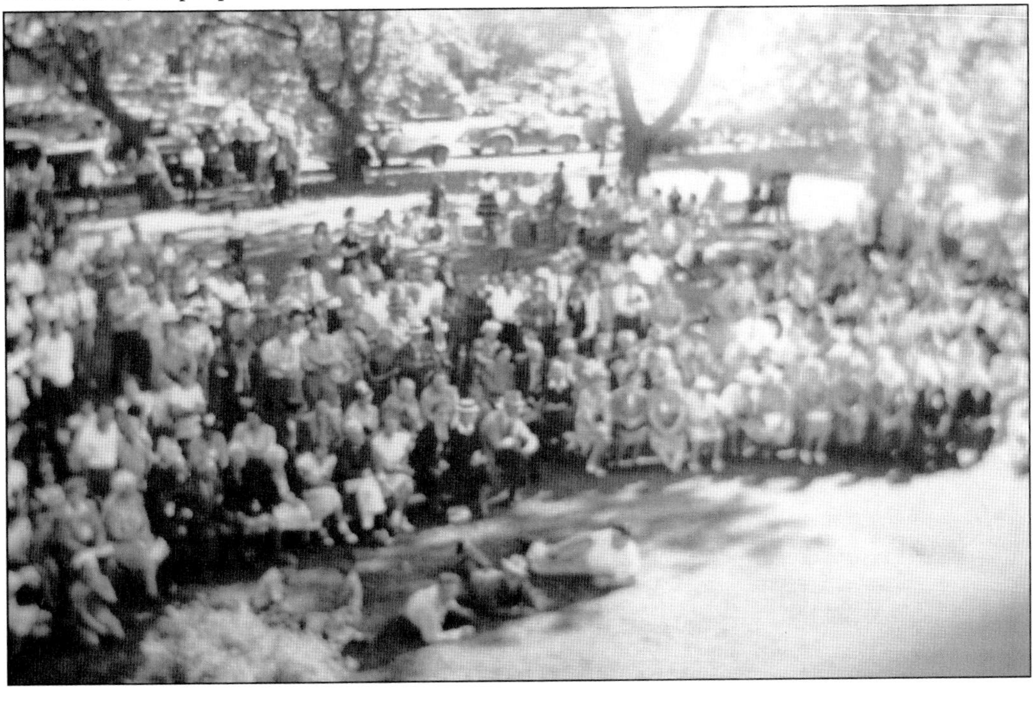

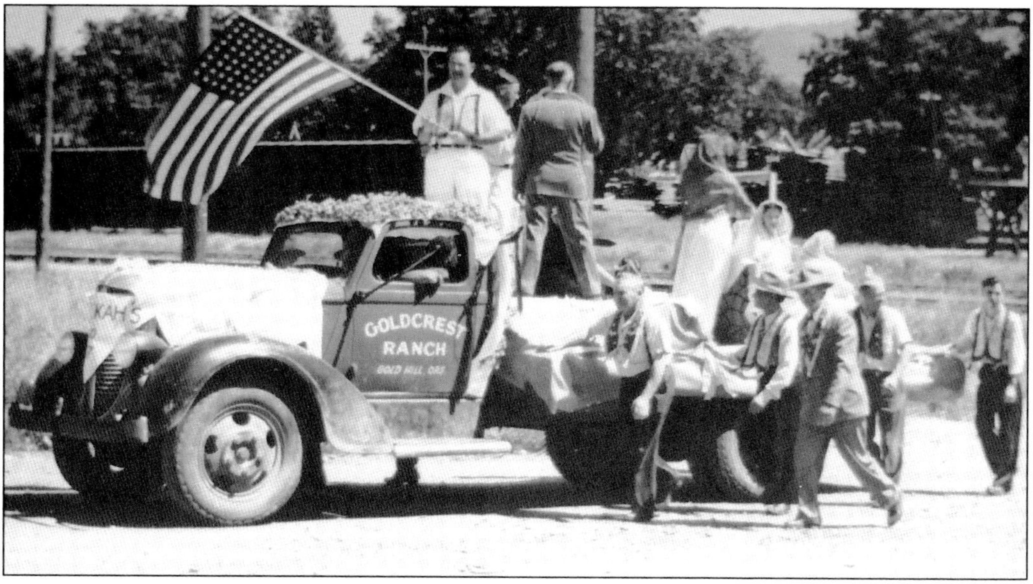

Among the parade goers were Damien Estremado's Gold Crest Ranch truck and, apparently, local Odd Fellows. A park on the Rogue River's bank opposite Gold Hill, a road, and a street are named in Lampman's honor. He died on January 24, 1954, and is buried in Portland.

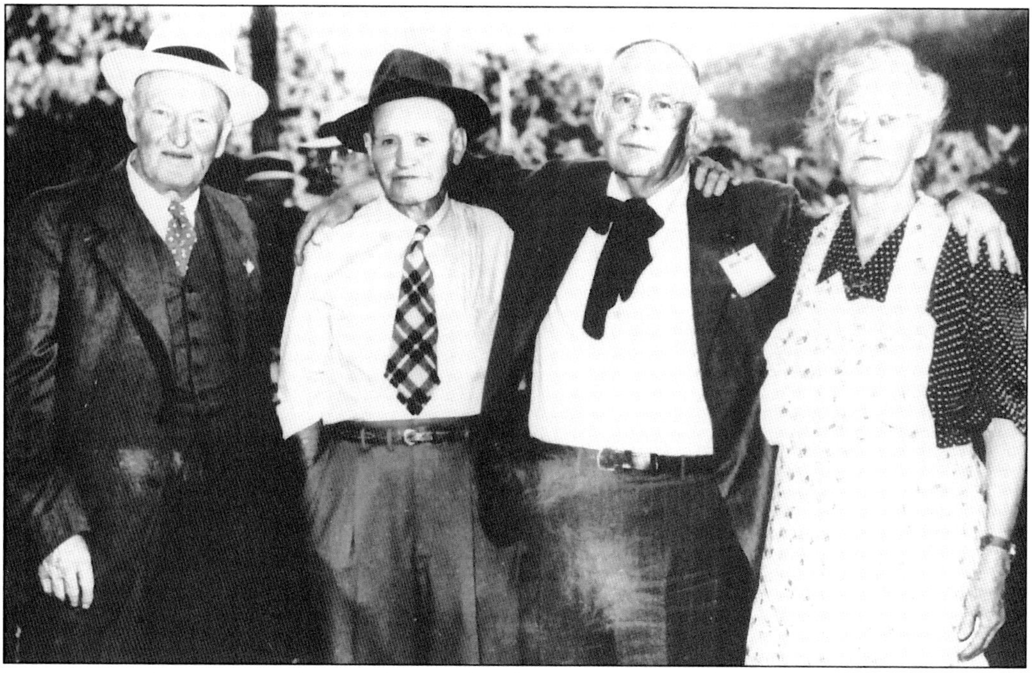

In a noteworthy essay on where to bury a dog, Lampman wrote, "On a hill where the wind is unrebuked, and the trees are roaring, or beside a stream he knew in puppyhood, or somewhere in the flatness of a pasture land, where most exhilarating cattle graze. It is all one to the dog, and all one to you, and nothing is gained, and nothing lost—if memory lives . . . The one best place to bury a good dog is in the heart of its master." The masterful piece should be read in its entirety. In this image are, from left to right, John Hays, Martin Bowers, Ben Hur Lampman, and Lily MacKay during Lampman Days.

Nine

From Gold Nuggets to Fine Wine

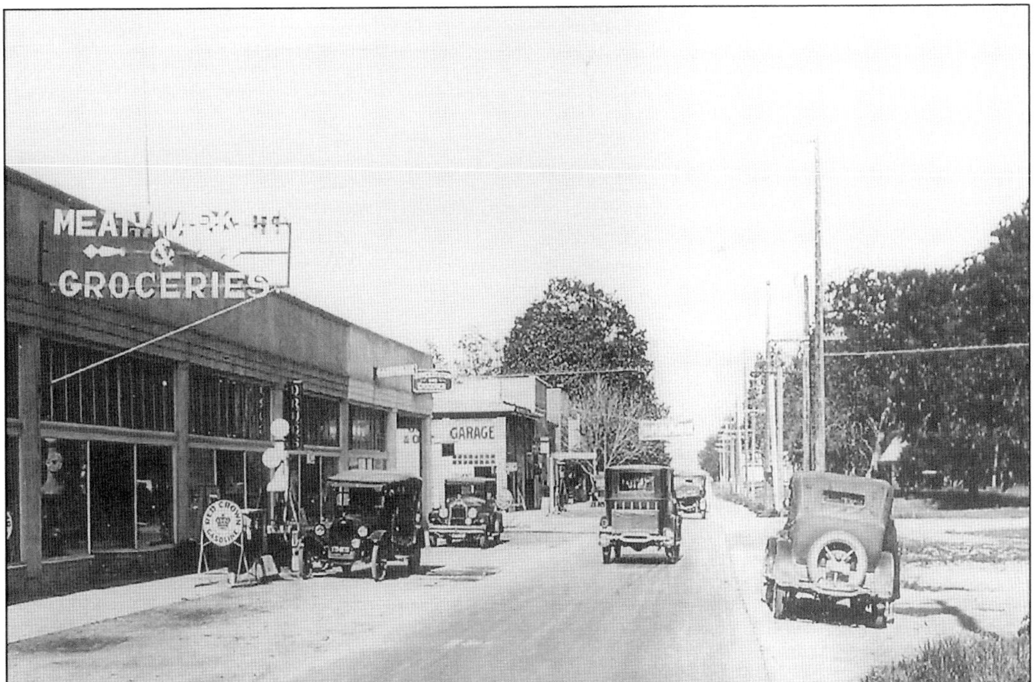

Second Avenue in the 1930s had cars in place of horses and gas stations rather than livery stables. The gas station on the left has changed hands a few times, but a filling station is still there. The park to the right, once used for picnics and baseball games, is now home to Sweed Machinery and the public library.

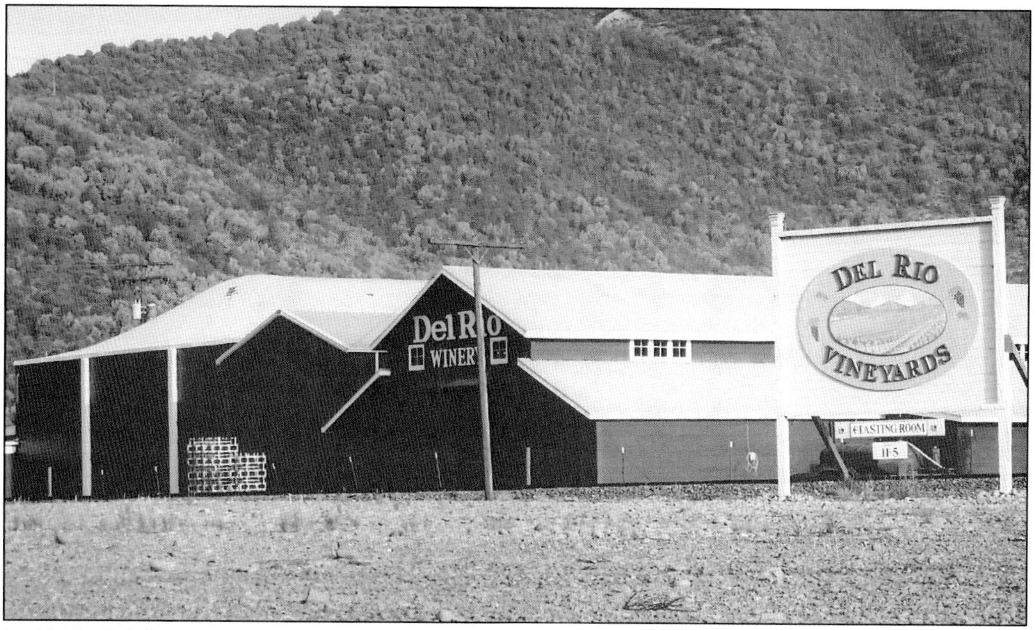

In 1997, Californians Lee and Margaret Traynham purchased Del Rio Orchards, with Jolee and Rob Wallace as managing partners. They transformed the third-generation pear orchard into one of Oregon's top-rated, premium vineyards in a decade. The 200-acres-plus—and constantly expanding—vineyard grows 14 different varietals, primarily warm-climate types, the most famous of which is a Syrah, with 40 acres now planted.

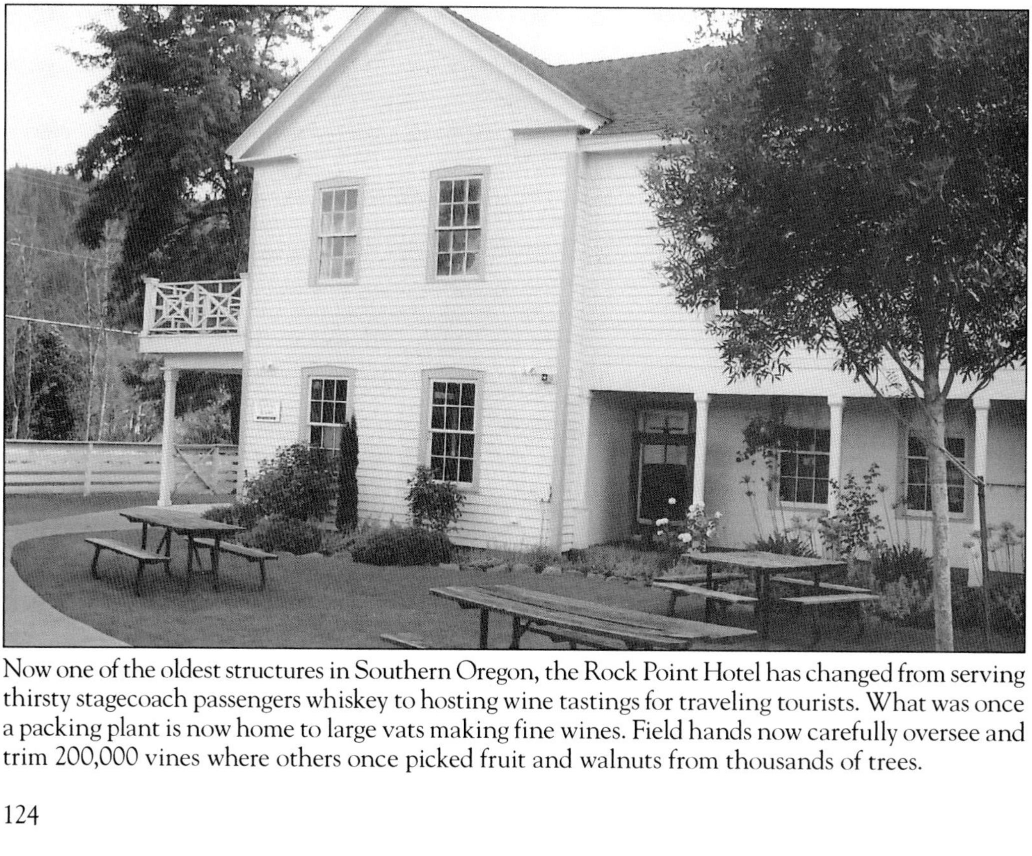

Now one of the oldest structures in Southern Oregon, the Rock Point Hotel has changed from serving thirsty stagecoach passengers whiskey to hosting wine tastings for traveling tourists. What was once a packing plant is now home to large vats making fine wines. Field hands now carefully oversee and trim 200,000 vines where others once picked fruit and walnuts from thousands of trees.

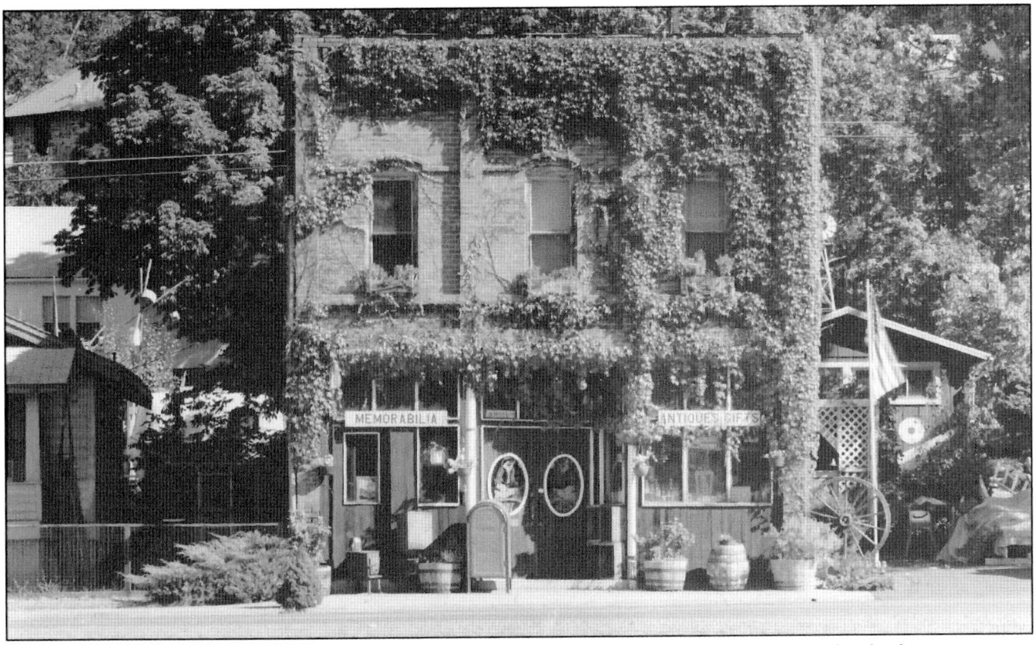

Thomas Chavner sold the underlying land to the railroad in 1894, which then built this two-story brick building and used it as a boardinghouse for its workers. Although it has been remodeled inside, the outside is untouched. Owned and used by the Gold Hill Grange for 18 years to 1935, it has had a variety of uses since. Presently, an antique store is on the first floor, and the owner lives on the second. (Bob Howe.)

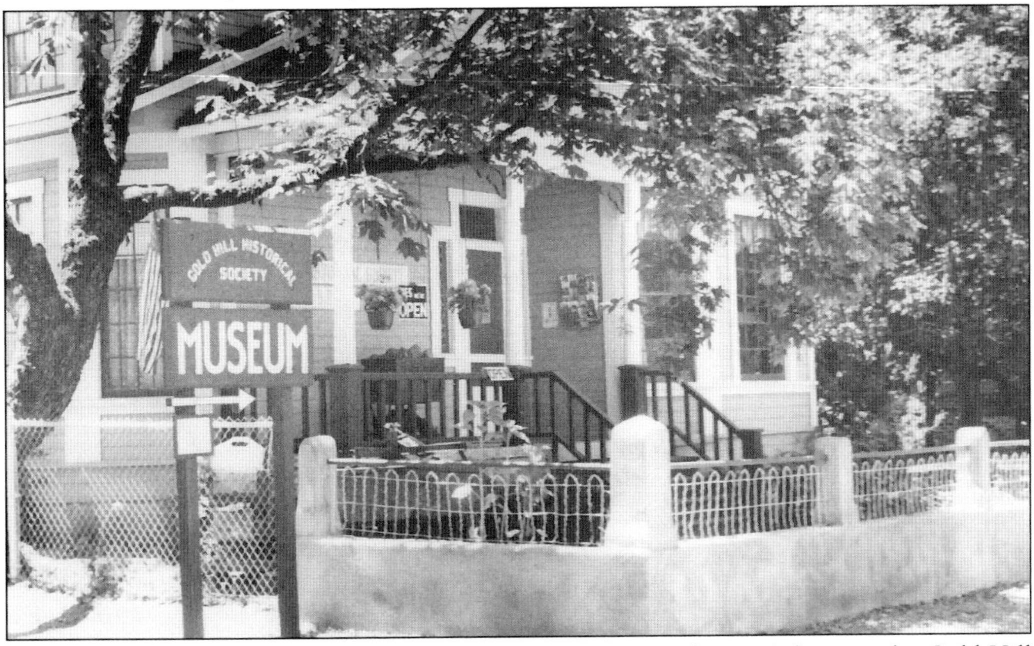

Continuing its important work of preserving and exhibiting the area's history, the Gold Hill Historical Society operates from the Beeman-Martin house, built over 100 years ago. Constructed from the profitable operations of the Lucky-Bart gold mine, the house is now maintained by the efforts of countless volunteers and by membership fees, donations, and gift shop sales.

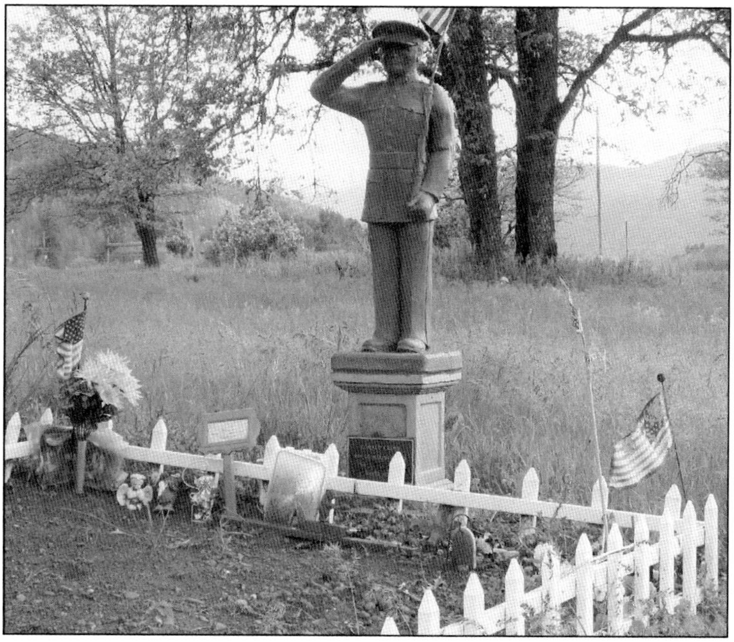

GHHS volunteers also serve on the board of the Rock Point Pioneer Cemetery adjacent to Del Rio Vineyards. Created over 135 years ago, this cemetery association and the local Independent Order of Odd Fellows have adjoining cemetery ownership and responsibilities. Striking monuments of late Victorian marble and sedate, weathered stone mark the graves of the founding families of Rock Point, stagecoach drivers, area residents, and soldiers who fought in different wars, all in a beautiful setting.

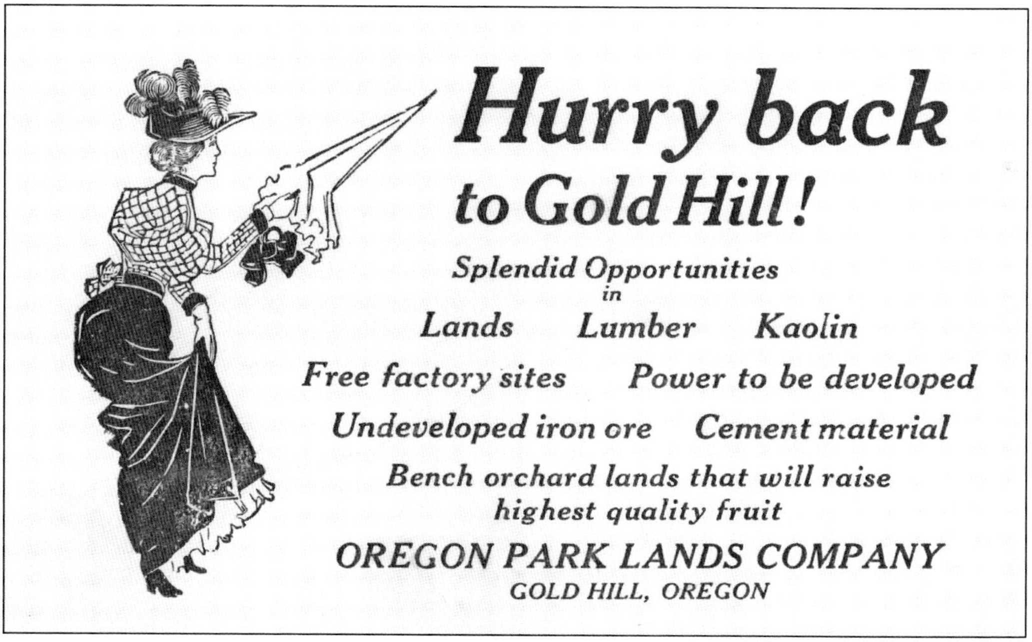

This 1900s postcard was handed out to prospective residents and businesses. Kaolin is a fine clay, rich in kaolinite that is found in ceramics and papermaking, among other uses. "Hurry Back to Gold Hill" applies today, but they are now mostly retirees and families looking for the small-town, easier life that it offers.

Bibliography

Brooks, Howard C. and Len Ramp. *State of Oregon, Department of Geology and Mineral Industries, Bulletin 61: Gold and Silver in Oregon*. Baker, Oregon: The Record-Courier Printers, 1968/1980.

Dufur, Lee. "Bill Hay: A Mix of Shrewdness and Nerve." *True West*, July–August, 1975, 32–34, 49–53.

Fitch, Ronald R. "History of Gold Hill, Oregon." Research paper for History 478(g), Department of History, Southern Oregon College.

Genaw, Linda Morehouse. *Gold Hill and its Neighbors along the River*. Central Point, Oregon: Linda Morehouse Genaw, 1988.

Gold Hill Historical Society. Calendars and papers. Gold Hill, Oregon.

Gold Hill Historical Society. *Nuggets of News*: Articles, columns, pictures, 1992–2010.

"Gold Mining: The Activity that Built Jacksonville: Gold Hill District." *Jacksonville Nugget*, July 29–August 2, 1986; August 5–11, 1986; September 9–15, 1986; September 23–29, 1986; December 6–18, 1990.

Hendricks, Mary Truax. "Gold Hill between 1911 and 1915: Events and Personalities." Gold Hill Historical Society files, 1986.

Throne, Dorothy Joanne. "A Brief History of the Gold Hill Area." Research paper for History 478(g), Department of History, Southern Oregon College.

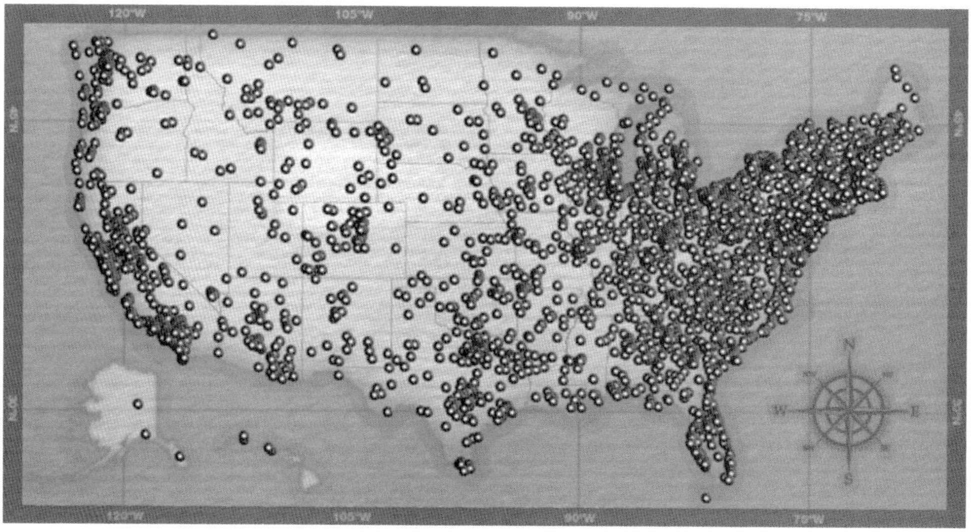